Mental Health of Athletes

Recent Titles in
Health and Medical Issues Today

Drug Decriminalization and Legalization
Aharon W. Zorea

Medical Tourism
Lydia Gan

Organ Donation
Sarah Boslaugh

Mental Health of Athletes

Christine L. B. Selby

BLOOMSBURY ACADEMIC
NEW YORK • LONDON • OXFORD • NEW DELHI • SYDNEY

BLOOMSBURY ACADEMIC
Bloomsbury Publishing Inc, 1359 Broadway, New York, NY 10018, USA
Bloomsbury Publishing Plc, 50 Bedford Square, London, WC1B 3DP, UK
Bloomsbury Publishing Ireland, 29 Earlsfort Terrace, Dublin 2, D02 AY28, Ireland

First published in the United States of America 2025

A catalog record for this book is available from the Library of Congress.

ISBN: HB: 978-1-4408-8112-1
ePDF: 978-1-4408-8113-8
eBook: 979-8-7651-1066-9

Series: Health and Medical Issues Today

Typeset by Integra Software Services Pvt. Ltd.
Printed and bound in the United States of America

For product safety related questions contact productsafety@bloomsbury.com.

This book is dedicated to all athletes who have struggled with, who are struggling with, and who may struggle with mental health challenges. You are not alone.

Contents

Series Foreword

Every day, the public is bombarded with information on developments in medicine and health care. Whether it is on the latest techniques in treatment or research, or on concerns over public health threats, this information directly affects the lives of people more than almost any other issue. Although there are many sources for understanding these topics—from websites and blogs to newspapers and magazines—students and ordinary citizens often need one resource that makes sense of the complex health and medical issues affecting their daily lives.

The *Health and Medical Issues Today* series provides just such a one-stop resource for obtaining a solid overview of the most controversial areas of health care in the twenty-first century. Each volume addresses one topic and provides a balanced summary of what is known. These volumes provide an excellent first step for students and laypeople interested in understanding how health care works in our society today.

Each volume is broken into several parts to provide readers and researchers with easy access to the information they need:

Part I provides overview chapters on background information—including chapters on such areas as the historical, scientific, medical, social, and legal issues involved—that a citizen needs to intelligently understand the topic.

Part II provides capsule examinations of the most heated contemporary issues and debates, and analyzes in a balanced manner the viewpoints held by various advocates in the debates.

Part III provides case studies that show examples of the concepts discussed in the previous parts.

A directory of resources and a glossary provide additional reference material and serve as the best next step in learning about the topic at hand.

The *Health and Medical Issues Today* series strives to provide readers with all the information needed to begin making sense of some of the most important debates going on in the world today. The series includes volumes on such topics as stem-cell research, obesity, gene therapy, alternative medicine, organ transplantation, mental health, and more.

Preface

Deciding to write a book on athlete mental health was easy. An increasing number of high-profile athletes are speaking out not only about their own mental health challenges but the importance of not ignoring those challenges when they arise. In addition, athlete suicide, particularly among high school and college athletes, has been in the news quite a bit in recent years calling attention to the pressures many athletes face when juggling expectations related to school and sport, and for some not being able to compete in their sport (e.g., due to social distancing mandates related to Covid-19). Despite all of this, there is still a prevailing attitude, among athletes and non-athletes alike, that athletes are immune to mental health struggles. When athletes do experience mental health challenges, they may not disclose their struggles out of fear of losing their spot on the team, being ridiculed by teammates and coaches, and generally being labeled as "weak." This ongoing stigma in sport often means athletes will ignore or "push through" their struggles until they cannot. When athletes get to this point, they may lose time with their sport or, depending on the severity of their concerns, may have to leave their sport altogether.

I am also a licensed counseling and sport psychologist, therefore, writing this book is personal in that I work directly with athletes who have struggled with myriad mental health concerns, some of which were severe and required the athlete to temporarily pause their sport participation. I have witnessed athletes at various levels of competition struggle with performance, and ultimately return to the level of competition they knew they were capable of once they addressed and understood the mental health challenges that were impeding their ability to perform. Healing is possible, and can occur relatively quickly when the challenges are identified early and formal support is received as soon as possible.

Mental Health in Athletes was written to educate and inform readers about the myriad factors that affect an athlete's mental health to include how not tending to mental health challenges when they arise can put an athlete at greater risk for injury and/or can lead to a decline in performance. The content in this book is based on current research (i.e., mostly within the last 5–10 years of publication) conducted by scientists who are invested in understanding the athlete experience and how they can be best supported in all ways including their mental health, and news stories about issues that have not yet received much scientific inquiry (e.g., name, image & likeness [NIL]).

The term "mental health" is often shorthand for "mental health problems" or a "mental health diagnosis"; however, as explored in the book, mental health exists on a continuum with optimal functioning on one end and being in a mental health crisis on the other end. Most readers know that their own mental health can fluctuate from one day, week, or month to the next depending on what is going on in their life. This is no different for athletes. Athletes, just like those in the general population, may be predisposed (i.e., have a genetic vulnerability) to developing specific mental health-related symptoms, and most of us, including athletes, under the right circumstances can be overwhelmed by life which can result in mental health-related symptoms. Sometimes these symptoms, regardless of the cause, require treatment, and sometimes they do not. This book will help readers learn more about common mental health challenges found among athletes and learn about when an athlete would benefit from speaking with a qualified mental health professional.

Athletes are an eclectic group of people that include different genders, abilities, sexual orientations, and different histories with respect to trauma. Athletes are now also categorized as "traditional athletes" and "e'athletes" (i.e., those who compete in esports). Understanding the unique issues faced by these different groups can help athletes themselves, and those who work with and care about athletes, ensure that all athletes have the general and unique support needed to thrive in sport.

My general hope in writing this book is to contribute to the growing awareness of the mental health challenges athletes face, and to normalize seeking support or treatment for a mental health concern. My more specific hope is that seeking support for mental health challenges will be viewed in the same way physical injuries are viewed: as an injury that requires treatment of some kind. Mental health symptoms may be the equivalent of a sprained ankle that requires some tape so the athlete can continue to practice and compete, or may be like a broken bone that requires much more significant treatment and time away from sport until the bone is fully healed. Either way, mental health injuries cannot and should not be ignored any more than physical injuries should be. Both can be treated effectively, especially when they are identified right away and treatment is administered shortly thereafter.

Strong mental health contributes to strong performance in sport and in life. Do not ignore any sign or symptom of a mental health challenge and seek help right away.

Acknowledgments

This book has been many years in the making, and I received tremendous support along the way.

My husband is and has always been my biggest supporter and cheerleader. A project like this cannot be completed without someone like that in your corner. I am grateful for his ongoing encouragement, his continued support when I struggled to find time and energy to write, and plying me with my favorite food and drink when I was in the midst of long writing and editing sessions.

I have had the pleasure and the privilege of working with Maxine Taylor, senior acquisitions editor, on several projects including this one. She has been a significant source of support including working with me when I was unexpectedly unable to make my deadlines. Her graciousness and flexibility have allowed me the opportunity to make this the best book possible.

I am also grateful to my employer, Springfield College, particularly the librarians. I have been able to access the resources I needed for this book quickly and easily. The librarians, of course, procured relevant books for me that our library did not have, and processed countless other interlibrary loan requests for journal articles and book chapters. Without this type of support, this book could not have been written.

Finally, I would like to thank all athletes with whom I have directly worked, and who participated in the numerous published research studies used to inform this book. Without your willingness to share your experiences, we would not know how best to support you when you need it the most.

Part I
Overview

1

Benefits of Sport on Mental Well-being

Exercise, physical activity, and sport are each different endeavors; however, they all involve movement. While the focus of this book is on sport, in this and other chapters, much of what we know about what is beneficial about sport has been learned from studying the impact of movement in general. However, when possible, experiences unique to sport will be the focus. In this chapter, we'll initially examine the benefits of movement (i.e., physical activity), then we'll turn our attention to self-esteem and self-confidence and how those are impacted by sport. Then we'll examine flow or "being in the zone" before taking a look at how physical activity and sport can help reduce symptoms of common mental health challenges.

General Findings on the Benefits of Sport and Physical Activity

It has long been known that physical activity has myriad benefits for both the mind and body. These benefits have been significant enough that in 2007 the *American College of Sports Medicine* (ACSM) established the *Exercise Is Medicine* (EIM) initiative. The purpose of this effort was to make exercise, or physical activity, something that was formally prescribed by healthcare professionals. Under this model, healthcare providers are encouraged to inquire about a patient's level of physical activity and make recommendations (or a prescription) as part of standard prevention and treatment for myriad physical and psychiatric maladies. Via their website, EIM publishes treatment recommendations on using exercise for things such as Alzheimer's dementia, asthma, cancer, hypertension, low back pain, osteoporosis, pregnancy, and many more. In addition to these physical conditions, there are recommendations for depression and anxiety. Since 2007 a great deal of research has been conducted to determine what type and amount of exercise are ideal for overall health and well-being. In addition, researchers have studied how participating in organized sports at various points in our development can provide physical as well as mental health benefits.

In a systematic review of the literature conducted in 2013 a group of researchers, led by Rochelle Eime, found myriad benefits for individuals who engaged in sport-related activities. The authors examined over 3,600 empirical studies and concluded that sport-related activities are recommended as a leisure activity that has many physical, psychological, and interpersonal benefits. Among the benefits listed include improved personal characteristics such as caring, confidence, emotional control, sense of well-being, and sense of self-efficacy. They noted personal benefits related to psychiatric symptoms such as less emotional distress, less hopelessness, fewer thoughts of suicide, and fewer symptoms related to depression. Social interactions can also be improved through sport participation including an increase in cooperation, better relationships with coaches and friends, better social skills and overall social functioning, and not surprisingly, an increase in sportpersonship. Even for preschoolers, participation in sport can enhance cognitive skills, specifically executive functioning skills which include things such as cognitive flexibility and working memory.

A study conducted by Petr Bedura and colleagues, with over 10,500 adolescents in the Czech Republic, examined the impact that playing sports may have on one's mental health. They categorized participants as inactive, team sports, individual sports, artists, or all-rounders. Those categorized as inactive were not engaged in any organized activity and those categorized as team sports were only active with a team sport. Those categorized as individual sports participated in an individual sport and half of this group also participated in team sports. Similarly, of those identified as artists half also participated in an individual sport and/or a team sport. Finally, among those classified as all-rounders, 85 percent participated in at least two activities and as many as six activities. Findings indicated that participation of any kind in what they termed "organized leisure-time activities" resulted in better overall health and higher feelings of satisfaction, regardless of age or gender. Where there were differences in gender (only the binary genders were included) boys tended to report better health if they participated in sport (individual or team), and girls reported better health if they participated in art.

Recently, prominent sport-based organizations such as the National Collegiate Athletic Association (NCAA), International Olympic Committee (IOC), and International Society of Sport Psychology and European Federation of Sport Psychology have released documents calling for greater identification and treatment of mental health issues within sport environments. In addition, interest regarding resilience within sport performers has increased within the past decade or so. Particular attention has been given to understanding the subjective experience and development of resilience within athletes, teams, and sport organizations.

Self-Esteem and Self-Confidence

Self-esteem can be defined as the confidence a person has in their own worth and in their skills and abilities. Although quite similar, self-confidence can be defined as the trust a person has in their abilities, personal qualities, and judgment or decision-making. High self-esteem would be reflected by someone who feels good about who they are and what they can do, whereas someone with high self-confidence is someone who trusts who they are as a person and would be someone who approaches most situations thinking "I got this." When binary gender is considered, both males and females experience a boost in self-esteem and self-confidence through participation in sport.

Much of the research in the area of the benefits of self-esteem and self-confidence as it relates to physical activity is in the area of exercise rather than sport specifically. In the context of sport, much of the information comes from studying the impact of youth sport participation. The President's Council on Sports, Fitness & Nutrition is a US federal advisory committee focused on promoting healthy behaviors for people of all ages, backgrounds, and abilities. In 2020 the Science Board of this Council produced a document entitled *Benefits of Youth Sports*. The document, of course, notes the myriad physical health benefits of sport participation to include improvements in bone health, better cardiorespiratory functioning and fitness of muscles, a reduction in the risk for serious diseases including cancer and diabetes, and an increase in quality of life. Psychologically based benefits, that the Science Board of the Council refers to as "mental, emotional, and social health," include greater satisfaction with one's life, enjoyment of physical activity in general, improved cognitive performance, lower rates or risk for common mental health challenges including depression, anxiety, substance use and suicide, and higher levels of self-esteem and self-confidence. Boosts in self-confidence, however, do not just occur in the context of physical activity or sport.

A study conducted with parents and their children from "low-income families" found that both parents and children noted an increase in confidence related to sport participation. One parent was quoted on what they saw in their child " … what's significant for me is the confidence of just being like trusting that I can step out and I can do this and even if I fall that's fine. I can try again … " (Holt et al., 2011, p. 495). One of the children interviewed for this study stated, "I think a really big part of sport is I learned how to be confident and that helps a lot, especially in school and like public places. If I need to give a speech, I know how to like calm myself down before I present. I can be confident … " (Holt et al., 2011, p. 495). As seen, particularly by the quote from a child who was interviewed, confidence that originated with sport permeated multiple aspects of their life, not just in sport.

Another study entitled *If You Let Me Play Sports* asked female-identifying collegiate athletes to think back on their sport participation prior to competing in college. These researchers found that the more these athletes participated in sport prior to college, the higher their self-esteem. They found that when female-identifying athletes participated in sport prior to college they felt better about themselves overall including feeling a strong sense of physical competence (trusting their body to do what they wanted it to do) and having a positive body image. They also reported feeling a sense of acceptance from their peers, and a sense of academic competence. Each of these factors was found to contribute to their overall level of self-esteem.

Additional research found that when elementary-aged children participate in team sports, they are more likely to experience higher levels of self-esteem compared to similarly aged children participating in individual sports. Importantly the self-esteem benefit did not differ between boys and girls (only the binary genders were included), between those with different levels of physical ability in sport, or between those who viewed the importance of sport differently. Performing in individual sports, however, has been shown to demonstrate more clearly a particular athlete's competence in sport which is one factor (i.e., a sense of competence) that contributes to self-esteem. It was suggested that younger children do not really have a sense of an internalized sport self-concept meaning that they don't really think of themselves as good or bad athletes. Researchers suggested that this is because young athletes rely primarily on feedback on things such as the outcome of a competition or direct feedback from parental figures to determine whether or not they are good at sport. Thus, these researchers theorized that the children in their study were more likely to have a positive sport self-concept when they considered how they contributed to their team's win rather than how well they actually performed individually. They also theorized that the team element of sport places a greater emphasis on relationships with teammates and coaches which in turn can positively contribute to an individual's positive self-concept and self-esteem. This research supports what other research has suggested about sport for children: it is not about individual accomplishments or achievements for youth athletes, but what the team can do and how an athlete contributes to the team.

In the late 1980s a model, the *Exercise and Self-Esteem Model*, was created in part because the developers noted that research findings at the time did not adequately explain why there was a connection between exercise and self-esteem. The elements of the Exercise and Self-Esteem Model include physical self-efficacy, physical confidence, physical acceptance, and self-esteem. The developers of this model suggested that people start out with a particular level of physical self-efficacy which refers to a person's sense of what they are capable of physically (e.g., I believe I can run 5 miles or I believe I can walk 5 miles). Physical competence refers to a person's sense of having an adequate level of fitness. Physical acceptance has to do with the extent to which a person is satisfied (or not) with how their body functions and how their body looks. And, as noted previously, self-esteem refers to the confidence one has in their skills and abilities, and overall worth. In terms of how the elements of this model fit together, the developers stated that a person's physical self-efficacy will lead to a sense of physical competence. This type of competence can impact self-esteem directly or influence physical acceptance which in turn directly impacts self-esteem. Therefore, our belief in ourselves that we are capable of specific physical activities will help us feel like we can do what we need to do physically. This ultimately leads us to feeling good about our body's abilities (and appearance) which positively impacts our overall self-esteem. So, when a person starts from a point of feeling like they are capable of some measure of physical activity, engaging in physical activity will improve a person's perception of their fitness level. This will bolster their self-esteem as well as their acceptance of what their body looks like and how it functions.

The Exercise and Self-Esteem Model has since been tested among various populations and an expanded version of this model was tested in 2022 with female-identifying adolescents. These researchers found support for the updated model which included the additions of body fat and cardiovascular fitness. Each element was found to contribute to physical self-esteem as well as overall self-esteem. The researchers concluded that "physical activity participation still remains the primary determinant to bring about the cascade of positive changes in physical self-efficacy and self-esteem" (Gothe et al., 2022, p. 8876).

Interesting research has been conducted in the area of confidence and sport. Specifically, research has shown that sport-specific confidence can be influenced by physical appearance such that if athletes believed they look good they would have greater confidence in sport. Although it may seem strange that how one looks would impact one's perception of how one performs, researchers have also found that athletes who engage in superstitious behaviors tend to feel more confidence and that in turn can improve performance. Whether we believe superstitions are the reason we perform better, or our belief that looking good will also lead to better performance it is clear that what we tell ourselves about what leads to good performance, matters.

Athletes with an amateur status reported that their inner confidence had a greater impact on their sport performance and subsequent success more so than their actual physical strength. Athletes new to their sport, however, believed physical strength was a more important factor for sport success compared to confidence. And finally, as noted in other studies these researchers found that participants consistently stated that participating in sport contributed to their confidence in other areas of their life regardless of their skill level in sport. Researchers clarified that participants were clear that it was participation in sport *not* success in sport that contributed to confidence in other life domains. This suggests as other researchers have noted for many years that what is learned in sport (e.g., cooperation, skill development, emotional control, etc.) are skills that can transfer to other areas of one's life.

Flow or "Being in the Zone"

The state of "flow" was first identified by psychologist Mihály Csíkszentmihályi in 1970 and was born out of his intent to understand artists who became so absorbed in their work that they lost track of time and would forgo basic needs (i.e., food, water, and sleep). Flow has become part of the lexicon of positive psychology which is focused on optimal functioning in all aspects of people's lives. When someone is in a state of flow, they are fully absorbed by the activity they are engaged in with an accompanying feeling of enjoyment. Part of the experience of flow involves a shift in the experience of time (i.e., time flies). Three decades after first describing this phenomenon, Csíkszentmihályi and his colleague, Jeanne Nakamura, identified six distinct factors that comprise the flow experience:

- Intense focus on the present moment
- Merging of action and awareness
- Loss of a reflective self-consciousness
- Sense of personal control over what one is experiencing
- Distorted sense of time
- The experience itself is intrinsically rewarding (aka., an "autotelic experience" which means we engage in the experience just to engage in it.)

Each of these six factors can be experienced by someone at any time; however, it is only when all six are involved that one will experience flow. Since first identifying this phenomenon in artists, Csíkszentmihályi and others studied the experience of flow in myriad contexts including school, business, and eventually sport.

When applying flow to sport, researchers found that athletes consistently described similar experiences to non-athletes. These experiences reflected nine distinct psychological factors. When athletes are engaged in sport and experience flow the activity they are engaged in has (1) an optimal balance between feeling challenging but within the athlete's skill level, (2) the athlete has clear goals they are working toward, (3) their concentration is acutely focused on the task at hand and is not easily derailed, (4) they experience a merging of action and awareness such that their sport-related activity is channeled through them (e.g., writers and composers talk about being a vessel for their work), (5) a sense of control (i.e., efficacy), (6) loss of self-consciousness (i.e., they are fully in the present moment but are not necessarily aware of themselves and what they are thinking), (7) unambiguous feedback (i.e., they *know* they are performing well), (8) what they are doing is intrinsically rewarding (i.e., they would play their sport regardless of praise and accolades from others), and (9) they experience a transformation of time (i.e., the "time flies" phenomenon).

Although anyone in a state of flow is not easily pulled out of it, flow can be interrupted by things familiar to most of us: feeling bored or anxious. Boredom typically accompanies activities we have little to no interest in or activities that are too easy for us. Being in a state of flow requires some measure of challenge, and, by definition, flow occurs when we are engaged in activities that are rewarding to us simply because we are doing them. By contrast, activities that feel too difficult can give rise to feelings of anxiety. Readers familiar with free solo climber (i.e., rock climbing without any ropes or safety equipment), Alex

Honnold, may also be familiar with the myriad documentaries that have been made on his free solo climbs; climbing the tallest rock faces in the world without ropes. In most of these films, while he is in the midst of a climb viewers can see his enjoyment, and the fluidity and certainty of his movements that seem to occur with ease. In one documentary, *Alone on the Wall*, Honnold climbed Moonlight Buttress (Zion National Park) and Half Dome (Yosemite National Park) that are 1,300 feet and nearly 5,000 feet tall, respectively. For perspective, Willis Tower (formerly Sears Tower) in Chicago is 1,450 feet high and the Empire State Building in New York is 1,250 feet high. At one point while standing on "Thank God Ledge" in the midst of his climb on Half Dome Honnold was hit with significant anxiety that left him stuck, mid-climb, for a matter of minutes. Since he was being filmed, videographers encouraged him to simply stop the climb and come back toward those who were filming (and harnessed in with myriad ropes and safety equipment). Alex is heard saying "Just a second I'm freaking out actually" (Mortimer et al., 2010, 1:20:00). He was clearly no longer in a state of flow that could easily be seen earlier on that climb. He characterized what happened as a "mini nervous breakdown" and was ultimately able to complete the climb, free solo. Essentially, anxiety, as predicted by researchers, decidedly pulled him out of flow and into a state of self-consciousness (i.e., fully aware of what he was doing and what was happening—not in a good way). It may be difficult to imagine anyone getting into a state of flow when the activity is that difficult and that death is certain if any mistake is made; however, it is important to remember that the type of activity that puts anyone in a state of flow requires that the activity is challenging but doable, and inherently enjoyable. For a highly experienced and elite climber like Alex Honnold that means climbing rock faces thousands of feet high without safety equipment when most of us would experience a good measure of fear and dread on a ladder that is too tall.

Flow is often described by those who have experienced it, in terms of things "just happening. I'm not thinking, I'm just doing" or "everything just clicked." Despite the subjective experience that things are happening flawlessly and without thought, as if executing a particular task was "easy," flow itself is a complex process with multiple facets that are not necessarily easy to activate. As noted earlier, flow is achieved only when someone pursues a personally meaningful goal that is realistically challenging for them to meet. In essence the activity is something they personally want to do, and is not too easy, nor too difficult for that person. This means, of course, that each person's experience of flow will occur under conditions unique to them. Overall, the experience of flow is that someone is "pleasurably absorbed" by an activity.

Flow has also been linked to other constructs important to athletes including mental toughness (see also Chapter 3 and the section on "Mental Toughness" for more information). Researchers interested in understanding what kind of relationship exists between mental toughness and flow also examined psychological factors that support someone being in flow. Prior research has shown that many characteristics connected with mental toughness (e.g., confidence, emotional control, and focus) are also connected to flow and may be prerequisites to flow. That is, in order to experience flow one must first have or must first develop the qualities connected to mental toughness. Psychological factors such as concentration, confidence, effective coping mechanisms, goal orientation, locus of control, optimism, and perfectionism have all been found to be connected to flow. Researchers examining these factors were curious to know if there were any differences between athletes who experienced flow and who were categorized as having either high or low levels of mental toughness. Both groups of athletes, as noted, experienced flow; however, those categorized as having a high degree of mental toughness experienced flow more regularly and in a variety of different contexts compared to athletes characterized as having low levels of mental toughness. Although the two groups experienced flow differently, including the fact that those lower in mental toughness who started an activity with a lower level of confidence took longer to get into a flow state, both groups noted that experiencing flow was not something entirely under their control. Those with a higher level of mental toughness, however, noted that being well prepared and working on their confidence were important factors for giving them a greater sense of control over flow. Concentration has independently been found to contribute to both mental toughness and flow such that athletes who were able to redirect their attention and concentration to the task at hand when things weren't going well (this is an element of mental toughness) were able to get themselves back into a state of flow.

Decreases in Symptoms of Common Mental Health Challenges

A long-standing finding related to sport participation is the benefit this activity can have on mental health-related challenges. Depression and anxiety have routinely been studied in the context of sport and physical activity; however, related issues have also been examined including levels of stress, self-esteem (see the section on Self-Esteem & Self-Confidence earlier in this chapter), and thoughts of suicide.

Although some physical activity is typically better than none, at least one study showed that a bit more engagement with sport does have greater benefits related to depression compared to less engagement. Readers who are already engaged with organized sport know that practices at the high school and collegiate levels can be 2–3+ hours each weekday outside of time spent on things like watching film or sitting in team meetings. This means 10–15+ hours a week are spent engaged in the physical side of sport. Those who have examined how time in sport can impact something like clinical depression found that increasing one's engagement with sport from two hours per week to three hours per week can result in lower scores on measures of depression. The authors involved with this study also included athletes who had a high level of involvement with sport (i.e., seven or more hours per week). Although they engaged in more hours per week in their sport, they did not show a greater benefit with respect to depression-related symptoms. The authors hypothesized that this finding might reflect a connection between overtraining and depression (see also Chapter 3 for more information on Overtraining Syndrome). To be clear, this does not mean that engaging in more or fewer hours per week will automatically result in higher or lower symptoms of depression. However, these findings do suggest that there may be an optimal level of engagement in sport that helps reduce signs and symptoms of depression, and, as is the case with most things, that optimal level will differ from one person to the next.

Related to depression is stress. Stress can be defined as "a state of worry or mental tension caused by a difficult situation" (World Health Organization, 2023, para. 1). Ongoing, unmanaged stress can lead to burnout, and burnout is a close cousin of depression. When burnout goes unmanaged, it can evolve into diagnosable depression. Physical activity has routinely been found to reduce stress levels, and is known to impact the chemicals in our brains called neurotransmitters. These brain chemicals, in particular dopamine and serotonin, both of which are active when experiencing positive emotions including pleasure, help lower stress levels and reduce symptoms of depression and anxiety.

Although athletes may be at greater risk for some mental health challenges in large part due to the demands associated with being a competitive athlete (see Chapters 2 and 3 for more information), they may also experience protective factors from these same mental health challenges *because* they participate in sport.

Conclusion

As with most chapters in this book, this one did not cover all known benefits of participating in sport. Some things such as resilience or mental toughness, and interpersonal connections are covered in other chapters. The benefits of sport participation and engaging in physical activity associated with sport can help build self-esteem and confidence, help people experience a state of flow, and reduce symptoms associated with common mental health challenges. Thus, it is reasonable to conclude that participating in sport, whether competitively or for fun, has myriad benefits that can enhance people's lives at any age.

2

Describing Mental Health and Common Mental Health Challenges in Athletes

Although there are myriad benefits to physical activity and participating in sport (see Chapter 1 for more information), participating in sport can also place some athletes at greater risk of health-related concerns including significant mental health challenges. In this chapter, we'll review what mental health is, including that it can be on a continuum from mental well-being on one end and mental illness on the other. In the context of understanding what mental health is, we'll also explore the importance of mental health literacy for athletes and all who support them. Finally, we'll review some of the more common diagnosable mental health challenges found among athletes.

Defining Mental Health and Mental Health Literacy

According to the World Health Organization (2022) "mental health is a state of mental well-being that enables people to cope with stresses of life, realize their abilities, learn well and work well, and contribute to their community" (Concepts in Mental Health section, para. 1). This means that when we are mentally well, we are able to effectively deal with whatever life throws at us, express who we are through our skills and abilities, learn and work effectively, and interact with the world around us in ways that give back to or enhance the people and places we encounter. In short, we are able to thrive in all aspects of life. Of course, many people have periods of time during which they do not feel mentally well. For some, those periods of time can extend for months and years. Some are able to appear to others as if they are functioning well but when alone or with others who know them well, they let their guard down and express how they truly feel. The reality, of course, is that there are varying degrees of being mentally well or mentally unwell.

Mental Health on a Continuum

As early as 1937, psychologist Gordon Allport noted that mental health and mental illness are not two different experiences with no relationship to one another, but that they represent the ends of a continuum. He suggested that each person may be on different points on the continuum depending on what they are experiencing in their lives. Over six decades later, in 2002 researcher Corey Keyes developed the *Mental Health Continuum* to account for the fact that mental health is not an all or nothing proposition (i.e., you are either mentally healthy or you are not). This dichotomous approach (i.e., all or nothing) has led many to believe that mental illness is the opposite of mental health. Instead, Keyes proposed that mental health is more nuanced than that and suggested that a mental health continuum included anchors of "languishing" and "flourishing," with "moderate mental health" in the middle. He noted that mental health necessarily includes feeling good and functioning effectively. Thus, someone who is flourishing in terms of their mental health would say not only that they are feeling well but that they are also doing well.

Since Keyes suggested mental health be placed on a continuum, others have identified additional markers on the continuum. For example, some continua include "thriving" on one end and "in crisis" on the other with "surviving" and "struggling" in between. Others have suggested, in order, "in crisis," "struggling," "surviving," "thriving," and "excelling." Regardless of which continuum anyone may consider to be the most useful, Allport's and Keyes' point was clearly made: mental health is not an all or nothing experience. We must understand that there are times when people struggle to function, other times when they are living their best lives, and many other times during which they are somewhere in between those two extremes.

Mental Resilience/Mental Toughness

When considering mental health and mental well-being among athletes, sport has long utilized terms such as "mental toughness" (see also Chapter 3 for more information on Mental Toughness). Having a high degree of mental toughness is considered a characteristic prized by athletes and coaches, and is thought to be necessary for success in sport. Attempts over the years to define mental toughness have led researchers to understand that this construct is multidimensional making a single definition for this construct difficult at best. Some researchers have characterized mental toughness as reflecting the ability to cope effectively with pressure so that an athlete's performance is not negatively affected, an ability to persist and not quit, being able to recover or rebound when an athlete experiences failure, having a psychological edge, and so on. Others have suggested that mental toughness is similar to the concepts of "hardiness" or "resilience."

Attempts to measure mental toughness have resulted in a theory that may capture some elements others have noted contribute to whether or not someone is mentally tough. A group of researchers led by Kostas Papageorgiou identified what they called the 4 Cs of mental toughness: control, commitment, challenge, and confidence. Others have considered whether or not mental toughness is a state-based characteristic. This debate explores whether an athlete's mental toughness is based on the situation they find themselves in, or whether mental toughness is a trait such that if someone is mentally tough they are always mentally tough, regardless of the situation. Another question associated with mental toughness reflects the ubiquitous nature vs. nurture debate: is mental toughness inherited (nature) or can it be learned (nurture)? Research on mental toughness from this perspective has not laid the question to rest; however, some researchers and practitioners have suggested that mental toughness, at least in part, can be learned and therefore taught.

However mental toughness is described, defined, or measured, and whether we're born with it or we can learn it, mental toughness does impact a person's overall well-being. Research has demonstrated that when someone is mentally tough, they are less likely to experience distress or depression-related symptoms, and are more likely to feel an overall sense of satisfaction with their lives. Research in this area has also shown, for example, that when someone who is mentally tough experiences a high degree of stress they are more likely to also experience two of the 4Cs of mental toughness: control and confidence both of which contribute to feelings of positive well-being.

When considering common mental health challenges among athletes, some may think this is oxymoronic, meaning that many people consider athletes as being examples of health (in both mind and body) and may be privileged such that they should not have much to worry about and are therefore "immune" to mental health problems. Indeed, many athletes also believe they should not have any mental health problems because it may be perceived as a sign of weakness; a long-standing taboo in sport. These perspectives may be the result of believing that competitive athletes, by definition, are mentally tough and therefore do not endure the same mental health challenges non-athletes endure, or that athletes don't deal with mental health challenges at all. This is untrue. Athletes are human beings, who are also athletes, and who encounter life struggles just as non-athletes do.

Adding to the mistaken view that athletes are automatically mentally tough and do not deal with mental health challenges is the belief that if an athlete is successful in sport, particularly at the highest levels, they must not have any mental health challenges. This belief suggests that success and mental health challenges cannot possibly coexist in the same person. The reality is that many athletes achieve a high level of success despite having significant mental health challenges. However, because some athletes achieve success while also dealing with a mental health challenge, this can contribute to the myth that any mental health challenge an athlete endures cannot be "that bad" or they would not have been able to achieve as much as they have. Michael Phelps, the most decorated Olympian of all time, revealed that he likely started experiencing signs and symptoms of depression as early as 2004 when he won six gold medals and two bronze medals at the Olympics in Athens. He capped off his Olympic competition by competing at the next three Olympic games winning a total of seventeen gold medals, and three silver medals. Michael Phelps publicly talked about "crippling" depression and anxiety experienced throughout his Olympic career including having thoughts of suicide. More recently, another storied Olympian, Simone Biles, considered by most to be the best gymnast of all time, famously removed herself from the 2020 Olympics in Tokyo due to mental health reasons that resulted in the "twisties" (a mental block experienced by gymnasts when they are in mid-air and do not have a sense of where their body is in space) which can be exceptionally dangerous. Though she received an enormous outpouring of support from fans and others who praised her decision, many were highly critical of her decision saying that she let her teammates down, that she was a quitter, and that she should not be considered a role model. These critics, many of whom were fans or journalists, essentially did not believe she needed to withdraw. These critics might be forgiven since they are not healthcare providers; however, even healthcare providers miss the mark when it comes to athletes and mental health challenges.

In 2000, physician Thomas Schwenk noted that far too often athletes presenting with the same symptoms as non-athletes were less likely to be diagnosed with a mental health disorder compared to their non-athlete counterparts. Using depression-related symptoms as an example he noted that a primary care provider of a non-athlete would likely recommend counseling and medication to help them resume their typical roles and responsibilities as they had been prior to the development of their symptoms. An athlete, with the same symptoms, on the other hand, treated by someone in sport medicine may see these symptoms as a sign of burnout or overtraining. Indeed, the similarities between burnout and diagnosable depression are many; however, such athletes are typically "prescribed" rest or a lighter workout/training schedule so they can resume performing at the level they had been. Certainly, this does not happen with all athletes and all sport medicine providers. Indeed, in the nearly two-and-a-half decades since Thomas Schwenk noted this contradiction much has changed in terms of how we see mental health generally and among athletes specifically. However, there still exist misconceptions and myths about high-performing athletes as being indestructible and that they are healthy in all ways at all times.

Although it has never been true that athletes do not and should not experience mental health challenges, in recent years, particularly since Covid-19 (see also Chapter 10 for more information on Covid-19 and athlete mental health), the mental health of all people, including athletes, has been a focus of worldwide attention. Mental health challenges have been taken more seriously by the populace, governments, and healthcare providers who may have previously overlooked signs and symptoms of mental health challenges. Among athletes, more and more high-profile athletes have publicly disclosed their own mental health struggles. In addition to the Olympians previously mentioned, other high-profile athletes who have competed in leagues such as the National Basketball Association, the Women's National Basketball Association, and the National Hockey League have come forward and publicly talked about mental health challenges that they may have been able to "hide" from fans but that impacted them significantly in and outside of sport. Athletes are not immune to mental health challenges any more than they are immune to physical injury.

Prevalence rates of mental health challenges in athletes are typically reported based on the level of sport competition (see also Chapter 5 for more information). For example, at the elite level the most common mental health diagnoses seem to appear at the same rates as they do among the general population. However, some researchers appropriately caution that not all athletes (indeed not all people) will exhibit all signs and symptoms of a specific mental health diagnosis but may still be negatively impacted by what they experience. As a result, these researchers encourage others to consider mental health as being on a continuum (see the section in this chapter "Defining Mental Health" for more information) so those who are struggling are provided the support they may need even if what they are experiencing does not conform to the criteria for a formal mental health diagnosis. Such experiences are often identified as being "sub-clinical" but still have a significant impact on a person's functioning.

Some studies have found that as many as 50 percent of athletes who perform at the highest levels have had a mental health challenge in their lifetime. A review conducted of many different studies examining the mental health of elite-level athletes concluded that those competing at the highest levels are at risk for a variety of mental health challenges that may include substance use disorders, eating disorders, depression, anxiety, and so on. This review also noted that contributing factors for these mental health challenges may be accounted for by sport-specific factors such as injury or overtraining (see also Chapter 3 for more information in Injury and Overtraining), and non-sport-related factors that can affect anyone.

Because a significant number of athletes experience signs and symptoms of myriad mental health disorders, researchers and professionals who work with athletes have encouraged athletes and others in an athlete's life (e.g., coaches, teammates, sport medicine personnel, family members) to learn about common signs and symptoms as well as how to best support their athlete generally and in getting the care they may need. This type of knowledge is part of what is called mental health literacy.

Mental Health Literacy in Athletes

Mental health literacy was first coined in 1997 and since then various programs have been developed and implemented to facilitate mental health literacy in both schools and communities. Mental health literacy is believed to include several different components such as the ability to recognize when someone's mental health is suffering (i.e., recognizing signs and symptoms), knowledge about what may cause mental health challenges including what may put someone at greater risk than others (e.g., participating in a specific sport), knowledge about what help may be available to someone including self-help and professional help, and knowledge about how to find helpful information about mental health. These components also include awareness of attitudes and beliefs about mental health, particularly with respect to the stigma that surrounds mental health generally, and in sport specifically.

As many readers know, mental health challenges in sport are historically not talked about, and if they are, they are talked about in a way that would leave many if not most athletes never wanting to admit that they are struggling in this way. Words and phrases around mental health in sport include things like referring to someone with a mental health challenge as "weak," "crazy," or a "head case." In addition, mental health challenges in athletes are viewed by some as something they should be able to easily "get over." In recent years there has been a shift in acknowledging and accepting that mental health challenges exist in sport. This is illustrated by (and perhaps because of) high-profile athletes such as Simone Biles and Michael Phelps talking about their significant mental health struggles, and in Simone Biles' case, withdrawing from Olympic competition because she knew (i.e., had a good measure of mental health literacy) if she continued to compete, she was putting her body at risk of serious injury or death (e.g., landing on her head while attempting an aerial element in a routine).

Mental health literacy programs have been implemented with sport populations with some success. One program, called *Ahead of the Game,* that was implemented with male-identifying adolescents (aged 12–18) found that this program was particularly effective with those in a low socioeconomic status who typically did not seek help when needed, and who reported having reasonably high levels of distress. When implemented with this population, the program was shown to increase overall well-being and reduce distress in athletes. Some have suggested that while improving mental health literacy among athletes is important, providing similar education to those in supporting roles is equally important.

One study implemented a mental health literacy program with "support staff" identified as either "team officials" or "staff members." The aim of the intervention was not only to increase individual's knowledge and awareness of mental health issues in athletes and to reduce mental health-related stigma, but also to improve their attitudes toward help-seeking and to improve their confidence in providing mental health support to athletes. Researchers divided participants into two groups. One group received the mental health literacy intervention, and the other group was on a waitlist meaning that they would eventually receive the intervention but not until after the study concluded. Not surprisingly the researchers found that those who received the intervention saw substantial improvements in their mental health literacy and attitudes toward help-seeking, and a reduction in mental health-related stigma compared to those who were on the waiting list. Interestingly, however, among those who received the intervention, there was no improvement in confidence in their ability to help an athlete struggling with a mental health challenge. Researchers suggested the reason for this may have been a limitation of the study itself, or that this finding may have reflected a true perception that mental health challenges should be addressed by qualified professionals (e.g., licensed sport psychologist) and therefore no amount of education for non-qualified personnel may meaningfully improve this type of confidence.

Another group of researchers focused on parents of athletes in community sports clubs. Parents took part in a brief educational program related to mental health in youth athletes. After the intervention, parents who participated in the program in comparison to those who did not, showed no difference in overall mental health literacy. However, those who participated in the program did report that they were more likely to seek help for themselves when needed, had a reduction in their own psychological distress, experienced greater support from fellow parents, and had greater confidence in themselves that they would be able to help someone who may be dealing with a mental health challenge. So, parents did not seem to learn any more about mental health as a result of the program, but what they did learn helped them personally feel better, and improved their confidence in helping themselves or others.

Another study of adolescent athletes (ages 12–15) found that a mental health literacy program improved participants' mental health literacy overall (i.e., they learned more about mental health in general), and intent to seek help when needed particularly among those who at the start of the study indicated they would not be likely to seek help for a mental health-related challenge. Another study examining the impact of a mental health literacy program among male-identifying adolescent athletes found improvements that reflect what other researchers have found with the exception of a reduction in mental health stigma. The researchers noted that some of the athletes did report a reduction in stigma as it relates to mental health whereas others saw no change. They noted that addressing mental health-related stigma may be an ongoing challenge for sport-related programs.

Coaches and athletic trainers have also been groups of focus for mental health literacy training since those in either role have a great deal of contact with athletes. Researchers have found that coaches and athletic trainers had levels of mental health literacy that were similar to those found among college students and community samples, but lower than mental health professionals. Those who identified as female among these two groups were found to have much higher levels of mental health literacy compared to those who identified as male which is consistent with studies examining mental health literacy in myriad populations (e.g., college students, social workers, and clergy members). They also found that if the coach or athletic trainer had many years of experience and/or were older in age, they had lower levels of mental health literacy. It is likely that age, rather than experience, may account for this finding since younger individuals generally are found to have much higher levels of mental health literacy.

Common Mental Health Challenges in Athletes

Although it is possible for any athlete to be diagnosed with any mental health disorder that can also be found in the general population, there are some mental health disorders that are far more common among athletes. These disorders, found in the Diagnostic and Statistical Manual of Mental Disorders, Fifth Edition, Text Revision (DSM-5-TR), are identified and described in the sections that follow.

Substance Use Disorders

Substance use disorders, according to the DSM-5-TR, involve using a legal or an illegal substance that negatively impacts a person's cognition, behavior, and physiology. Moreover, a substance use diagnosis requires that a person will continue to use the particular substance despite the fact that it is causing problems for them in one or more areas of their life (e.g., relationships, sport, work or school, trouble with the law, etc.). In this context, and according to the DSM-5-TR (2022), use of a substance results in an "underlying change in brain circuits that may persist beyond detoxification, particularly in individuals with severe disorders" (p. 483). This means that using a substance can literally change one's brain in ways that may be permanent, regardless of whether or not the person continues to use the substance.

Athletes are not immune to using substances in ways that can lead to a formal diagnosis. Sometimes the reasons an athlete may use a substance are the same as why anyone else might (e.g., as a coping strategy, or to numb thoughts or feelings); in other instances, the substances are used to gain an advantage in competition (i.e., performance enhancing). Substances may be used by athletes for myriad reasons including self-medicating for pain or anxiety, or simply to socialize. In some sports the use of substances may be part of the culture itself. Alcohol is the most commonly used substance by athletes particularly at the collegiate level, and among adolescent athletes studies have found that participating in sports may be more likely to lead to alcohol use but the opposite has been found for marijuana use.

With respect to collegiate athletes specifically, a study conducted by the National Collegiate Athletic Association (NCAA) compared substance use between athlete and non-athlete college students and reported binary gender differences in substance use. The NCAA reported in 2018 that although alcohol use among student-athletes was down from previous years, 77 percent of student-athletes reported consuming alcohol. Forty-two percent of athletes surveyed (down from 55% in 2009) stated that they engaged in binge drinking which can be defined for adults as consuming 4–5 drinks in a two-hour period. Although athletes use smoke and smokeless tobacco/nicotine products (over 10% use cigarettes; over 13% used spit tobacco), they smoke cigarettes at a rate lower than non-athlete college students. Similarly, fewer student-athletes (25%) report using marijuana products compared to their non-athlete counterparts (over 30%). Illegal substances such as cocaine (5.2%; 1.7%), ecstasy (2.4%; 1.1%), amphetamines (2.1%; 0.7%), and heroin (0.3%; 0.0%) are reportedly used by male and female (only binary genders were reported) athletes, respectively, at a rate much lower rate than the substances already mentioned: alcohol, nicotine, and marijuana. Athletes' use of prescription drugs reported by the NCAA includes narcotics (10.5%; 2.9%), and stimulants used to treat Attention-Deficit/Hyperactivity Disorder (ADHD; 6.6%; 7.5%) which were reportedly used with or without a prescription, respectively.

At the elite level the most commonly used substances include legal ones such as alcohol, nicotine, and marijuana (as of 2024 marijuana is legal for recreational use in twenty-four states plus the District of Columbia, and thirty-eight states plus three US territories and the District of Columbia have legalized the medical use of marijuana). In addition, elite athletes are likely to use stimulants that may or may not be legal, and prescription opioids which are typically used in relation to pain. Generally speaking, elite-level athletes use substances at a rate lower than the general population.

Organized athletics often deploy screening tools to identify those who are at risk for or who are currently using substances in ways that suggest a substance use problem (e.g., addiction). Recommendations include that when a substance use problem is identified the athlete should also be screened for other diagnosable mental health challenges since it is common for substance use disorders and other mental health disorders to co-occur. Athletes who screen positively for substance use or mental health challenges can then be referred to appropriate treatment professionals (see Chapter 4 for more information) for help.

Use of Performance-Enhancing Substances

The use of performance-enhancing substances (aka. doping) does not necessarily reflect a substance use disorder though one could argue that if an athlete continues to use these substances even after getting caught such a diagnosis may be considered. The use of substances to enhance performance is not a recent phenomenon. Records involving the use of substances to enhance performance date back to the time of the Ancient Olympics (i.e., 776 BCE to 292 CE) when athletes consumed figs which have been shown by modern science to aid multiple systems of the body including the respiratory, cardiovascular, and metabolic systems. During the 1800s, the use of performance-enhancing substances started to more closely mirror a mixture of compounds used by some athletes today. A number of high-profile athletes have, in recent years, been found guilty of doping, such as Alex Rodriguez of Major League Baseball, former world number one women's tennis player Maria Sharapova, and Lance Armstrong who captured seven consecutive Tour de France victories only to have them stripped years later after he was found guilty of using performance-enhancing substances over the course of his cycling career. Alex Rodriguez was banned from baseball for one year without pay, and Maria Sharapova was suspended from tennis for two years.

The World Anti-Doping Code developed by the World Anti-Doping Agency (WADA) provides a framework for policies developed and adopted by sport organizations (including the US Anti-Doping Agency [USADA]) and includes a list of all banned substances updated annually. Some prescription medications are on this list including medications for attention deficit/hyperactivity disorder (ADHD) and beta-blockers which can be used to treat hypertension (i.e., high blood pressure). Any substance on the banned list, when used by athletes, is believed to give them an unfair advantage in their sport; however, if the medication is medically necessary athletes can seek a "therapeutic use exemption." Random drug testing at certain levels of competition is thought to be a deterrent to athletes for using banned substances; however, research has not clarified whether athletes are not using substances out of fear of getting caught or if they have found more sophisticated ways of avoiding detection.

Gambling Disorder

Gambling disorder is a condition that can be formally diagnosed and treated by a licensed mental or medical health professional. Generally speaking, for someone to be considered as having a diagnosable challenge with gambling they engage in recurrent gambling that causes significant distress or impairment in the person's life. Distress or impairment can refer to things such as needing to gamble with larger sums of money in order to get the feeling they are after, feeling a high degree of discomfort if they try to stop or cut back on their gambling, being preoccupied with gambling (e.g., most of the person's thoughts are about past or future gambling including how to get money to gamble with), losing one's job or an important relationship due to their gambling behavior, and so on. Those familiar with diagnostic criteria for substance use disorders will see similarities between addiction to a substance and addiction to gambling. In fact, gambling disorder is classified along with substance use disorders in the DSM-5-TR.

Gambling among athletes at the highest levels of competition has garnered increasing attention in recent years. This is likely due, in part, to the legalization of gambling and the proliferation of online-based gambling platforms. One aspect of gambling in sport is related to "match fixing" or when an athlete or team may do certain things to ensure a particular outcome (e.g., win, or loss). If the outcome is predictable and therefore known, then gamblers can place wagers assuring they will win their bet. Even if an athlete is not intentionally "throwing" a competition (i.e., ensuring they or their team will lose), betting on one's own sport is a serious violation in most professional leagues. For example, in 2024, for the first time in over 100 years, a Major League Baseball (MLB) player, Tucupita Marcano, who played in the MLB for three years for the San Diego Padres, was banned from baseball for life because he placed over 380 bets on baseball. Contributing to an increased risk for problem gambling among athletes is the fact that in the United States sports betting businesses have established formal partnerships with several professional sports leagues including the MLB, NBA, NHL, and the WNBA. When major leagues such as these and others endorse gambling, betting on sport can seem more benign than it may be for many people who are at risk for gambling disorder.

Elite-level athletes are thought to be at greater risk for problem gambling compared to the general population due to sport being dominated by young men, athletes being highly competitive in general, an increased likelihood of engaging in risky behaviors, and a high degree of sensation seeking. Each of these characteristics is a risk factor not only for gambling but also for other risky behaviors in and outside of sport. High levels of competition tend to attract athletes who also have these other traits.

Problematic gambling at the collegiate level occurs in at least 2.9 percent and perhaps as high as 15 percent of college student-athletes. The NCAA identifies gambling activities as purchasing lottery tickets, playing card games for money, playing the stock market, gambling in a casino, betting on sports, and so on. Collegiate student-athletes who gamble, whether it is problematic in and of itself or not, were also more likely to engage in other high-risk behaviors (e.g., unprotected sex, or heavy substance use) and have symptoms of other mental health challenges. Between 2004 and 2016 rates of gambling have decreased for this population; however, overall, about 55 percent of athletes who competed in men's sports engaged "consistently" in gambling activities which was significantly higher than the rate found among athletes who competed in women's sports (38%). However, gambling behaviors in and of themselves do not necessarily indicate a problem requiring intervention. The percentage of athletes with problematic gambling behavior has decreased for athletes who compete in men's sports from 4 percent to 1.8 percent and remained under 1 percent for athletes who compete in women's sports. Thus, although gambling behavior occurs among larger percentages of all college athletes, very few gamble in ways that may be diagnosable and require treatment.

Regardless of whether or not gambling threatens the integrity of any particular sport, the reality is gambling, when it turns into an addiction, can be devastating. The financial consequences can be severe whereby people may lose their homes and important relationships, may suffer from other mental health challenges, and are at a higher risk for death by suicide. In sport, the consequences can be the same but can also include sport governing bodies which may intervene and bar an athlete from competing in their sport for some period of time or for life.

Depression and Anxiety

Depression and anxiety are mental health disorders that often coexist, meaning that if someone is diagnosed with one of these disorders, they are at greater risk of also being diagnosed with the other. Depression and anxiety are the most commonly diagnosed mental health disorders in the United States.

It has long been known that physical activity, including sport, is a protective factor for both depression and anxiety (see also Chapter 1 for more information). We know that those who engage in regular episodes of moderate physical activity have lower rates of depression and anxiety suggesting that physical activity may help to prevent these disorders from developing in the first place. Moreover, mild-to-moderate levels of depression and anxiety have been shown to decrease when individuals with these diagnoses engage in regular, moderate exercise suggesting that physical activity may be an effective form of treatment for these disorders (see also Chapter 1 for information on *Exercise Is Medicine*). Some studies have demonstrated that exercise may be as effective as antidepressant medication, and that regular exercise may prevent symptoms of depression and anxiety from returning once the individual's symptoms have waned. Exercise has not been studied in the context of anxiety to the same degree as it has been with depression. What is known to date, however, is that the impact exercise has on anxiety is not quite as profound as it is for depression. Anti-anxiety medications, for example, generally outperform exercise in reducing anxiety-related symptoms.

Although depression and anxiety can impact individuals at all ages, being in college has been identified as an "at-risk" context in which as many as 30 percent of college students have reported signs and symptoms of depression. Researchers have found that although collegiate student-athletes do not generally report low levels of self-esteem, they are at risk for developing depression- and anxiety-related symptoms suggesting that something other than low self-esteem is at play. Compared to the general population, college student-athletes may be three to four times more likely to develop depression. According to the NCAA, over 30 percent of those who compete for men's sports and nearly 50 percent of those who compete for women's sports have reported symptoms of anxiety and depression. Some have suggested that the demands of being a competitive athlete along with managing the demands of academics and relationships may account for the higher levels of these disorders among student-athletes.

Among elite-level athletes over one-third of those competing at the highest levels of sport may have diagnosable mental health challenges, and about one-third are believed to experience diagnosable levels of depression. At the high school level, it has been found that over 60 percent of athletes experience significant levels of stress that can contribute to both anxiety and depression. Regardless of the level of sport competition, it is clear that depression and anxiety among athletes can be fairly high. It is therefore important to know what to look for so athletes can receive the care they may need as soon as possible.

General signs and symptoms to look for in athletes include any changes in behavior (i.e., behavior that is different from how they usually are and is "not like them"), a decrease in performance, nonspecific physical complaints (e.g., general aches and pains that may surface as stomachaches or headaches), academic difficulties (e.g., difficulty keeping up with homework, declining grades), social isolation (e.g., avoiding social gatherings including team gatherings), and changes in eating habits (e.g., over- or under-eating). Given the relatively high prevalence of these psychiatric concerns among athletes, it is recommended that screening for depression and anxiety is conducted. Identifying mental health challenges early and getting individuals referred to qualified, licensed mental health professionals lead to a shorter duration of symptoms, lower severity of symptoms, and a quicker recovery. A process like this is beneficial for all, regardless of whether or not the person is an athlete; however, for athletes, this also means they can get back to the level of performance they know they are capable of.

Eating Disorders

Athletes are typically well aware of their bodies in terms of what they look like and how they function. For some this focus can spiral into an unhealthy pattern of eating designed to manipulate their body weight, shape, or size, and that may develop into an eating disorder. Like so many things, eating behaviors can be placed on a continuum with anchors such as "healthy" or "normal" eating and "disordered" eating. Disordered eating technically refers to eating patterns that are not healthy but are "subclinical" meaning these eating patterns may cause the individual some problems, but are not diagnosable. Other eating patterns are diagnosable and require specialized treatment.

Eating disorders are serious mental health disorders that have one of the highest mortality rates (primarily accounted for by anorexia nervosa) of any psychiatric illness. Eating disorders are currently categorized as Feeding and Eating Disorders in the DSM-5-TR; however, the focus of this section is on the traditional eating disorders: anorexia nervosa, bulimia nervosa, and binge eating disorder. Eating disorders have historically been associated with young (i.e., adolescent or young/emerging adults), white, females; however, eating disorders do not discriminate and impact all genders, all races and ethnicities, and all ages. And, in the context of sport: all sports.

When comparing the prevalence of eating disorders in sport compared to the general public, some research has shown the rate is about the same whereas other research suggests athletes are at higher risk for developing an eating disorder. The rationale for the latter is believed to be connected to the dual pressures athletes face relative to conforming to society's standard of beauty or attractiveness, as well as conforming to the expectations of their sport. This can be particularly challenging for athletes whose sport requires a physique for performance excellence that differs from what society expects for attractiveness. For example, women's rugby star Ilona Maher helped her team win a Bronze medal at the 2024 Olympics in Paris, the first Olympic medal for US women's rugby sevens, by an upset victory over Australia. Ms. Maher has also garnered attention for her lip sync videos posted on a popular social media site. After posting a video during the Paris Olympics a commenter noted, "I bet that person has a BMI [BMI stands for body mass index] of 30" (Anbouba, 2024, para. 2). Ms. Maher confirmed that was pretty close to accurate, adding that "I've been considered overweight my whole life" (Anbouba, 2024, para. 2). She further added that "I chatted with my dietician. Because I go off of facts. BMI actually isn't helpful for athletes because it just goes off of height and weight and what that equals" (Anbouba, 2024, para. 4). She noted that she has 170 pounds of lean muscle mass which artificially inflates her BMI. She ended her comment with "But BMI doesn't tell you what I can do on the field or how fit I am" (Anbouba, 2024, para. 4). She is 100 percent correct. Many professional athletes (think basketball and American football players) have BMI numbers that would place them in the "ob*se" category. For example, in 2016 it was reported that the average BMI for the entire Denver Broncos football team fell into the ob*se range. Ms. Maher is an excellent example of two things: (1) having a body type that greatly benefits her for her sport is not what society views as attractive, and (2) understanding that one's body can do amazing things, and that one does not need to manipulate it or change it because of something like BMI. It is important to note that using one's BMI as an indicator of health is highly flawed for myriad reasons including those Ms. Maher identified. There are more and more articles published, both professionally and in online media outlets, revealing the flawed nature of this measure and how it should no longer be used as an indicator of one's health.

When athletes, however, struggle to accept that the type of body they need to perform well in their sport either does not match society's standards of attractiveness or does not match the athlete's natural body type, some will manipulate how much they eat and how much they train or exercise to get the "right" body. With respect to specific sports, participating in some sports may place athletes at a higher risk of developing an eating disorder.

Eating disorders, in the context of sport, are more likely to surface in sports that are categorized as lean (e.g., distance running), aesthetic (e.g., gymnastics), having revealing uniforms (e.g., swimming), having weight classes (e.g., wrestling), and/or are judged (e.g., figure skating). Some sports can be categorized by more than one of these aspects which is believed to place athletes at even greater risk of developing an eating disorder compared to those competing in sports that only have one of these elements. For example, gymnasts (particularly those who compete for women's teams) are expected to be lean, perform aesthetically, wear revealing uniforms, and are judged. Not surprisingly, athletes who compete in gymnastics have a higher rate of eating disorders compared to other sports that have fewer of these sport-related risk factors.

It is imperative to identify athletes at risk for an eating disorder and/or who are showing signs of an eating disorder as soon as possible. The longer an eating disorder goes unidentified and untreated the much more difficult it is to recover from. For athletes this can mean a significant decline in performance, or in extreme cases, the necessity to leave their sport altogether. In some instances, it can be quite difficult to identify who may show signs of an eating disorder. Many years ago, practitioners, Ron Thompson and Roberta Sherman, working in the specialty area of eating disorders and athletes, noted that it can be difficult to identify some athletes with an eating disorder because they have characteristics that reflect both being a "good" athlete and having an eating disorder such as anorexia nervosa. For example, an athlete with an eating disorder may engage in excessive exercise but to others they may appear to be highly committed to their training. Coaches may look for athletes who respond to their suggestions and criticisms indicating that these athletes have high coachability; however, for an athlete with an eating disorder this may be less about being coachable and more about being overly compliant. Individuals diagnosed with anorexia nervosa often deny any discomfort, which means they may be inaccurately viewed as a highly committed athlete who can perform despite physical pain. These attributes in and of themselves are not specific symptoms of any eating disorder but are commonly associated with anorexia nervosa, specifically, and can make quickly identifying an athlete at risk for this diagnosis quite difficult.

The historical focus on those who identify as female (athletes and non-athletes) in the context of eating disorders has meant that male-identifying athletes are frequently overlooked. Symptoms that would lead to an eating disorder diagnosis in an athlete competing in girl's/women's sports may be dismissed as a phase or as another diagnosis such as depression (e.g., under-eating can be associated with depression) for those competing in boy's/men's sports. A by-product of this focus on biological females as it relates to sport was something called the "female athlete triad:" menstrual irregularities, low bone density, low caloric intake. The idea was that if one element of the triad was identified the other two should be assessed. The female athlete triad, of course, could not apply to biological males, nor could it apply to pre-pubescent or menopausal biological females. Following the female athlete triad some researchers identified a male athlete triad replacing, for example, menstrual irregularities with low testosterone. Both syndromes were still lacking in terms of the breadth and depth of what can happen in athletes of any age and any sex who do not consume enough calories. Researchers and practitioners in the area of eating disorders in athletes eventually identified a number of signs and symptoms reflecting a syndrome that can sometimes be connected to an eating disorder and can also exist outside of an eating disorder. This syndrome, called relative energy deficiency in sport

(REDs), can still be quite problematic for the health, well-being, and level of performance of an athlete of any sex, any age, and competing in any sport.

Relative Energy Deficiency in Sport (REDs)

In the last decade, myriad researchers identified what is called relative energy deficiency in sport which is often known by its abbreviation and moniker: REDs. The initial element is low energy availability (LEA) (i.e., relative energy deficiency) based on what is needed to be a competitive athlete (the syndrome can also be found in exercisers who are not competitive athletes). Essentially, the athlete is not eating enough to account for how much fuel their body requires to be a competitive athlete. Michel Phelps famously consumed approximately 12,000 calories a day while training for and competing in the Olympics. His body required that amount of fuel to maintain his training regimen and to be able to perform at his best. Had he consumed less than his body required there is an excellent chance he would have experienced many of the symptoms associated with REDs including a decrease in performance.

Originally identified in 2014 through a consensus statement of the *International Olympic Committee* (IOC), what was known about REDs was updated in 2018. Since that time over 170 research studies were conducted contributing to the most up-to-date knowledge about REDs and how to identify it. The IOC published their most recent consensus statement in 2023 based on the wealth of knowledge gleaned from this body of research. When athletes (or anyone) consume less than what their body needs, all systems of the body can be negatively impacted. That is not hyperbole. All systems of the body are negatively impacted when an athlete regularly does not consume what their body requires to function each day and to perform at a competitive level. This can result in myriad problems that athletes and their coaches will likely notice and include: decreased power, decreased recovery, decreased response to training (i.e., they are not seeing expected improvements as a result of training), decrease in specific skill execution, decreased muscle strength, decreased endurance, and a decrease in an athlete's availability. Decreased athlete availability refers to the fact that the athlete is literally not available to train or compete because they are unwell, have chronic injuries, or do not have the energy to do what they need to do. Although REDs is not a mental health diagnosis found in the DSM-5-TR, early identification of REDs is critical for athlete well-being and performance. It is important, therefore, that athletes work or occasionally consult with a registered dietitian who specializes in sport and is knowledgeable about REDs so they can help the athlete ensure they are fueling for optimal performance.

Body Dysmorphic Disorder (BDD)

Body dysmorphic disorder including a specific type, muscle dysmorphia, has been linked to eating disorders but does not always lead to an eating disorder. However, since an unhealthy preoccupation with a specific element of one's body is the hallmark symptom of body dysmorphic disorder, it is not surprising that someone may also develop an eating disorder (see the previous section Eating Disorders for more information).

Body dysmorphic disorder is a diagnosable mental health disorder classified in the DSM-5-TR in the category of *Obsessive-Compulsive and Related Disorders*. Body dysmorphic disorder is primarily characterized as someone having a "preoccupation with one or more perceived defects or flaws in physical appearance that are not observable or appear only slight to others" (APA, 2022, p. 242). Essentially what this means is that the individual believes there is something significantly, physically wrong with some part of their body; however, no one else sees what they see. For example, someone with this disorder may see a freckle on their face as being "huge" and overtaking their face while others barely or do not notice it. Individuals with body dysmorphic disorder often scrutinize the perceived flaw in a mirror for an extensive period of time, may pick at the perceived flaw, and are likely to repeatedly ask others for reassurance about their appearance. The reassurance, however, typically does little to quell the person's concern. Some people diagnosed with body dysmorphic disorder may also undergo multiple medical procedures to fix what they see as wrong with their body, and, like with reassurance seeking, the medical procedures do not typically placate the person's concerns.

Many diagnosable mental health disorders have what are called "specifiers." A specifier is intended to provide additional information about the diagnosis and may include things like the severity of the symptoms, when the symptoms appeared in the person's developmental trajectory, or specific features that further clarify the nature of the person's symptoms. A specifier for body dysmorphic disorder reflects whether or not the person's primary concern with their body has to do with their musculature. In that case, the diagnosis would be *body dysmorphic disorder, with muscle dysmorphia*. This specifier typically reflects a person's fixation on feeling like their musculature is insufficient (i.e., their muscles are too small and/or are asymmetrical). Additional non-clinical terms used to describe body dysmorphic disorder, with muscle dysmorphia are "muscle dysmorphia" and "bigorexia."

Although a number of studies have been conducted to examine the prevalence and nature of *body dysmorphic disorder, with muscle dysmorphia*, a published review of the literature in this area noted that many studies did not acknowledge the fact that *muscle dysmorphia* is a type of body dysmorphic disorder, and in some cases, did not accurately indicate the presence of *muscle dysmorphia*. Nonetheless, there are findings consistently found across these studies that apply to athletes.

As has been previously discussed in this book, physical activity generally has a positive impact on people's self-esteem as well as their overall body image. However, those diagnosed with *body dysmorphic disorder, with muscle dysmorphia* often have poor body image meaning that they do not have positive thoughts and feelings about their physical appearance. This specific form of body dysmorphic disorder is typically found among weight lifters and bodybuilders, and is consistently found at a higher rate among those identifying as male compared to female. Recently, researchers have noted that this specific diagnosis shows up with more regularity among adolescents identifying as boys or girls. Moreover, although most research has focused on studying those in Western cultures, additional research in recent years reveals that *body dysmorphic disorder, with muscle dysmorphia* is "a growing, global mental health dysmorphic concern" (Sandgren & Lavallee, 2023, p. 316) that extends into non-Western countries.

For some people, this disorder may develop because they are already involved with bodybuilding- or weightlifting-oriented sports. Others may participate in these sports *because* they have this particular disorder. Excessive time and other resources spent on weightlifting activities are believed to be an attempt to calm the concerns and anxiety surrounding the person's perceived flaws with their muscles. As one study noted "despite their intense training, [these individuals] perceive themselves as having less *sport ability* and *physical condition* to practice sports, and with less *strength* and *physical attractiveness*" (González-Martí et al., 2014, p. 6). These researchers found that weightlifters and bodybuilders who do not have symptoms reflective of this diagnosis are able to engage in weightlifting- and bodybuilding-related activities in a psychologically healthy way, and have a positive perception of their physical abilities and appearance.

Although *body dysmorphic disorder, with muscle dysmorphia* is overwhelmingly found among bodybuilders and weight lifters, it is not exclusive to these activities and like all other disorders can be found in any sex, any sport, and any age.

Conclusion

Mental health is believed to exist on a continuum and should not be thought of in terms of the presence or absence of a mental health diagnosis. Developing one's mental health literacy can help individuals understand, recognize, and support those who may be struggling with a mental health challenge, including themselves. Despite the various benefits associated with participating in sport, athletes are not immune to mental health challenges and in some cases participating in sport may be the cause of a mental health challenge or make an existing challenge worse. Early identification of signs and symptoms of any mental health challenge is important for the athlete's overall well-being and for their performance in sport.

3

Biopsychosocial Factors Affecting Mental Health in Athletes

This chapter introduces a common paradigm for understanding human behavior called the biopsychosocial approach. A brief discussion of what this approach is and generally how it is used is the preface for a more in-depth discussion on athlete-specific factors categorized as biological, psychological, or social (to include cultural factors). As is the case in many areas of this book, this chapter does not address all possible athlete-specific factors but provides a starting point for readers to consider the ways in which the three elements of this approach can impact athletes, and offers at least a partial understanding of what they may experience.

What Is the Biopsychosocial Approach?

The biopsychosocial approach involves considering three factors to help explain behavior: biological, psychological, and social/cultural factors; all of which interact with one another. Biological factors can include genetics (what someone inherits from their biological relatives), how a person's body processes information that comes in through our senses, medical illnesses that in and of themselves may impact mood or mental health (e.g., hypo- or hyper-thyroidism), and so on. Psychological factors involve how we each uniquely process our experiences to include how we think and feel about our experiences and how we interpret them. For example, someone who is diagnosed with anxiety is likely to have very different thoughts, feelings, and interpretations of a situation that causes them anxiety (e.g., giving a speech in front of an audience) compared to someone experiencing the same event but does not have diagnosable anxiety. Finally, social/cultural factors refer to our relationships with others and how the culture in which we live and/or were raised impacts our well-being. For example, do the people in our lives reliably provide support when needed? What belief systems does our culture expect us to have that may impact our overall well-being (e.g., what is considered to be "good" behavior or "bad" behavior). According to the biopsychosocial approach, understanding a person from each of these three perspectives is essential to understanding who they are and why they behave the way they do.

Biological Factors

Biological factors are certainly important for understanding who and why a person may experience what they experience. In recent years there has been a shift to finding the biological explanation for most everything that can be studied which has led some to rely exclusively on biological factors to explain why someone behaves as they do. However, researchers have noted that while understanding how biology plays a role in our experiences, including mental health, biological factors do not provide the whole picture. This means that biological factors must be considered but stopping there is not sufficient for fully understanding a human being and their experiences. Following this section on biological factors will be separate sections on psychological and social/cultural factors.

Genetics

When talking about biology in the context of genetics, we're talking about what we inherit from our biological relatives. Scientists who study genetics have, in recent years, found genetic explanations for many diagnosable mental health challenges. Critics have noted that genetics themselves do not create well-being or illness. The *National Institute of Mental Health* (NIMH) noted that the majority of genetic markers associated with one mental health disorder or another do not directly *cause* that mental disorder to appear. If genetics did cause such disorders that would mean that every human being with a particular genetic marker would have the disorder in question—this is not the case. Even identical twins (who have identical genetics) don't always develop the same physical or mental health disorders or illnesses. It is known that many mental health disorders run in families (who are genetically related) therefore knowing your biological family history as it relates to mental health can help you understand that you may be at greater risk for a particular mental health challenge due to this genetic family history. However, as noted above, just because a family member is diagnosed with a particular disorder does not mean you will be too. The reverse is also true. If your biological family history is silent for any mental health challenges, that does not mean you will not develop a mental health challenge.

Beyond genetics, researchers and clinicians understand that psychological stress can impact how our hormones are deployed throughout the body which can subsequently negatively impact our physical and psychological well-being. We also know that when our immune system (i.e., the system that helps us fight off infection and disease) is active we experience inflammation. If our immune system is overactive and we experience too much inflammation for too long, we are much more susceptible to diagnosable mental health challenges. Inflammation has also been linked to problems with our cardiovascular system which in turn can negatively impact our mental health. A full examination of how the body's systems impact mental health is beyond the scope of this book. However, it is clear that there are myriad systems in the body that when not functioning optimally can impact certain diagnosable mental health challenges including things such as depression and anxiety.

The sections that follow will briefly explore some of our body's systems and how they function in the context of physical activity or sport.

The Gastrointestinal System, or Your "Gut"

One system of the body that has received a great deal of attention in recent years is the "gut" or the gastrointestinal system also known as the gastrointestinal tract. This system includes a long tube-like structure that processes food after it is consumed, and is made up of your stomach, intestines, and colon. This system is responsible for getting important nutrients into your body, and for getting rid of waste. When we think of our gut or our gastrointestinal system, we usually think of how our food is digested and processed. We rarely consider the impact of how the design of this system may impact the rest of the body including the brain. The gut-brain connection (aka, the gut-brain axis) was identified in the 1840s. The gut is believed to contain as much as 80 percent of all immune cells in the body. As noted previously, effective immune system functioning is critical for fighting illness, infection, and injury which includes diagnosable mental health challenges. Thus, a well-functioning gut is critically important for the mind and body to function at its healthiest.

It has long been known by researchers and healthcare providers (including mental healthcare providers) that a healthy body leads to a healthy mind (and vice versa), and regular physical activity contributes to this benefit. Most of what is currently known about the positive impact exercise has on the gut-brain axis is predominantly accounted for by aerobic exercise (i.e., a form of exercise that uses large muscle groups and is rhythmic and repetitive such as walking or running) compared to anaerobic forms of exercise (e.g., strength training). However, many people, athletes included, tend to think that when something is known to be good for us, then as we do more of that thing, we should experience more and more benefits. This is not always true including in the context of the gut-brain axis. In some cases, strenuous or prolonged physical activity has been found to negatively impact blood flow to the gastrointestinal system and is implicated in something called *endotoxin susceptibility*. Endotoxin susceptibility causes things such as fever, nausea, low blood pressure, and shock. In studies with rodents (which are often studied to understand how human systems function) that engaged in "exhaustive exercise" several days in a row resulted in an increase in inflammation, fatigue, and problems with learning and memory. Research like this suggests that human beings can experience a similar, problematic outcome.

Diet/Nutrition

Most people, including athletes, know that what we put into our bodies matters. Many athletes also know that how well an athlete fuels their body can impact their performance; however, it can also impact risk of injury and overall well-being.

Recent research conducted with college athletes has shown that high quality and sufficient quantities of food are not always readily available. One study found that collegiate athletes' "dietary quality was poor based on US dietary guidelines for the general population" (Werner et al., 2024, p. 1309), whereas another found a high rate of food insecurity among female-identifying athletes (they reportedly did not have enough male-identifying athletes participate to make a comparison). Research on the impact of diet and nutrition on athlete performance is extensive and many athletes, particularly those competing at the highest levels, have their dietary intake down to a science. Athletes at elite levels typically know (or someone knows for them) precisely when they need to fuel and precisely what they need to replenish (e.g., specific nutrients) and in what quantities. They know this based on a typical day of training, harder days of training, and what is needed to properly fuel during a competition. In addition to all other factors that contribute to high performance, being properly fueled puts the athlete in the best position possible to perform at their very best. Much less is known about how adequate or inadequate fueling may be related to mental health in athletes (see also the section on REDs in Chapter 2).

A study conducted in 2021 examining factors that impact mental health in collegiate athletes noted that diet (i.e., what someone eats) was one of several factors that have been examined in terms of their respective impacts on physical health but not on mental health. These authors found, for female-identifying athletes only, that unhealthy eating habits (i.e., eating fast food, candy/cookies, chips or salty snacks, drinking caffeinated soda and/or energy drinks, and frozen food meals) and not paying close attention to their nutrition (e.g., how often did the person make sure they were eating healthy proteins) contributed to high levels of psychological distress. The researchers speculated that this finding (in those who identify as females but not those who identify as male) may reflect the fact that female-identifying athletes tend to have more significant concerns related to body image compared to their male-identifying counterparts, and that female-identifying collegiate athletes have been found to have higher-quality knowledge about nutrition than male-identifying athletes.

Even though there is not much research in the area of dietary intake and mental health among athletes, we know that what we eat impacts our overall well-being, and there is extensive research noting that the health of our "gut" impacts our brain which impacts our overall well-being (see the preceding section: The Gastrointestinal System, or Your "Gut"). Thus, what is in our gut matters and therefore what we eat matters.

Sleep

Adequate sleep is necessary for things such as the body's ability to repair itself and recover. Sleep is certainly impacted by how well our body is functioning; however, it is also impacted by psychological and social factors. Despite this, the importance of sleep on a person's mental health will be discussed here in the biological section of the biopsychosocial approach.

Athletes can require more sleep than non-athletes due to the high need for recovery from training (see also the section on Overtraining Syndrome in this chapter). It is believed that adolescent athletes, for example, require ten hours of sleep when they are in the most rigorous episodes of training. Although this is on the upper end of what is recommended for people aged 13–18 years old according to the Centers for Disease Control and Prevention (CDC), it is still more hours than we typically think are needed. Of course, the amount of sleep needed from one person to the next will vary based on what their body needs including how much recovery time is needed related to training for competitive sport. Not getting enough sleep and having poor quality sleep have been linked to myriad mental health challenges, including depression, anxiety and stress, and have been linked to lower social support. In addition, not getting enough sleep impacts our ability to think clearly and make good decisions, and can lead to poorer performance in sport.

One group of researchers presented a case study of an adolescent athlete who experienced sleep problems and overtraining. A number of issues affecting the athlete's sleep were identified (e.g., insomnia, restless leg syndrome) and treated; however, the athlete continued to report fatigue and "sleep attacks." What was found to help was to reduce the athlete's training load, specifically the intensity level, and when this was implemented, the athlete saw reductions in daytime sleepiness. Thus, sometimes, for competitive athletes, difficulty with sleep may not be about a diagnosable sleep disorder (though in this case that was also present), and fatigue may not be about not getting enough sleep. Sleep difficulties and fatigue may be connected to overtraining in sport.

Overtraining Syndrome and Overreaching

Normal training for an athlete means that their body is intentionally overloaded to disrupt the balance, or homeostasis, that the body is in. The result is that the body is temporarily, and expectedly fatigued but ultimately benefits from this effort in terms of improved performance. Training can vary in volume and intensity, and high-level athletes carefully construct training plans to maximize performance improvements which involve incorporating adequate fueling and rest. Overtraining, however, can result in tissue damage to the body and can result in injuries to bones and tendons.

Researchers out of California, Nekisa Haghighat and Todd Stull, suggest that overtraining syndrome can be placed on a continuum. This can be helpful since overtraining syndrome is the "last stop" on the continuum. Thus, there are earlier indications that something might not be quite right and therefore can be identified and corrected prior to getting to the deleterious effects of overtraining syndrome. These researchers suggest two points on the continuum prior to hitting overtraining syndrome that have to do with "overreaching." Overreaching refers to feeling run down, likely with muscle soreness, and typically occurs when there is not sufficient recovery between workouts. However, if caught early, the effects of overreaching can be reduced and eliminated with adequate rest and a temporary reduction in training load. The two types of overreaching that can occur prior to an athlete developing overtraining syndrome are functional overreaching (FOR) and non-functional overreaching (NFOR). Functional overreaching is characterized by a period of two weeks or less during which the athlete experiences a decrease in performance. That period is then followed by "supercompensation" when the body rebounds briefly with improved performance in order to compensate for training-related stress (on the body). The second spot on the continuum toward overtraining syndrome, non-functional overreaching, is characterized by a decrease in performance that exceeds two weeks up to 3–4 weeks after which there is not a period of supercompensation. Once an athlete gets to the end of the continuum and is dealing with overtraining syndrome the recovery time can take months and in extreme cases years for the body to sufficiently recover.

There are myriad signs that an athlete may be overtraining and are noticeable in a variety of ways. Signs of overtraining syndrome include muscle soreness that is not typical or is not what would be expected (e.g., soreness after increased weight on lift days may be expected, whereas soreness with the same weight would likely not be expected) following a workout, the inability to keep training at the level one has been training (e.g., intensity level, duration, etc.), performance levels that seem to be going backwards or not advancing, "heavy legs," and frequent thoughts about shortening training or thoughts of skipping training. Non-sport-related signs of overtraining include ongoing fatigue, more tension than usual, greater irritability or a lower mood than what the athlete typically experiences, difficulty relaxing, sleep problems, overall low energy levels and low motivation, and loss of enjoyment in activities. Health-related signs of overtraining include frequent illness, increases in blood pressure and heart rate at rest, missed or irregular frequency of menstruation, loss of appetite and weight, and gastrointestinal issues that may include constipation or diarrhea.

Estimates suggest that at elite levels of competition 20 to 60 percent of athletes experience overtraining syndrome at some point during their competitive careers, and the risk of overtraining over one's lifetime is estimated to be 64 percent for male-identifying athletes and 60 percent for female-identifying athletes. As with most diagnosable concerns, once an athlete experiences overtraining syndrome, they are much more likely to experience it again in the future. One study found, for example, that among athletes who already experienced an episode of overtraining syndrome, 91 percent experienced another episode within a year. In youth athletes, risk factors for overtraining syndrome include training volume, overscheduling (i.e., doing too many things/engaged in too many activities), pressure to perform by parental figures, coaches or peers, having a high athletic identity, and not having basic psychological needs met (i.e., autonomy, competence, relatedness). The result of all of this can be athletes leaving sport altogether out of necessity due to the negative impact on their bodies and minds.

Multiple factors can contribute to overtraining syndrome including training load, quality of sleep, medical ailments, environmental stressors such as heat or cold, humidity or altitude, interpersonal stressors, and work- or school-related stress. Thus, it is important for athletes to take stock of all areas of their lives, not just that which is sport-related, to determine how much they are asking of their bodies and to determine how much time for rest and recovery is truly needed for their performance, as well as their overall well-being.

Injury

Sport-related injury is exceptionally common among athletes and it is often a matter of when, not if, an athlete will be injured. Of course, not all injuries are created equal. Some sport injuries are relatively minor and may require a brief assessment and treatment on the sidelines by athletic trainers or other sport medicine professionals with the result being the athlete immediately returning to practice/competition. On the other end of the continuum are severe injuries that are career ending. Just as sport injuries can vary so can an athlete's reaction to injury.

Most athletes would rather not get injured and if they do, they do everything they can to return to play as soon as possible. Sometimes that may mean not providing the entire truth about the impact of the injury to sport medicine staff and/or to themselves. The desire to return to competition can so strongly override telling the truth of the impact of the injury that major sport organizations have hired independent medical professionals to assess the nature and severity of an athlete's injury. The National Football League (NFL), for example, uses independent neurologists to assess brain injury (i.e., concussion; see Chapter 11 for more information on Concussion).

The more severe the injury, regardless of the type of injury, the more likely it is that an athlete will view the injury as a significant and negative life event. Researchers have determined that an unexpected injury that requires a lengthy recovery process is an important factor contributing to a decline in the mental health of the athlete. It is important to consider that some reactions to sport-related injury would be expected whereas other reactions can become problematic for the athlete. For example, an injury that keeps an athlete out of practice or competition for some measure of time is likely to result in frustration, anger, or impatience for an athlete. This type of reaction would not be surprising to anyone who knows or works with athletes. Problematic reactions to a sport-related injury are those that do not seem to subside and get worse over time. In short, it is expected that injured athletes would not be happy about any injury; however, if their reaction keeps getting worse and negatively impacts other important aspects of their life (e.g., academics/work, relationships) the athlete may require additional, specialized support (see also Chapter 4 for more information on treatment).

It is not uncommon for athletes who experience injury to develop concurrent mental health challenges, such as depression, anxiety, and eating disorders. Researchers examining the connection between injury and return to sport have found that athletes who experience high levels of stress and anxiety around their injury and have strong worries about getting reinjured when they do return to play may not fully recover from their injury. Injured athletes who are also diagnosed with depression, for example, have been found to experience higher levels of pain, and if their injury required surgery, are likely to have more complications following surgery compared with athletes who are not diagnosed with depression. For some athletes, having a high level of athletic identity (see the section on Athletic Identity later in the Psychological Factors section of this chapter) may fuel them to participate fully in their recovery and follow recommendations so they can return to their sport as soon as possible.

The biological systems and factors discussed in this section are highly complex and the brief surface-level descriptions do not do them justice; however, it is clear that these systems and factors clearly affect and are affected by one another. This means, of course, that when any one system is not functioning properly there is a very good chance that other systems of the body will be negatively impacted and may ultimately lead to mental health challenges and/or exacerbate existing ones. Finally, many if not all of these biological factors are impacted by some of the psychological and social factors discussed in the following sections.

Psychological Factors

Psychological factors refer to our internal thoughts and feelings about our experiences in sport and in life that in turn impact how we think, feel, and behave. What follows is an overview of some psychological factors found specifically among athletes.

Mental Toughness/Resilience

Mental toughness can be defined as a person's ability to continue to pursue a goal despite significant obstacles and barriers that make it more difficult to achieve. Resilience refers to a person's ability to effectively cope with adversity. Although the definitions of these two concepts are not identical, they are very closely related and the terms are often used interchangeably. Specific training programs to help people develop the skills to withstand difficulty and to persevere are typically referred to as resilience programs or resilience training. However, when training around this is specific to sport, more likely than not "mental toughness" or "grit" will be used in place of resilience. For that reason, the term "mental toughness" will be used throughout this section.

Knowing what mental toughness is can help athletes identify and cultivate it; however, it can also be important to know what mental toughness is not. Given that the pervasive climate in sport is to not show weakness and to "tough things out" mental toughness can be misunderstood to mean that a mentally tough person shows no emotion or "weakness," never fails, has no fear, and has never wavering self-confidence. In fact, mental toughness refers to the ability to experience things like perceived "weakness," failure, or fear but understanding why those things are experienced and to learn from them. A mentally tough person can be identified by their ability to experience something unpleasant, such as unpleasant emotions, and allow that experience to teach them about what is going on and how they are responding to it. Mental toughness is about recognizing obstacles, understanding their impact, then figuring out what to do next so an athlete can continue to effectively pursue their goals. This might include bulldozing through an obstacle, but it might also involve a systematic dismantling of it, or finding a way around it.

Researchers examining the importance of mental toughness as it relates to mental health and performance in athletes have used the basic psychological needs mini-theory that is part of self-determination theory developed by Edward Deci and Richard Ryan. Deci and Ryan proposed, and have found substantial evidence for, the notion that when our basic psychological needs are met, we will perform at our best. The basic psychological needs mini-theory includes three components: autonomy, competence, and relatedness. If our need for autonomy is met then we believe, or perceive, that what we do is self-governed. That is, we believe our decisions are our own and that we are free to choose. When our need for competence is met, we believe that we can do what we need to do in order to reach our goals. And, finally, if our need for relatedness is met, we believe that we have relationships in our lives that are meaningful and satisfying. Deci and Ryan note that since mental toughness can be construed as also supporting optimal human functioning, then considering mental toughness in the context of meeting these basic psychological needs makes a great deal of sense. For example, researchers have found that developing mental toughness in an athlete requires that they receive support to make self-directed decisions (i.e., autonomy support). When they are allowed to explore various options and make decisions that fit them (autonomy) they are able to develop desired skills and challenge themselves (competence). When this is allowed to happen, athletes also feel supported by those within that environment (e.g., coaches and teammates) and tend to feel valued and respected (relatedness). When an athlete's basic psychological needs are met, they have greater mental toughness.

An additional and interesting area of inquiry around mental toughness was pursued by researchers who wondered: "Can athletes be tough yet compassionate to themselves?" (Stamatis et al., 2020). In short, the answer is yes. These researchers found that athletes who reported higher levels of self-compassion (i.e., being kind to one's self) also had higher levels of mental health/wellness. Higher levels of mental health/wellness were, in turn, also associated with higher levels of mental toughness. They noted that athletes struggling to persist in the face of adversity benefitted from being compassionate with themselves during the struggle (e.g., not beating oneself up for struggling), and this was found to enhance athletes' mental health. The researchers tied their findings to what this may mean for the NCAA's guidelines outlined in the *Mental Health Best Practices* document. The newest version of this document was released in 2024 and in this version the authors' findings are most relevant to NCAA's Best *Practice 1: Create Healthy Environments That Support Mental Health and Promote Well-Being.* The researchers noted that institutions that support and teach mental toughness and self-compassion in athletes will bolster athlete mental health and well-being by encouraging athletes to learn how to manage stress in all forms, and to learn skills that promote their overall well-being and self-care.

Additional research in the area of how mental toughness may interact with mental health in athletes found that higher levels of mental toughness were not only connected to higher levels of well-being, as found in other studies, they also found that mental toughness helped athletes resist the stigma associated with seeking help for one's mental health. Although these researchers did not examine whether these athletes actually sought help for their own mental health when needed, the implication is that the more mentally tough an athlete is, the more likely they are to seek their own help and perhaps encourage teammates to seek appropriate help when needed. Others have suggested that having a high level of mental toughness may lead to athletes viewing help-seeking as a form of weakness; however, this presumption is likely connected to a view of mental toughness as exemplifying a "no pain no gain" or a "man up" mentality which, as noted at the start of this section, does not accurately represent what mental toughness truly is.

Overall, there appears to be ample evidence that mentally tough athletes have a high level of resilience that translates to better mental health for themselves, a greater likelihood of seeking mental health support when needed, and encouraging others (including teammates) to seek similar help if they, too, are struggling with their mental health. To that end, it is important that those who interact with athletes (e.g., coaches, sports medicine professionals, sport mental health professionals, and so on) understand what mental toughness is and what it is not. When everyone understands what mental toughness truly looks like, we are better able to teach athletes what mental toughness really is, what it looks like, and how to develop it. Helping athletes become mentally tough will help them face fewer mental health challenges and be better equipped to manage them if they do occur.

Performance Enhancement and Mental Skills Training

Performance enhancement or mental skills training refers to skills an athlete can develop with or without the aid of a mental skills consultant (e.g., a sport psychologist, or certified mental performance consultant®). Working with a mental skills consultant can help athletes acquire skills more quickly and understand the nuances of these skills when used by a specific athlete in their specific sport, during a specific point in the competitive season, and so on. Mental skills involved in sport that help to improve or enhance performance can include goal setting, self-talk, imagery, relaxation, team building, emotional regulation, pre-participation/pre-skill routines, concentration and focus, and so on.

Yogi Berra, a former Major League Baseball manager, was (in)famous for quotes that made sense and didn't make sense at the same time. For example, he has been quoted as saying "Baseball is 90% mental. The other half is physical." Peyton Manning, a former quarterback in the National Football League, was quoted as saying "Pressure is something you feel when you don't know what the hell you're doing." And, Michael Jordan, former National Basketball Association player, and for some, the GOAT of men's basketball, has said "Obstacles don't have to stop you. If you run into a wall, don't turn around and give up. Figure out how to climb it, go through it, or work around it." Each of these quotes points to the importance of managing the mental aspects of sport and competition. Managing pressure, learning to control what is controllable, and effectively dealing with adversity are key mental skills that serve athletes well at all levels of competition. Another way of looking at this, particularly at the highest levels of competition, is that the physical talent at elite levels is nearly the same. Generally speaking, elite athletes are among the best athletes in the world. Thus, it can be, and has been, argued that what differentiates good athletes from great ones is mastering the mental side of the sport.

Robin Vealey, a highly regarded professional in the world of performance enhancement, recently proposed a model that depicts how mental training and mental health fit in with sport. Dr. Vealey advocates for the newly proposed model in part because mental health has become a recognized outcome of effective mental performance consulting and gains in mental wellness can be seen in work with non-licensed professionals (non-licensed professionals in the United States cannot ethically or legally diagnose or treat mental illness). Dr. Vealey argues that the field of mental performance consulting should identify and deploy interventions that support and enhance both an athlete's mental health and their mental health literacy (see Chapter 2 for more information on mental health literacy).

Performing at one's best in sport (or other domains in one's life) can result in feeling a sense of satisfaction or enjoyment, and possibly a state of flow (see also the section on Flow/Being in the Zone in Chapter 1 for more information). Essentially, the relationship between mental skills and mental health is reciprocal in that developing strong mental skills can contribute to better overall mental health, and better mental health can contribute to more effective development and use of mental skills designed to enhance sport performance. Thus, it can be reasonably argued, as Dr. Vealey does, that helping an athlete enhance their performance via mental skills training can contribute to mental well-being.

Athletic Identity

A group of researchers, led by Britton Brewer, formally defined and developed a measurement of athletic identity in the early 1990s. These authors defined athletic identity as "the degree to which an individual identifies with the athlete role" (Brewer et al., 1993, p. 237).

Athletic identity can be considered a complicated sport-related factor. A high athletic identity, for example, can help an athlete with performance such that with a high athletic identity an athlete is much more likely to devote as many resources (e.g., time, money) as they can to their sport. The more an athlete spends learning as much as they can about their sport including how elite athletes train and prepare for competition, reviewing film, honing their skills, developing team-related relationships and so on, the more likely they will see an improvement in their performance. On the other hand, when an athlete highly identifies with this role and the role is threatened in any way such as through injury, retirement, performing poorly, or a career-ending injury, such athletes often struggle with their mental well-being in large part because they do not know who they are without their sport. Some researchers have found that when athletes have what they perceive to be a poor season they may distance themselves from the athlete role thinking that their sport was not really that important to them. It is suggested that this attitude shift may be adaptive by reducing the negative emotional impact of having a poor season.

An additional downside of having a strong athletic identity is that it is often accompanied by "foreclosure." Foreclosure in the context of identity means that someone has decided who they are (i.e., what their identity is) without taking time to explore other possible roles or versions of themselves. Essentially, someone who is foreclosed in their identity decides prematurely who they are and who they will be. Although this may sound like a good recipe for high achievement in sport (and it can be), problems arise when that identity is threatened in some way or removed altogether. Most athletes have a very short "shelf life" in sport which means they have to retire from sport very early in life since the body is only capable of high-level performance for a very limited time.

Regardless of the why or how an athlete may experience their athletic careers in the context of athletic identity, it has been recommended that athletes, before their athletic career is threatened in any way, consider who they are outside of sport. Certainly, this process can be fraught since athletes cannot necessarily predict when their athletic career may unexpectedly come to an end and therefore may resist considering life-after-sport. Athletes who are able to plan for the end of their athletic career tend to fare better and typically have time to explore who they are outside of their sport. The Covid-19 global pandemic (see also Chapter 10 for more information on the impact of Covid-19 on athletes) was one such circumstance in which athletes suddenly found their access to sport was either severely limited or cut off altogether resulting in negative consequences for many athletes.

Given the substantial, and for some, devastating, impact Covid-19 had on competitive seasons, many athletes struggled to be mentally and emotionally okay due to the loss or significant disruption to their lives as athletes. Researchers in the United States and Canada surveyed collegiate student-athletes on athletic identity, mental health, and social connectedness or isolation in the context of Covid-19 and found that some athletes reported a stronger athletic identity following campus closures and cancellation of competitive seasons. They explained this by noting that these athletes were able to maintain social connections with teammates, albeit via physical distancing thereby preserving their athletic identity. Retaining this connection and preserving their athletic identity were linked to a lower degree of mental health challenges indicating that staying connected to the athlete role by staying connected to those involved with their sport (e.g., teammates) meant that athletes were more likely to fare better in terms of their mental well-being compared to those whose athletic identities waned due to disconnection from their sport. For some athletes, the disruption to sport due to Covid-19 was devastating and many felt lost without sport. An international group of researchers examining the impact of the end of a sport career identified ways in which some athletes who were highly identified with their role as an athlete were able to effectively weather that particular storm.

The definitive end to a sport career can be very difficult to manage for many athletes, particularly those whose sense of self revolves around their sport. An international team of researchers from Australia, China, and Belgium examined what happens to athletes when their competitive careers end. In particular they examined athletic identity, interpersonal relationships, psychological resources, and adjustment to determine what factors contribute to athletes who fare better than others when they retire from sport. They found that the loss of athletic identity contributed to difficulty with adjusting to their new reality (i.e., life without competitive sport) such that athletes reported a loss of meaning in their lives, and the sense that things in general felt beyond their control. However, when athletes maintained important social networks following retirement from sport or established new social networks the impact of the loss of athletic identity was not as profound. Keeping already established social networks can help athletes feel a sense of control, and establishing new relationships can help athletes identify a sense of meaning in their lives outside of sport.

Burnout in Athletes

Burnout occurs when someone undergoes ongoing stress that is unmanaged. Symptoms include energy depletion or exhaustion, negativism or cynicism, reduced effectiveness, loss of empathy, social withdrawal, and cognitive impairment. Essentially when someone is burned out, they feel it physically and mentally. Burnout can happen to anyone at any time; however, the impact of burnout received a great deal of attention during Covid-19 and since.

The impact of burnout is expensive. Estimates of healthcare-related costs (physical and psychological) in the United States due to burnout during the time of Covid-19 were $125–$190 billion; worldwide estimates were $150–$350 billion. Although burnout is not an official medical or psychological diagnosis, it has been included in the 2019 publication of the *International Classification of Diseases-11* (ICD-11) as an "occupational phenomenon." This means that burnout may be noted in someone's medical record as a factor that impacts their overall well-being and that may worsen symptoms associated with any diagnosed diseases or disorders.

When someone endures unmanaged, ongoing stress their body responds with the fight-or-flight response. The body's fight or flight response is activated when the brain registers a threat of any kind. Although stress may not seem like a "threat" per se, the reality is that the brain cannot differentiate between a mortal threat that would require someone to literally fight or flee, and a psychological threat such as giving a public speech or performing in an important competition. Any threat is registered as a potentially mortal threat by the brain and activates the body's protective system that mobilizes us to take action by directing blood flow to the extremities. When this system is chronically activated, as it is with unmanaged, ongoing stress, the body's immune system is compromised making it more difficult to fight off illness resulting in inflammation throughout the body that is typically linked with chronic illness (e.g., cardiovascular disease, diabetes, autoimmune disease, and cancer). In addition, there can also be measurable changes to the brain's structures and functions.

An entire issue of the *Sport Psychiatry* journal published in 2024 was devoted to the problem of burnout in athletes. In this issue researchers noted that examining burnout in athletes started in the 1980s and has since been characterized as a multidimensional phenomenon including experiences similar to those noted in the description of burnout in general: athletes may start to resent their sport or begin to see it as not as important as it used to be (i.e., a reduction in athletic identity), and they may experience exhaustion both physically and emotionally. Current estimates of burnout among athletes may be as high as 15 percent; however, researchers predict this percentage to climb as increasing expectations of athletes also climb in terms of training load, competition, and performance-based pressure in general.

Causes of burnout in sport are not likely surprising for those who have competed in or who are an avid fan of competitive sport. These causes include the pressure to consistently perform at a high level, meeting expectations that an athlete has for themselves or others have for the athlete (e.g., coaches, teammates, family), consistently striving for goals, and the demands of performing in sport including the hours required for training. In addition to these performance-related stressors, if relationships among teammates and between athletes and coaches are not good, then the negativity associated with these relationships can contribute to burnout. For younger athletes, the pressure to participate in sport year-round can reduce or eliminate recovery time and contribute to overtraining syndrome (see also the section on "Overtraining Syndrome and Overreaching" earlier in this chapter)—all of which can be factors in burnout.

A study conducted examining the nature of the coach-athlete relationship found athletes who characterized their relationship with their coach as "negative" reported higher levels of burnout-related symptoms in general and in sport specifically. Symptoms associated with sport-specific burnout include athletes feeling "wiped out," feeling like they are not as invested in their sport as they previously have been, feeling less motivated to perform well, feeling exhausted by the demands of their sport, feeling like they want to use the energy spent in sport in other areas of their life, and so on. These researchers also examined what role, if any, mental toughness may have on burnout and found that, overall, the more mentally tough an athlete was the fewer burnout related symptoms they had. However, when the relationship between the coach and athletes was poor, mental toughness did not seem to alleviate burnout symptoms in these athletes. Therefore, if an athlete perceives their relationship with their coach to be a negative one, mental toughness is not likely to prevent or help manage burnout (see also Coaching Style in the Sociocultural Factors section of this chapter).

Burnout in athletes has also been examined in the context of the basic psychological needs (i.e., autonomy, competence, and relatedness) proposed by self-determination theory. When athletes do not have these needs met by their coach, in particular the need for autonomy, they are less likely to experience positive emotions and more likely to experience burnout. The good news is that coaches can learn how to support athlete's basic needs and when they do, athletes do not show an increase in burnout.

A unique examination of burnout in sport explored the impact of what the researchers refer to as "savoring." Savoring in sport occurs when athletes do things that allow them to keep feeling positively about their sport. This may involve sharing positive experiences in sport with others (e.g., being selected for a team, or winning), fully being in the moment and being fully aware of a positive experience in sport, showing how happy the athlete is, and thinking about the importance of and meaning of the positive experience they had. Savoring positive experiences has been associated with increased happiness immediately following a positive experience, improved life satisfaction, less stress, lower levels of depression, and less burnout. Essentially this means that athletes who are able to fully experience, share, and appreciate what they love about their sport are far less likely to experience negative psychological effects including burnout. An additional factor that is related to how athletes experience their sport is called psychological flexibility.

Psychological flexibility refers to the ability of being aware of one's thoughts and feelings in an objective, curious manner, rather than being judgmental or critical. This type of flexibility can help people better understand their internal experiences by noticing them, not judging them, and responding to them in a non-defensive way. Researchers have found that athletes who have a high degree of athletic identity and who are also able to be psychologically flexible with their sport-related experiences will be less emotionally exhausted (an important element of burnout) because they can accept and cope with negative experiences in sport. Whereas athletes with a high degree of athletic identity and low psychological flexibility are much more likely to experience emotional exhaustion which can lead to burnout.

Although burnout in athletes has garnered more attention over the years from researchers and practitioners (e.g., sport psychologists), some have suggested there is much more to learn about what burnout in athletes looks like and how it can be prevented and managed. Specifically, some researchers have called for a greater understanding of burnout as a multidimensional syndrome in athletes, the impact of burnout on athletes, how recovery fits in with burnout, the importance of athletes' relationships with others, and how to develop effective prevention and treatment programs for burnout (i.e., most burnout-related interventions were developed in the context of occupational burnout).

As previously noted, the impact of burnout can be extensive and therefore burnout in an athlete will probably lead to a decline in performance and overall well-being. Athletes can become exhausted both physically and psychologically, and they can experience a drop in motivation for their sport. The impact of burnout in athletes also places them at risk for injury and illness (e.g., they may be more susceptible to things like colds and the flu, or Covid-19). However, athletes who are able to savor their sport, have psychological flexibility, who feel supported by their coach, and feel a sense of community in sport are likely to experience less burnout.

Sociocultural Factors

As previously noted, the social part of the biopsychosocial approach involves social interactions and influences that can also involve the culture(s) in which we were raised and in which we live. Culture can be defined as the beliefs, values, expectations, and behaviors that are shared and that define a particular group. Any group can have its own culture and can include nations, religious groups, families, neighborhoods, and sport.

Sport Culture

Athletes have consistently underutilized mental health services and one of the most significant factors for that has to do with sport culture and the stigma associated with mental health. Terms such as "head case" are used when athletes struggle either with their mental game or with their mental health specifically. Athletes who acknowledge struggling with their mental health have been called "weak." When Simone Biles, the most highly decorated gymnast in the sport's history, withdrew herself from competition at the Summer Olympics in Tokyo in 2021 she received an enormous amount of support for her decision; however, there were many who were less than impressed that she prioritized her mental health and physical well-being (she experienced the "twisties" which can be exceptionally dangerous for gymnasts performing routines with aerial elements) over competing at the Olympics. Disparaging comments about Simone and her decision were made by those in and outside of sport; however, most if not all seemed to reference how athletes are "supposed" to be: immune from mental health challenges of any kind.

An article proposing a mental health intervention program tailored specifically for athletes noted that contributing to athletes underusing mental health services was the concern that mental health providers would not understand the importance of sport nor the culture of sport and therefore many athletes felt like any services received would be a "waste of time." The authors noted that anyone providing health-related services to athletes should be familiar with sport culture, and the needs that are unique to athletes that may differ depending on the developmental age of the athlete, the gender of the athlete, and at what level of competition the athlete performs. For athletes, sport and their associated competitions are not "just a game" and many athletes engage in behaviors that reflect an often prevailing element of sport culture: win at any cost.

Of course, the negative elements of sport culture as they relate to mental health are not present within all sport programs, organizations, or teams. Whether or not these stigmatizing elements are present has to do with the values and beliefs of the coaches involved as well as the organization that supports the athletes. The NCAA, for example, has recently enacted legislation that requires all Division I programs to make mental health services available to athletes. Professional sport organizations in the United States and around the world employ sport psychologists who are licensed to provide mental health treatment when needed. Many high-profile athletes have publicly disclosed their own mental health struggles and treatment they received. Those who have done so have not escaped ridicule but have, in various ways, clearly stated that struggling with one's mental health and seeking help does not mean the athlete is weak. Time will tell if acknowledging that mental health challenges occur with athletes will become fully integrated into sport culture, and whether seeking mental health support will be as routine as going to the athletic trainer to get one's ankle taped.

Coaching Style

Coaching style is a factor that has been linked to the overall well-being of athletes. Myriad coaching styles have been identified over the years, including controlling, autocratic, democratic, reciprocal, problem-solving, and so on. The nature of the coach-athlete relationship is critical and can impact whether an athlete continues in a specific sport or in sport at all, and how invested the athlete is in training and competition. Thus, the athlete-coach relationship can impact the well-being of the athlete. Depending on the coaching style implemented with their athletes, coaches can bolster all of the aforementioned factors or diminish them.

A controlling style of coaching means that a coach is likely to use coercion and threats to impose on their athletes what they want to have happen, and are likely to ignore any input from or reactions of their athletes. This style, however, results in the loss of autonomy for athletes which means that they will not feel like they have a say in anything that occurs to them in the context of their sport. An autocratic coaching style eliminates coercion and threats but the coach will make definitive decisions without much, if any, input from athletes and is likely to result in lower team cohesion and impaired communication. This approach can be effective when there are strict guidelines to follow, and can benefit a coach who needs to make a decision quickly without time for input from others; however, there is also an accompanying loss of autonomy as seen with the controlling style of coaching. Since both of these coaching styles contribute to a loss of autonomy for athletes, neither style is recommended. There is a good deal of research examining the importance of autonomy support in sport and the benefits that has for the athlete's performance and overall well-being. Autonomy support can be found in the democratic style.

The democratic style of coaching can leave athletes feeling valued and empowered to have a say in what happens in their sport and on their team (i.e., they have autonomy support). Ideally, time can be taken to solicit input from athletes; however, when input is solicited and welcomed it can take a good deal of time for a decision to be made making this style inefficient and not ideal for situations in which a quick decision must be made. When there is time to gather input from athletes, this style is highly recommended.

There are many more styles of leadership that have been applied to and studied in the context of sport. Generally speaking, leadership that thwarts athlete autonomy (i.e., athletes do not feel as though they have a say in what happens to them), such as the controlling coaching style, can negatively affect athletes. One coaching style that has been found to have a positive impact on athletes specifically is referred to as "authentic leadership." This approach to coaching has been associated with positive mental health in athletes. Various researchers have offered explanations of what authentic leadership is and have characterized this style as one in which the leader or coach engages in behaviors that accurately reflect what they truly value and ground those values in a code of ethics. This style is believed to comprise four elements. First, the coach understands what their own strengths and weaknesses are and how what they do and say impact their athletes. In addition, the coach does not disguise their genuine thoughts and feelings while also minimizing showing "inappropriate" emotions (e.g., explosive anger). Coaches who are authentic leaders also engage in thoughtful consideration of all information available to them, including ideas from athletes, prior to making any decisions. Finally, authentic coaches use their "internal moral standards" as a compass to help direct their behaviors. A study that examined authentic coaching and its impact on the mental health of athletes found that such a style can be exceptionally beneficial for athletes. This style encourages athletes to work cooperatively rather than being focused on what they can accomplish individually and discourages athlete behavior that can be considered "antisocial" such as any behavior that may harm or negatively impact their teammates.

Coaches adopting an authentic leadership style can indirectly and positively impact athlete mental health challenges by enhancing what researchers referred to as "psychological capital." Psychological capital has been defined as "a collection of four healthy psychological states that enhance well-being and performance—hope, efficacy, resilience, and optimism" (American Psychological Association, 2023, para. 2) and has been found to result in things such as performing at a higher level, being more engaged and satisfied with what someone is doing, lower levels of burnout, and higher overall well-being. When a coach is able to enhance athletes' psychological capital, they facilitate the athlete's self-belief that they have what it takes to perform well, the athlete's sense of optimism and hope, and their ability to cope with and effectively endure difficulty (i.e., resilience). Coaches who value these things in their athletes are likely to adopt an authentic leadership style with their athletes.

Teammates

There is no doubt that an athlete's teammates, whether in an individual or team sport, are important and can influence an athlete's overall well-being. The research on the importance of social support in general (e.g., support by friends, family, dating partners) is substantial and is regularly tied to better mental health overall. When someone is experiencing mental health challenges a strong supportive social network can help individuals, athletes, and nonathletes, more effectively cope and heal. Research examining the positive impact of supportive teammates on athlete well-being has found that athletes are less likely to experience burnout (see also the section on "Burnout" in this chapter), experience greater enjoyment from their sport, and feel better emotionally. By contrast, teammates who are generally negative and critical can contribute to the development of anxiety and low self-esteem, and may exacerbate these and other mental health challenges including problematic eating behaviors.

Although teammates in any sport context can be helpful or harmful, researchers did find that among adolescent athletes, those who participated in team sports (e.g., soccer) were more likely to feel better about themselves, have fewer depression-related symptoms, and feel a sense of belonging compared to those who participated in individual sports (e.g., distance running). Researchers have speculated that by participating in sport within a team context, athletes are more likely to experience social support when something goes wrong or a mistake is made simply because there are literally more people involved in the performance. Individual athletes, however, have been found to have a better ability to focus and concentrate compared to their team sport counterparts. Individual athletes have also been found to be more self-reliant which can contribute to developing mental toughness (which has been linked to good mental health; see the section on Mental Toughness/ Resilience earlier in this chapter).

There is no doubt that athletes benefit from support from myriad relationships beyond coaches and teammates. Families, sport medicine personnel, sport psychology professionals, and so on all can support or detract from an athlete's overall well-being. Coaches and teammates, however, spend the most time with the athlete in the context of sport and therefore can have a significant influence on how well an athlete is doing in sport and in life.

Bullying in Sport

The quote at the top of the page on "Bullying and Sports" on the *StompOutBullying.org* website is: "In the sports world, there is a fine line between competitive play and bullying." Televised coverage in the United States of the 2024 Summer Olympics in Paris saw a controversial advertising campaign. A very well-known sports company, most famous for their shoes, produced a commercial with a quote throughout "Am I a bad person?" In it they flashed high-profile athletes competing in all manner of sports at various ages with aggressive and dismissive looks on their faces with the voiceover saying things like "I have no empathy," "I want to take what's yours and never give it back," "I don't respect you," and, "I have zero remorse and have no sense of compassion." These comments may reflect an attitude of bullying and many have criticized this advertisement as glorifying a win-at-all-costs mentality, no matter who may get hurt, and argue that this advertising campaign moves dramatically away from competitive play and the competitive spirit. Though, of course, many would argue this campaign precisely embodies the competitive spirit of sport. Regardless of one's opinion about the appropriateness of the message in this advertising campaign, there is no doubt that bullying in sport is a problem.

Bullying in sport can be defined to include instances where one or more members of a team intentionally do or say something to hurt another teammate. This can take the form of verbal bullying that involves things like taunting or name calling, and may include threatening language. Physical bullying may involve physical violence that is not part of the sport and that is unwanted. And, bullying in sport can include relational or social bullying. This type of bullying involves exclusion from relationships or gossiping about a teammate or saying things about the teammate publicly that are embarrassing for that teammate. Bullying in sport is a global problem and can have significant consequences on the person being bullied. A group of researchers who interviewed Spanish athletes aged 17–27 found that victims of bullying in sport generally characterized the impact of bullying as "suffering." The athletes described feeling sad, helpless, angry, lonely, and anxious. In at least one case, the athlete described what can be characterized as panic attacks (a severe anxiety reaction characterized by things such as difficulty breathing and chest pain). Another athlete described declines in motivation and concentration which, not surprisingly, negatively impacted their sport performance.

Consistent with other research on bullying in general, the athletes who were interviewed often used ineffective coping strategies such as feeling resigned to the situation, and not asking for help. The authors noted that not asking for help is in line with traditional sport culture that defines the need for help in any way as a sign of weakness. Researchers have called for sport organizations, and all those involved in athletes' lives, to devote resources to raising awareness of bullying in sport and the impact it can have not only on the well-being of the athlete but also their performance. Moreover, they noted the importance of taking this type of education a step further by creating protocols to help prevent bullying altogether, and to outline how bullying will be dealt with when it occurs so all athletes feel safe in sport. Bullying can, of course, occur via social media which in and of itself can contribute to mental health-related challenges.

Social Media

Social media (e.g., platforms such as Instagram®, TikTok®, WhatsApp®, X® [formerly Twitter®], etc.) is believed to be used by nearly 5 billion people, as of 2023, and anywhere between 70 and 90 percent of social media use is accounted for by those who live in the United States. Research conducted on the impact of social media use on well-being has clearly and consistently shown that the longer someone uses social media the greater the risk for developing things such as depression, anxiety, and body image disturbance.

Social media certainly has benefits to include being able to connect with others one might not otherwise be able to connect with (e.g., geographically distant family members), and to be exposed to helpful and informative content one might not otherwise be exposed to. The latter, ideally is accompanied by the ability to discern helpful, accurate information from that which is not. The ability to do this is referred to as social media literacy. Any type of media literacy (e.g., digital literacy) involves a person's ability to identify information relevant to what someone is looking for and to be able to critically evaluate how accurate and credible that information is. Researchers attempting to describe and define social media literacy recognized that although literacy skills for social media could fall under other types of literacy (e.g., media or digital literacy), there is enough that is unique about social media that developing unique skills for using such products is important. Researchers, for example, emphasize the interpersonal communication that occurs on social media that does not occur with other forms of media (digital or otherwise) and have identified competency areas that can demonstrate when someone is literate in their use of social media. These competencies are targeted toward preventing both mental and physical health problems that can arise from use of social media and other negative consequences such as cyberbullying, spreading of harmful information, etc. These competencies include the technical knowledge and skills need to effectively use a social media platform (e.g., posting content, and sharing others' content), the ability to analyze the relevance and reliability of information encountered via social media, morality-related competences equivalent to "do no harm" to others when using these platforms, critical thinking related to the persuasive impact of social media platforms and content, and so on.

Athletes, of course, are not immune to the negative aspects of social media and not to the fact that the use of these platforms may impact their mental health. There are some factors associated with the usage of social media that are unique to athletes. Social media can help athletes connect with their fans by posting videos of what they do, offering their thoughts about issues important to them, making others aware of organizations and causes that are important to them, and so on. Social media, however, also opens the door to athletes' critics and online "trolls," and opens the door to those who might use an athlete's fame or future earning potential against the athlete (see also Chapter 12 on Name, Image, and Likeness [NIL]). A review of the published literature on social media use among athletes notes how social media use impacts athletes' "body image, stress, sleep quality, performance, social connection, and financial implications" (Merrill & Faustin, 2023, p. 153). The researchers noted that there is very little research in this area but enough to conclude that athletes as well as those who regularly and directly interact with athletes (e.g., athletic trainers, coaches, sport psychology professionals, etc.) should be trained to recognize how social media can be harmful, and to learn how to use social media in ways that are healthy and ultimately life-enhancing for athletes (i.e., they need to develop social media literacy).

There are additional negative aspects of social media and athletes. For example, stress and burnout among athletes can come from the pressure to perform and live up to their own and others' expectations. More and more athletes are feeling the pressure to "perform" on social media by posting content, providing "behind-the-scenes" looks at what their life as an athlete is like, etc. They also have to be exceptionally careful about what they post, since their content can be construed to not only represent themselves, but also their team, their institution (e.g., college, professional team), their sport as a whole, or sponsors who may have entered into an NIL contract with the athlete (see also Chapter 12 on Name, Image, and Likeness [NIL]). All of this can contribute to higher levels of stress for athletes which can lead to anxiety, burnout, and depression.

Social media use among athletes has also been shown to negatively impact sleep. Sleep can be affected by how long someone uses social media as well as the time of day they access and use social media. Studies in this area have found that using social media for more than five hours or using social media within one hour of sleep negatively impacts sleep quality. Sleep issues can negatively impact most areas of our lives and for athletes that include their sport performance (see also the section on Sleep earlier in this chapter). In addition, inadequate sleep can affect the effectiveness of recovery for an injured athlete; they can experience mental fatigue and overall cognitive functioning both of which can lead to mistakes including those in practice, competition, or the rehabilitation process. One study tracked late-night social media posting with sport performance the following day and found that late-night social media use was connected to a decline in performance the next day. Another study found that as little as a half an hour of social media use prior to sport-related training contributed decreased response times, an increase in mental fatigue, and problems with effective decision-making during training.

Despite all of these negative aspects of social media, there are some benefits for athletes specifically in terms of financial incentives and the ability to socially connect with others. In terms of financial benefit, some athletes, particularly those with lucrative NIL deals (see Chapter 12 on Name, Image, and Likeness [NIL] for more information), can use their social media platforms for self-promotion and attracting sponsors (i.e., those who would sign NIL deal with an athlete). The more followers an athlete has, the more likely they are to benefit financially. Even high school students can benefit financially in that the more they post to social media (specifically X®—formerly known as Twitter®) the more collegiate scholarship offers they may receive.

In terms of social media and personal connection, social media platforms can be effectively used to facilitate communication among teammates and with coaches. This can help with strengthening in-real-life (IRL) relationships and overall support, particularly with respect to rookie athletes or athletes who cannot compete due to injury. Athletes can also use social media to promote causes and issues that are important to them. Using social media to foster positive social interactions can serve as a buffer against mental health challenges. The key, however, is to be sure an athlete knows how to navigate and use social media to avoid harmful content and harmful use, which brings us back to the importance of social media literacy training for all who support athletes, and for the athletes themselves.

Going beyond the Biopsychosocial Approach

Although the biopsychosocial approach to understanding athlete behavior can be useful, a special issue of the *Sport Psychiatry* journal suggests that health-care providers should move beyond the biopsychosocial model in the ways it is traditionally used, and to consider social issues that impact society as a whole including how these broader societal issues directly impact individual athletes or teams. For example, it was suggested that healthcare providers, of any kind (i.e., mental health, or physical health), be aware of and speak out about racism in sport. The authors noted that racism within sport includes expression of racism in violent ways, ways in which racism is systemic or woven into an entire system such that established policies and procedures may present obstacles or barriers to some athletes who want to participate in sport, and so on. A poignant example involves a world-renowned golf club, Augusta National Golf Club (aka, Augusta National) a prestigious club on the Professional Golfers' Association of American (PGA) tour, allowed the first Black golfer to play in 1975; however, being a Black *member* of Augusta National was not allowed until 1990.

An editorial published in the special issue of *Sport Psychiatry* led by Adres Schneeberger refers to "hidden" forms of racism also known as covert forms of racism that are woven into systems and policies so effectively that they don't obviously appear to be racist which allows those who support such systems to deny that there are any problems. Microaggressions are an example of more covert forms of racism and other forms of prejudice and discrimination. For example, someone might say "Wow! You're really a good quarterback [American football]; I had no idea gay people could play football let alone be good at it!" Some readers may immediately see the problems inherent in such a statement whereas others might not. It is highly likely that someone who makes such a comment believes they are complementing the athlete. Similarly, some readers may be familiar with a phrase that shows up in many contexts: "You (throw, catch, run, etc.) like a girl." Recently advertising campaigns have attempted to turn such statements on their heads by demonstrating what female athletes look like when they are engaged in sport. Spoiler alert: they look like athletes. Just as racism may be systemic throughout sport, so can sexism and other forms of prejudice.

The idea behind awareness of these and other significant societal issues is that they should not be ignored and should be discussed with athletes in terms of the ongoing impact racial and other issues continue to have on athletes. Including these broader social issues when considering athlete behavior enhances the biopsychosocial perspective in explaining why an athlete may behave the way they do.

Conclusion

There are a multitude of factors associated with one of the three facets of the biopsychosocial approach that impact athlete well-being, and mental health specifically. Some of these factors can be both positive or negative (e.g., social media), depending on the circumstances, while other factors can only be seen as negative (e.g., bullying). Overall, those who research and work with athletes have consistently called for more awareness of issues related to athlete mental health, and the development of programming that specifically tends to the unique needs of athletes. In addition, some have suggested that as comprehensive as the biopsychosocial approach is including a consideration of how broader social issues (e.g., racism, sexism) may impact athlete behavior will contribute to a more thorough understanding of an athlete's behavior.

4

Determining Whether an Athlete Has a Mental Health Challenge

Athletes encounter unique stressors and challenges that can make them vulnerable to mental health challenges that may require diagnosis and treatment. They also encounter stressors and mental health challenges that mirror those found among the general population. Regardless of the source of any stressor or specific mental health challenge, identifying signs and symptoms of existing or developing mental health disorders is critical so the athlete may receive the support and treatment they need to keep them at practice and able to compete. Moreover, being on the lookout for this type of information can also help athletes return to sport should their symptoms be significant enough that pausing their sport participation is indicated. For athletes, the pre-participation examination required at most levels of sport competition is an ideal process in which mental health screening can be included. By including mental health screening in this process, those conducting such screenings can make a referral to a qualified, licensed mental health professional who can determine if a mental health diagnosis is warranted and who can recommend the best course of treatment.

Pre-participation Examinations/Screening

Pre-participation examinations (PPE) of athletes are strongly recommended at every level of competition. The purpose of such an assessment is to identify any existing medical problems that may require attention prior to the athlete participating in sport. In addition, these types of assessments can identify risk factors for specific conditions (e.g., cardiac disease) so the athlete can be appropriately monitored and referred for treatment when indicated. Historically, PPEs focused on physical health exclusively. Over the years those working in sport have recognized that mental health challenges are quite common among athletes. Therefore, evaluating the presence or risk of developing a mental health challenge has been deemed as equally important. Thus, screening for mental health challenges is regularly included as part of the pre-participation examination process.

The *International Olympic Committee* (IOC) developed the *Sport Mental Health Assessment Tool-1* (SMHAT-1) to be used with athletes so signs and symptoms of common mental health challenges can be identified early. This particular tool was developed for use by licensed medical or licensed mental health professionals. Those who are not licensed are directed to use the *Sport Mental Health Recognition Tool-1* (SMHRT-1). Non-licensed people who can use the SMHRT-1 include the athletes themselves, loved ones of the athlete, coaches, teammates, and so on. The purpose of this tool is to identify the possibility of a significant mental health challenge without diagnosing anything.

The *National Collegiate Athletic Association's* (NCAA) *Sport Science Institute* developed the *Mental Health Best Practices* document that identifies four specific best practices including:

1. Clinical Licensure of Practitioners Providing Mental Health Care
2. Procedures for Identification and Referral of Student-Athletes to Qualified Practitioners
3. Pre-Participation Mental Health Screening
4. Health-Promoting Environments that Support Mental Well-Being and Resilience.

In "Best Practice 3," *Pre-Participation Mental Health Screening*, the NCAA recommends but does not mandate that mental health screening be included in the PPE process. They emphasize that if this type of screening is conducted, a clear procedure for when a referral to appropriate professionals should occur and who those professionals are should be identified. The NCAA (2024) further notes that decisions about which screening tools to be used "should be made in consultation with the primary athletics healthcare providers and the licensed practitioners who are qualified to provide mental health services to student-athletes" (p. 13). Those who are qualified to provide mental health services are those who are licensed to do so and can include licensed psychologists, licensed counselors, licensed clinical social workers, and so on. Ideally, these licensed professionals will also have education and training in working with athletes. For example, the *Society for Sport, Exercise, & Performance Psychology* (also known as Division 47 of the American Psychological Association) developed the *APA Sport Psychology Proficiency* and notes that this proficiency "recognizes specialization in sport psychology" that includes "training in psychological skills of athletes, in the well-being of athletes, in systemic issues associated with sports organizations and in developmental and social aspects of sports participation" (Society for Sport, Exercise, & Performance Psychology, 2012, Abstract section). Whatever procedure is used to screen for mental health challenges among athletes, the procedure should be appropriate to the age of the athletes.

Finally, it is recommended that screening for mental health challenges strategically occur throughout an athlete's season and off-season. For example, screening at the start of an athlete's season can provide a baseline measure of their mental well-being. These scores can then be compared to later screening when, for example, the athlete experiences a significant injury or a sport-related transition (e.g., career-ending injury, or the end of their high school or collegiate athletic career). For high school and college students, screening again around mid-term exam and final exam times can also help identify when an athlete may be struggling with their mental health related to ongoing stressors outside of sport.

General Signs and Symptoms of Mental Health Concerns

It is not within the scope of this book to outline signs and symptoms for all possible mental health disorders that can be diagnosed (see also Chapter 2 for some commonly diagnosed mental health disorders in athletes); however, this section will briefly describe common signs and symptoms that indicate a person is or may be dealing with a mental health challenge. As you will see in the descriptions below, noticeable changes in a person's behavior tend to be a hallmark signal that something is not okay for the individual regardless of whether or not they are an athlete. They may simply need some additional support from friends, family, and teammates, or they may require some measure of treatment with the help of a licensed professional.

Social Withdrawal or Social Isolation

Social withdrawal means that the athlete is no longer as social as they have previously been. They may stop hanging around friends or teammates outside of practices and competitions, they may stop engaging in activities they usually participate in, or they may no longer enjoy those activities. Social isolation refers to having very few if any social contacts. It is important to note that having a small group of friends or one to two good friends does not constitute social isolation, just as having a lot of friends does not mean an individual has strong social connections. What matters is the quality of those relationships. If an athlete cannot identify anyone they feel connected to, that is a sign that they may need support. It is possible that some athletes may not feel particularly connected to their teammates but have strong relationships outside of sport; thus, it is important to understand the nature of the athlete's myriad relationships beyond how many relationships they may have.

Changes in Behavior

A change in behavior is a somewhat nebulous sign since changes in behavior can refer to nearly anything, and does not always mean there is a problem. However, if an athlete starts acting in ways that are odd or erratic for them (e.g., they are regularly committing fouls or penalties when they historically do not), if they stop meeting obligations or responsibilities that they typically meet (e.g., not showing up on time for practices or missing them altogether), or if you know them quite well and they just seem "off" in some way it is worth reaching out to them and possibly help them get connected to a licensed mental health professional. A licensed professional can determine if there is a common explanation for what is going on with the athlete, or if the changes in behavior may reflect a mental health challenge that would benefit from treatment.

Changes in Mood

Changes in mood can constitute dramatic mood swings that may leave people around the athlete feeling like they do not know which "version" of the person they will interact with and feeling like they are "walking on eggshells" around them. Dramatic changes in mood can also include the athlete feeling depressed or in such a state of optimism or elation that you feel concerned about them since their mood does not seem to fit with or match what is going on in their life. Being consistently or increasingly irritable with or without outbursts of anger is also an indication that the person may be struggling with their mental health. Certainly, there can be myriad explanations for such changes in mood that make sense and do not require diagnosis or treatment; however, athletes who are struggling with their mood for any reason can still benefit from support whether from a professional or someone trusted in their life.

Changes in Sleep and Eating Patterns

Although it is not unusual for people to have trouble sleeping at times or find that on occasion, they sleep a lot more than normal for them, ongoing sleep problems can in and of themselves be problematic. Of course, most people have times in their lives in which their sleep is negatively impacted. These times can include periods of high stress or being ill. Ongoing sleep difficulties are frequently tied to the worsening of both mental health and physical health concerns. Thus, if an athlete consistently complains about not getting enough sleep, sleeping a lot but not feeling rested, or simply sleeping far more hours than they think is needed, it can be helpful to refer them to a licensed medical or mental health professional to determine what may be going on and if treatment is necessary.

Similarly, temporary changes in eating patterns can predictably occur around things like holidays, increase in stress, or significant life changes. Ongoing changes in eating patterns (i.e., not eating enough, overeating, or binge eating), however, can be an indication of any number of mental health disorders some of which can be quite serious if not identified and treated quickly (e.g., restricting forms of eating disorders). Some athletes, for example, may be at higher risk for developing an eating disorder (see Chapter 2 for more information), therefore changes in eating behaviors could reflect something serious like that. Changes in eating can also occur with the presence of depression, anxiety, and other mental health disorders.

Neglect of Basic Self-Care

Another indication that someone is suffering (physically or mentally) is when a person's basic self-care is erratic or neglected. Basic self-care or basic hygiene refers to ensuring that one's body is clean and healthy and involves bathing or showering, brushing one's teeth, tending to one's menstrual hygiene for biological females, getting enough sleep, and getting enough to eat. Of course there are times when someone may be directed by a healthcare professional, for example, to not brush all or some of their teeth for a certain period of time (e.g., oral surgery), or the person cannot or should not bathe entirely or a certain area of the body for a period of time (e.g., surgical areas that cannot get wet); however, barring that kind of healthcare-related instruction the ongoing or periodic neglect of one's hygiene is a sign of a possible mental health challenge. Athletes, for example, may show up to practice or competitions more disheveled than is typical for them, they may not have laundered their competition or practice kit in a long period of time, and so on. Of course, it is not unusual for athletes (and non-athletes) at certain ages to not pay attention to things like this. What is important, as it is for other signs and symptoms, are noticeable changes that suggest that what is happening is not typical for this athlete.

Changes in Thinking and Speaking

Changes in thinking are impossible to know about unless someone tells another person they are aware of changes in their own thinking. Changes in thinking, however, can be discerned from things such as noticing illogical or unusual speech patterns which typically reflect illogical or unusual thoughts. Some people are eccentric and may think differently than most, and have likely experienced this most of their lives. Whenever the person themselves, or you, recognizes a noticeable change in how they talk with others or the ideas they have, this may be a sign of a mental health challenge that requires intervention.

Similarly, difficulty focusing or concentrating can be a sign of myriad diagnosable mental health disorders (i.e., many difficulties with focus or concentration are not explained by attention-deficit/hyperactivity disorder [ADHD]). Such difficulties can be noticed in conversations when someone seems to have no idea what the other person was just saying, when reading and not knowing or comprehending what was just read, and so on. An athlete, for example, may seemingly not hear or pay attention to what a coach or fellow teammate has instructed them to do, or may feel like they were paying attention and start to execute a skill only to realize they are not sure what they were supposed to do. Of course, these kinds of experiences are not uncommon in our everyday lives since there are a lot of distractions around us. However, the key is a noticeable change; something that is not typical for the person.

Suicidal Thoughts

Anytime someone says they have suicidal thoughts, they should be strongly encouraged to go to or they should be brought to a licensed mental health professional. Suicidal thoughts are far more common than most people know and for most people these thoughts remain thoughts only and do not result in a plan or the person acting on that plan to attempt to die by suicide. However, only a licensed mental health provider (or someone otherwise specifically and thoroughly trained in suicide assessment and referral) can determine whether the person is a danger to themselves.

All thoughts of suicide should be taken seriously and a proper referral to a licensed mental health provider should occur immediately. If there is any concern that the person is an immediate threat to themselves, they should be taken directly to a licensed mental health provider, to a hospital emergency room (ideally one that has a psychiatric emergency department), or someone should call 911 and indicate that the call is about a mental health emergency and ask to have someone sent who is trained in handling mental health emergencies. Another possibility is to call 988 (in the United States) which is the *National Suicide and Crisis Lifeline*. This Lifeline also has an option (option number one) specifically for veterans of the United States military who have an alarmingly high rate of death by suicide. In addition, option number two is for Spanish-speaking people, option number three is used to reach the LGBTQ+ youth network, those who use American Sign Language (ASL) can call 988 through a video phone, and those who use teletypewriter (TTY) devices can use the service they normally use or dial 711 then 988. It is also possible to text 988 or to engage in an online chat by going to chat.988lifeline.org.

Athletes can experience suicidal thoughts for reasons similar to non-athletes, and there are some circumstances that are relatively unique to athletes (see Chapter 7 for more information on suicide in athletes). If you are concerned about an athlete in this regard, you can encourage the athlete to call the National Suicide and Crisis Life line, a local crisis line, a mental health provider, or a trusted friend or family member for support and stay with them until they get the in-person support they need. You can also offer to call someone on their behalf and stay with them until they get the in-person support they need.

Psychotic Symptoms

The term "psychotic" or "psychosis" has a very specific definition that is much different than how people may use these terms in everyday conversation. In the context of mental health, a psychotic symptom, or psychosis, refers to a detachment from reality, and can include hallucinations or delusions. Hallucinations are false sensory experiences meaning that a person senses something that does not exist. The most common hallucinations are auditory (i.e., hearing sounds or voices that do not exist) and visual (i.e., seeing something or someone that does not exist); however, any of our basic senses can be involved. Delusions refer to false beliefs that can be seeming outlandish (e.g., the person claims to be God) and sometimes may seem realistic (e.g., someone is out to get them or trying to kill them). If anything an athlete does or says seems to suggest they are not in touch with reality it is important to get that person to a licensed healthcare provider immediately since they may be or may become a danger to themselves or others. It is important to note that someone dealing with psychosis is highly unlikely to be a danger to anyone else. They are far more likely to be a danger to themselves or a victim of violence perpetrated by someone else. Psychotic symptoms are relatively rare and the previously discussed signs and symptoms are far more common; however, any hint of psychosis should not be ignored.

Screening Tools for Specific Mental Health Challenges

There are myriad screening tools that can be used to identify possible mental health challenges. Many are non-population specific in that they can be used with athletes and nonathletes. Some tools have been developed specifically for athletes because athletes may show unique signs and symptoms of specific disorders. Whenever possible, it is ideal to use a screening tool with athletes that has either been designed specifically for this population, or has been studied and determined to be effective for use with an athlete population. Many tools are also age-specific, and some are sex specific, and therefore should be used only with the appropriate population.

Screening tools in general should be relatively brief and easy to administer, and any screening tools used should only be administered to populations that have been studied with that specific tool. The point of any screening tool is not to diagnose; therefore, it is not necessary for a licensed professional to administer these tools. Anyone who does administer screening tools, however, should have some measure of training in how best to administer the tools (e.g., individually or in a group setting, electronically or on paper) as well as how to make sense of the results. Well-developed screening tools have guidance on how to identify low, moderate, or high scores and typically indicate at what point someone should be referred to a licensed professional.

Since screening tools do not provide enough information for a diagnosis, and those who administer screening tools often do not have the education and training to render a diagnosis, referral to a qualified professional is necessary when scores on a screening instrument are high enough. Referrals to licensed professionals who can diagnose specific mental health disorders are necessary to determine if the signs and symptoms endorsed on the screening instrument reflect the presence of a diagnosis or merely a temporary state. For example, it is not uncommon when screening collegiate athletes who are in their first year of college to endorse anxiety and/or mood-related symptoms. Often, these experiences diminish relatively quickly as the athlete gets comfortable with their new setting, new team, and new responsibilities. As always, however, if there is any concern that the signs and symptoms endorsed by the athlete may indicate something more serious, referral to a properly trained and licensed professional should occur so they can determine what the athlete's symptoms may reflect.

Screening tools used with athletes are ideally selected by professionals qualified to identify which ones are appropriate for the age, sex, and competition level of those to be screened. What follows is a brief description of some mental health screening tools commonly used with athletes.

Sport Mental Health Assessment Tool-1 (SMHAT-1)

Developed by the *International Olympic Committee's Mental Health Working Group*, the SMHAT-1 includes several screening tools as part of the entire screening process and involves three stages of assessment depending on how an athlete responds to each stage. As noted in the previous section of this chapter, the SMHAT-1 can only be used by appropriately credentialed professionals. The Sport Mental Health Recognition Tool-1 (SMHRT-1) can be used by non-professionals to identify signs and symptoms indicating that additional support is needed.

Patient Health Questionnaire-9 (PHQ-9)

The PHQ-9 is a nine-item screen for depression and includes a question about suicidal thoughts. This screening tool yields results suggesting the possible severity level of depressive symptoms from minimal to severe. A recent study examining this screening tool with male-identifying and female-identifying collegiate athletes concluded that it is a valid measure of depression-related symptoms in student-athletes.

Baron Depression Screener for Athletes (Baron)

As noted in its name, this depression screening tool was developed specifically for athletes. The higher the score on this measure, the greater the severity of depression-related symptoms. This tool has been recommended by the IOC for use with athletes.

Generalized Anxiety Disorder-7 (GAD-7)

Generalized anxiety disorder (GAD) is a specific mental health diagnosis. This screening tool, composed of seven items, is designed to measure common symptoms associated with anxiety. Although GAD is one of several possible anxiety-related diagnoses, GAD-7 can provide information about the presence of common symptoms that can then be further explored, if needed, by a licensed professional. The GAD-2 is an even briefer anxiety screen and uses only the first two items of the GAD-7. Both screening tools have been examined with an athlete population and cutoff scores have been identified specifically for athletes that can differ in comparison to non-athlete populations. In this case, the cutoff scores are lower for athletes suggesting that when athletes endorse anxiety-related symptoms, they may underreport these symptoms and therefore lower cutoff scores for referral are indicated.

Brief Eating Disorders in Athletes Questionnaire (BEDA-Q)

A commonly used brief screening tool for eating disorders is the SCOFF. The letters in this acronym stand for Sick, Control, One Stone (a measure of weight in the UK and Ireland), Fat, and Food. This screening tool has been widely used in a variety of settings, including with athletes; however, more recently an athlete-specific tool called the Brief Eating Disorder in Athletes Questionnaire (BEDA-Q) was developed and has since been used with myriad athlete populations. In addition to its development and use specifically for athletes, this screening tool was also developed with male-identifying athletes in mind. This is important since many eating disorder tools have been developed and studied only with those who identify as female or as a female athlete specifically.

Compulsive Exercise Test for Athletes (CET-A)

Compulsive or excessive exercise is a possible sign of an eating disorder. Assessing this in the general population is relatively straightforward; however, determining whether an athlete or regular exerciser is engaged in "compulsive" exercise can be much more difficult to determine. What is excessive exercise for a non-athlete or non-exerciser may reflect a normal practice or workout schedule of competitive athletes. Researchers have found that exercise rigidity and lack of enjoyment of exercise (commonly found among non-athletes) were not relevant to an athlete's experience of compulsive exercise. Athletes, therefore, were found to show compulsive exercise when exercise was used to avoid negative feelings when they do not exercise, when exercise was used to manipulate body weight shape or size, and the extent to which exercise resulted in an improvement in mood. Therefore, the CET-A should be used when assessing excessive or compulsive exercise in an athlete population.

Athlete Sleep Satisfaction Questionnaire (ASSQ)

The ASSQ is another tool designed specifically for athletes, in this case, to measure the quality of sleep an athlete gets. The tool was specifically developed to identify symptoms associated with significant sleep problems that may impact an athlete's ability to function during the waking hours. Information from this screening tool can indicate whether an athlete has no sleep problems, or mild, moderate or severe sleep problems.

Alcohol Use Disorders Identification Test—Concise (AUDIT-C)

This screening tool, modified from the *World Health Organization's* ten-item screening tool called the Alcohol Use Disorders Identification Test, is used with a wide variety of populations including military veterans and athletes. The concise version, AUDIT-C, tool has only three questions and different cutoff scores for biological males and biological females. Higher scores reflect increasingly problematic and likely hazardous drinking patterns.

CAGE & CAGE-AID

The CAGE tool was developed to assess problems with alcohol use. Each letter in the acronym stands for an element associated with the four screening questions. C refers to cutting down on drinking, A for feeling annoyed by others who criticize their alcohol use, G for feeling guilty about their use, and E stands for "eye opener" referring to using alcohol first thing in the morning. The CAGE-AID screening tool added "drug use" to each question. So, for example, the C question referring to cutting down on drinking adds cutting down on drug use. The CAGE-AID is embedded in the IOC's SAMHAT-1 professional screening measure, and therefore has been used and studied with athletes.

The screeners briefly discussed above reflect tools that can screen for common mental health challenges found among athletes. Additional screening tools can be used to assess symptoms associated with a variety of other diagnosable mental health disorders including bipolar disorder (previously known as "manic-depressive" disorder), social anxiety, personality disorders, obsessive-compulsive disorder (OCD), ADHD, and symptoms associated with psychosis. As noted previously, whenever possible, any screening tool used should ideally have been used and studied with the athlete population.

Making a Referral

Referring an athlete for mental health concerns starts with recognizing that an athlete may be dealing with a mental health challenge. Thus, providing education and training to those who have a great deal of contact with athletes (e.g., coaches, athletic trainers, teammates) so they can recognize common signs and symptoms of mental health challenges is important. As discussed in the previous sections of this chapter, screening for mental health challenges as part of the PPE process for competitive athletes is one way to identify common signs and symptoms among athletes. Screening only prior to an athlete's competitive season, however, will not capture any changes in mental health experienced by an athlete. Athletes may, for example, have very few or no signs and symptoms of mental health challenges at the start of the season, but may experience life stressors (in and outside of sport) that change how they feel. Therefore, it is important to engage in periodic mental health screening and/or to remain vigilant for changes in an athlete that may suggest they are struggling with their mental health. Regardless of when a possible mental health challenge is suspected, getting the athlete referred to the proper professional(s), as soon as possible, is important.

Although a delay in getting an athlete referred to the proper medical provider when a physical injury is known or suspected can occur, this tends to be less common than delays in referring athletes for mental health challenges. Athletic trainers and other highly trained professionals are not able to diagnose and/or treat all possible physical injuries or disorders. For example, while they may be able to temporarily set a broken bone, they would not be the one performing surgery for a fracture requiring surgical intervention. Similarly, coaches, athletic trainers, teammates, and others can provide emotional and psychological support for a struggling athlete; however, knowing when to get them to a professional who can do the mental health equivalent of conducting surgery on a fracture is equally as important.

One of the things that can be challenging when making a referral is knowing who to refer the athlete to. This consideration may involve whether an athlete may need psychotherapy, medication, and/or have a suspected diagnosis or set of symptoms that are best treated by a specialist. For example, eating disorders commonly occur in athletes and the treatment of these disorders is a specialty area requiring specific education and training. Similarly, although trauma itself is not a diagnosis, a traumatic experience whether recent or in the past often requires treatment by someone who specializes in working with trauma. One uniquely complicating factor in terms of to whom an athlete may be referred is how the term "sport psychologist" is used. This term is often used to refer to a variety of professionals who may or may not have the education and training to diagnose and treat mental health disorders.

In the United States, the term "psychologist" is protected by law in many states. This is like the protection afforded to the term "physician." A psychologist is licensed to diagnose and treat mental health disorders and has undergone specific education and training to be qualified as a psychologist. Adding "sport" to the title of psychologist means that the sport psychologist has specific education and training to work with athletes *and* who can diagnose and treat mental illness. The term sport psychologist, however, is often used (legally in some states but illegally in others) to refer to professionals who have a high level of education and training for working with athletes in mental performance. This means that they are adept at helping athletes perform at their very best by training the mental side of sport, but are not qualified to diagnose and treat mental health disorders.

The purpose for mentioning this is that what someone calls themselves (appropriately or not) does not necessarily accurately reflect what they are able to do. In the context of mental health, the professional must be licensed to diagnose and treat mental health disorders. This includes psychologists, psychiatrists, clinical counselors, clinical social workers, psychiatric nurse practitioners, and so on. Therefore, it is recommended that a list of professionals to whom an athlete can be referred for mental health includes only licensed professionals, and a short list of those who are not only licensed but who also have specific education and training in working with athletes.

The first step, as has been noted repeatedly, is to recognize possible signs and symptoms of a mental health challenge. It is not a coach's, teammate's, family member's, or athletic trainer's job to determine if the symptoms warrant a diagnosis. The job is to recognize the *possibility* of a mental health challenge. The next step in the process is having a conversation with the athlete. Such a conversation should involve several considerations not the least of which is when and where this conversation will occur.

Ideally, the conversation will take place in a private setting allowing for an environment in which the athlete feels more comfortable talking about personal and sensitive information. It is also recommended that, if possible, the conversation occurs when the athlete is not already in a stressful situation (e.g., they feel like they just performed poorly in competition). It is not always possible to get the timing "right," however, some more ideal times may include before or after practice, or asking the athlete to join you in your office or for a cup of coffee somewhere relatively private.

Once the location and timing are determined, it is important to share with the athlete what your concerns are. It is important to have specifics in mind prior to starting the conversation. Sometimes athletes may know exactly what you are talking about when you express concern, and others may have no idea or may feel defensive and minimize what you noticed that has caused you concern. One way to start such a conversation may be: *Thank you for taking a few minutes to talk. How are you doing?* [Allow the athlete to answer]. *I've noticed that you don't seem like yourself lately.* [See if the athlete has a response]. *I usually see you joking around with the team and spending time at meals with them but lately it seems like you've withdrawn from the team. I'm worried about you. Do you know what might be going on?*

As illustrated, it is important to be specific in your observations rather than simply saying that you are concerned about the athlete or that they do not seem like themselves. Being specific can help the athlete understand what you are seeing that has caused you concern and they may be less likely to deny that there are any issues. It is also important to know that, unless the organization or institution where you work has specific policies about sport participation and what an athlete may be required to do to keep participating, all anyone can do is express care and concern to the athlete and offer support including referral to a qualified professional. Parents of minors can effectively "force" their child to get treatment; however, an adult athlete (or non-athlete) can refuse treatment.

Treatment Options

This section describes the levels of care an athlete may receive or have recommended to them. These include outpatient treatment, intensive outpatient treatment, partial hospitalization, hospitalization, or residential treatment. It is important to note that the vast majority of those referred for mental health support will get what they need in an outpatient setting (e.g., a school's counseling center, a psychologist in private practice) and therefore will not need the other forms of treatment which are identified as "higher levels of care." This chapter will not describe specific treatments themselves such as cognitive-behavioral therapy (CBT), dialectical behavior therapy (DBT), eye movement desensitization and reprocessing (EMDR), psychodynamic psychotherapy, motivational interviewing, and so on. Many common mental health disorders can be effectively treated using more than one specific treatment. The "right" treatment in this respect typically involves the type of treatment a specific professional is trained to provide, if that form of treatment is known to be effective for the athlete's specific concerns, and whether that approach is a good fit for the athlete. Therefore, it is recommended that anyone seeking care from a licensed mental health professional inquire about what type of treatment they provide, how that treatment will help with the concerns in question, the providers' experience working with athletes, and what can be expected in terms of the length of treatment. Ultimately, what matters most when selecting a licensed mental health professional is the degree to which that professional and their approach are a good fit. This refers to the extent to which the athlete feels comfortable with the professional, and that the professional's approach makes sense to the athlete and feels like it would be helpful.

Since mental health exists on a continuum (see Chapter 2 for more information) from mental ill-health that interferes with daily functioning to mental wellness and thriving, not all mental health challenges require treatment. However, when in doubt it is always a good idea to refer an athlete to a properly licensed mental health provider who can determine if an athlete's challenges require diagnosis and treatment. While an athlete's primary care provider may be a reasonable referral source, it is recommended that the athlete is ultimately referred to someone with specialized education and training in identifying and treating mental health disorders. Such professionals can include licensed psychologists, licensed clinical mental health counselors, licensed clinical social workers, psychiatrists, and psychiatric nurse practitioners. An additional consideration is whether the licensed mental health provider also has specific education and training in the unique needs and experiences of athletes. Ideally the community in which an athlete lives and competes would have licensed mental health providers who have this specialty; however, this may not be the case for many communities.

Once an athlete is referred to and meets with a licensed mental health provider, depending on the nature of the athlete's concerns, the provider may recommend regularly scheduled appointments (e.g., weekly, or biweekly) so the athlete has the support they need, and can continue to participate and thrive in their sport. It can be useful, in fact, to reassure the athlete that anyone who works with them will be invested in their overall well-being along with keeping them engaged with sport. The latter point is an important reason why a provider with education and training in working with athletes can be critical. Some providers without this education and training may unintentionally minimize the importance of sport by recommending the athlete leave the sport when it may not be indicated to do so. Collegiate student-athletes, and athletes participating at the high school or middle school level will likely have access to counseling services of some kind. Depending on the resources available at the school there may or may not be providers who specialize in working with athletes. Larger colleges and universities often have at least one provider who is a sport psychologist (i.e., someone who is licensed to diagnose and treat mental illness, and who has education and training in working with athletes), and in some cases may have an entire office or department that is staffed with people who only serve athletes.

As will be discussed later in this section, there are circumstances in which a recommendation to discontinue sport for some period of time, or entirely, is an appropriate recommendation. Depending on who is involved and where the athlete competes (e.g., college/university) there may be a policy in place indicating the circumstances under which an athlete *should* be pulled from sport participation as well as the conditions under which they are cleared to return; not unlike what is seen with physical injury.

When regular meetings with a licensed mental health professional in an outpatient setting are not working, it is likely that there will be a recommendation for a higher level of care. Although clearly defining what constitutes a situation in which treatment is "not working" is difficult at best, licensed mental health providers are trained to determine when treatment is working and when it is not. When treatment is not working, providers have an ethical obligation to bring this to the athlete's attention as well as anyone legally allowed to have information about the athlete's treatment (e.g., parental figures if the athlete is a minor) or for whom the athlete has given permission to share information about their treatment (e.g., parental figures if the athlete is an adult, or coaches), so that informed decisions can be made regarding the best path forward for the athlete. In some cases, the best way forward may involve a higher level of care.

Higher Levels of Care

Higher levels of care are often needed with severe forms of disorders that place the athlete's life in danger (e.g., suicidal thoughts), or that involve symptoms that are so disruptive to their lives that they are unable to adequately function as they would like to or as they need to. For example, a student-athlete may deal with such severe anxiety that not only does it impact their sport performance, but they are also unable to attend classes and complete assignments, or are unable to leave their room/apartment. An athlete in such a circumstance may benefit from weekly meetings with a licensed mental health provider but that may not be enough.

Intensive Outpatient Programs (IOP). There are some institutions such as those called "community mental health centers," hospitals, or stand-alone treatment programs that can offer what is often referred to as IOP programs or "intensive out-patient programs." These programs require several hours a day multiple times a week of counseling and related programming (e.g., learning coping skills in a group setting). Depending on the circumstances, the athlete may still be able to live at home/school and attend this programming which tends to take place over the course of a few to several weeks. In recent years, more and more institutions have been able to offer IOP programming virtually so there is less disruption to the athlete's (or non-athlete's) life.

Partial Hospitalization Programs (PHP). Another level of care that may be indicated for athletes (and others) is called partial hospitalization programs or PHPs. PHPs provide more structure than intensive outpatient programs and typically involve a larger time commitment. In addition, since PHPs are affiliated with hospitals the implication is that there may be medical monitoring that occurs as part of a PHP that an intensive outpatient program cannot provide.

Hospitalization or Residential Treatment Centers. Both hospitalization and residential treatment centers constitute the highest levels of care. Hospitalization for mental health is indicated when someone is an imminent threat to themselves or others, when medication requires significant adjustment and medication monitoring is important (e.g., withdrawal or the possibility of severe side effects), or when there is some other medical issue that requires monitoring for the individual's safety and well-being (e.g., nutrition). Those who may require hospitalization for mental health typically remain in hospital until they are considered "medically stable." Generally, this means that the medical emergency or crisis has abated and the medical care being provided is either no longer necessary or can be safely monitored outside of a hospital setting.

Residential treatment centers, for mental health, are facilities where someone will live for a period of time (e.g., several weeks or months) and have access to care twenty-four hours a day, seven days a week. Some residential treatment centers have medical staff who can do some of what might be done as part of hospitalization or partial hospitalization; however, it is often the case that if constant medical monitoring is needed as described in the previous paragraph, then the person may need to be temporarily hospitalized until they are medically stable and can return to the residential facility. Residential facilities tend to offer myriad forms of treatment to include individual psychotherapy, family therapy, art therapy, animal-assisted therapy, and so on. Residential treatment facilities are typically designed and set up to treat specific disorders. For example, there are residential facilities for eating disorders, substance use disorders, posttraumatic stress disorder (PTSD), severe anxiety disorders, and so on. Some facilities may indicate they can treat more than one disorder at one time. For example, since it is common for those diagnosed with an eating disorder to have a trauma history and/or to engage in harmful substance use, many residential eating disorder treatment facilities will treat the eating disorder and another disorder at the same time. Finally, many residential treatment facilities are for the general population (i.e., anyone with a particular diagnosis) and do not specifically provide programming for athletes. However, there are, for example, a growing number of residential eating disorder treatment facilities that have specific programming for athletes given their unique needs and how differently these disorders may present in athletes compared to non-athletes.

Overall, it is highly recommended that any athlete known to have a mental health challenge or who may be at risk for one is referred, as soon as possible, to a licensed mental health professional who can determine if a diagnosis is warranted and what type of treatment may be recommended, including a higher level of care. When a higher level of care is recommended it can feel scary and perhaps like the athlete is being punished for seeking treatment at all. The reality is, when a higher level of care is recommended, it is done so for the purpose of making sure the athlete has the right care at the right level and at the right time so that they can stay with or return to sport as soon as it is safe for them to do so.

Conclusion

There are myriad ways to determine whether or not an athlete may be dealing with a mental health challenge. Mental health screening, for example, is strongly recommended as part of an athlete's pre-participation examination. Similarly, those close with an athlete may take notice of uncharacteristic behaviors that warrant attention. It is important that when an athlete is suspected of dealing with a mental health challenge that they are referred to an appropriate professional as soon as possible who can determine if treatment is necessary and what level of care is indicted.

5

Unique Issues Related to Age or Competition Level

Athletes at any age can deal with mental health challenges for myriad reasons. Some mental health challenges begin during the childhood years (e.g., neurodevelopmental disorders such as autism spectrum disorder), and others can develop at any time (e.g., depression or anxiety disorders). This chapter does not review specific mental health challenges (see Chapter 2 for some common disorders found among athletes); rather, it reviews factors that can impact an athlete's mental health during specific developmental periods or level of competition.

Youth Athletes (Under Age 14)

The age range for what is considered to be "youth" varies depending on the country and context in which age is considered. Many organizations consider youth sports to include athletes age eighteen or younger. Since sport participation in the United States can look substantially different between high school sports and younger, this section will focus on ages younger than high school (typically around age 14–18).

As noted in the opening chapter of this book, there are myriad benefits for anyone engaging in physical activity in general, and participating in sport specifically. Since childhood is a critical period in one's life for learning new skills and developing healthy habits (physically, psychologically, and spiritually), helping children see and experience the benefits of sport as early as possible can be helpful.

The *American College of Sports Medicine* (ACSM) produced a document in 2012 entitled *Designed to Move: A Physical Activity Action Agenda* to address the widespread issue of a lack of physical activity in the United States and in many other countries around the world. The focus of the document is on youth, specifically those under the age of ten. In this document the authors talk about benefits related to physical activity in terms of "human capital" which refers to the skills and abilities a person has that may ultimately benefit society. Often "capital" is measured in terms of the economic value of these skills and abilities, or how much are these things worth. The ACSM identifies six separate forms of capital which are ultimately discussed in terms of how these various forms of capital can be leveraged to benefit overall well-being. These six forms of capital are: physical, emotional, individual, social, intellectual, and financial. The authors specifically point to the critical developmental period prior to adolescence wherein motor skills are developed, and significant development in brain structure and function occurs. They note that childhood is a "critical intervention point" while the brain is not fully formed and certain connections in the brain are not yet "hardwired" after which these connections are difficult to change. When children are exposed to the benefits of physical activity and sport early on, they are much more likely to benefit significantly even if they do not pursue sport after their childhood years.

Depending on how exposure to sport occurs and what may happen during sport participation, there can also be some unique challenges to be aware of. Below are challenges that may have a unique impact on the youth athlete.

Athletic Identity

Although identity development is typically associated with adolescence, theories of how identity is formed often point to the importance of childhood in later identity formation. Erik Erikson developed one of the most well-known theories of how people develop psychologically and socially throughout their lives and emphasized the importance of identity formation. He noted that during adolescence we sort through the various versions we had of ourselves when we were a child to determine what still fits and what does not. In this way, the extent to which a child may or may not identify themselves as an athlete (i.e., their athletic identity) may impact later exploration and commitment to who they are "now." Do they still consider themselves an athlete? How important is this role? What else is important in their lives? Children, of course, are not expected to have their identities figured out. Indeed, who we are and what is important to us change throughout our lives including much later in life during our older adulthood years. Encouraging children to engage in sport will likely result in some measure of their identity being associated with sport, and helping children recognize that they are more than an athlete is critical for later identity development since our overall well-being can be impacted by how we define ourselves and whether or not we exclusively identify with a single role such as "athlete." The various sources of our identity also contribute to our sense of self-worth. When we only have one source of identity to which self-worth is tied, and that identity source is threatened in any way we experience mental health challenges related to not knowing who we are and our worth without this specific role (see also Chapter 3: Biopsychosocial Factors Affecting Mental Health in Athletes for more information on athletic identity).

Impact of Injury

Over 3.5 million athletes aged fourteen years or younger sustain a sport- or other physical activity-related injury annually. Injuries can occur as a result of contact with other athletes (these injuries will be more common in, but not exclusive to, contact sports), and overuse or misuse of a part of the body used during sport. When an injury is severe, death is a rare occurrence but when it does occur it is most likely to occur as a result of a brain injury. Much of what is written about injury in the context of sport can be categorized as either orthopedic- (i.e., bones and muscles) or brain- (i.e., traumatic brain injury to include concussion) related injuries.

Concussion is considered a type of injury but is typically classified and studied as a separate from musculoskeletal injuries due to the potential impact a brain injury can have on all systems of the body (see Chapter 11 for more information on concussion). A significant difference between a similar concussion endured by adults compared to children and adolescents has to do with how long concussion-related symptoms last. In comparison to adults who may need about a week to recover, children aged 5–7 years old may recover in about two weeks time, and adolescents are likely to need four weeks of recovery time. Up to 31 percent of children and adolescents may endure symptoms that require more than four weeks recovery time.

A group of researchers in Michigan examined head, neck, and brain injuries among children ages 9–10. Head injuries included what they referred to as TBI-LOC which stands for traumatic brain injury-loss of consciousness. The good news is that the rate of TBI-LOC in this age group is considered to be low; however, they noted that the risk increases for this type of injury the longer the athlete participates in sport, and when they participate in contact sports (e.g., American football).

Researchers in Canada compared the impact of brain-related or orthopedic-related injuries on mental health in nearly 450,000 child and youth athletes (age range was 5–18 years old) and found that concussion compared to an orthopedic injury was far more likely to be associated with a greater risk for mental health challenges that in some cases lead to psychiatric hospitalization and self-harm. Another study conducted in Australia noted that the connection between mental health and concussion may be that concussion makes existing mental health challenges worse or concussion may occur first and mental health challenges develop following the head injury. Either way, it is clear that mental health and concussion are connected.

Injury of any kind leaves an athlete at any age at risk for mental health challenges since they are no longer able to participate in sport for a brief or extended period of time, or permanently depending on the nature and severity of the injury. Anxiety and depression are common mental health challenges experienced in the context of injury; however, the risk of developing other concerns such as disordered eating patterns can increase since an athlete may feel like they have to eat differently (usually eating less) to compensate for the decrease in physical activity. In addition, things such as fear related to moving the injured body part or fear related to reinjury once the athlete returns to play can impact recovery and have been shown to lead to not fully recovering from injury. It is also important to note that not all psychological reactions to injury can lead to a mental health challenge. For some youth athletes, an injury that keeps them from participating in sport may feel like a relief particularly if they feel like there is too much pressure to perform, or if they are experiencing burnout related to how many activities they are involved in. Another factor that can be related to sport-related injury at a young age is specializing in a particular sport when the athlete is still a child.

Sport Specialization

According to a review of the existing research on sport specialization conducted by a group of sport medicine specialists in the United States and led by Neeru Jayanthi, sport specialization involves three components. The first is that the athlete selects one main sport to focus on with the second component being that they quit all other sports they may have participated in. The final component is that they engage in eight or more months of training and competition for the main sport. Oftentimes both parents and athletes feel pressure to specialize in a particular sport as early as possible with the hopes of competing at an elite level in the future. Therefore, families may find as many opportunities as possible for the athlete to train and compete in a specific sport all year. Many prominent medical and/or sport-related organizations (e.g., American Academy of Pediatrics, American Orthopaedic Society for Sports Medicine, National Athletic Trainers' Association) discourage sport specialization. These organizations provide this caution since they have concluded that early sport specialization can lead to burnout, overuse injury (see Chapter 3 for more information), mental stress and psychosocial concerns, and an increased likelihood of dropping out of sport. Additional concerns related to sport specialization include sleep difficulties, lower quality of life, and being at greater risk for depression- and anxiety-related symptoms.

Non-adolescent youth athletes are at greatest risk for injury related to sport specialization at a young age. As such pediatric physician Kristin Whitney and colleagues noted that when athletes and their families are contemplating early sport specialization they must consider the impact that a sport-related injury would have at such an early stage of life. The youth athlete's body undergoes significant maturational changes and care must be taken when developing a training regimen (ideally by someone knowledgeable about pediatric development) so the athlete is not put at undue risk for injury. Whitney and her colleagues also discuss what is known about recommended developmental programs for athletes. They suggest, for example, that training for competition should not start until around age fourteen, and training to win to occur no earlier than age eighteen. Prior to these ages, learning the fundamentals of physical activity and sport (e.g., balance and coordination), then training to learn sport-specific skills and appropriate recovery are reasonable and developmentally appropriate goals. Taking a slower approach to sport development can prevent, or at least reduce the risk of known issues that come with early specialization.

High School Athletes

High school athletes in the United States are typically aged 14–18 years old. For some high school athletes, their participation will end after their senior year. Athletes who are invested in sport and who show promise for competing at higher levels (e.g., college, elite amateur, professional) may forgo a public education and seek a specialized high school designed to nurture athletic talent in preparation for the next level of competition.

The *National Federation of State High School Associations* (NFHS) published a two-article series addressing how mental health challenges impact high school athletes. This Association noted that high school may be a time when athletes are pressured to compete through pain often leading to the mantra "no pain, no gain." Some of this pressure to perform despite pain can come from sources external to the athlete (e.g., coaches, teammates, parents) and may come from within the athlete themselves due to their own expectations.

High School Sport Participation and Later Mental Health

A study conducted in Canada examined the experiences of over 850 high school athletes. The authors surveyed students every three months throughout their high school years and followed up with them again three years after graduation. Overall, they found that students who participated in sport throughout their high school years were much more likely to have fewer symptoms related to depression and stress, and rated their overall mental health higher in comparison to those who were never involved in sport during their high school years. Additional research in this area suggests these mental health-related benefits may be derived from the cooperative and collaborative nature of sports, specifically team sports. The Canadian researchers noted that the mechanisms explaining why sport participation in high school may function as a protective factor for later mental health are unclear and speculate that the positive benefits are likely due to how the brain develops when engaged in sport. Another group of Canadian researchers expanded on the connection between high school sport and later mental health concluding that when students continued to participate in sport while transitioning from high school (i.e., adolescence) into adulthood they had better mental health in comparison to those who do not continue to participate in sport. This finding was specifically noted among those who continued to participate in team sports suggesting that continued social connection through a shared activity may account for this finding.

Elite-Level High School Sport Participation

Elite-level high school sport participation typically refers to high school athletes who matriculate into high schools designed specifically for athletes. These schools provide high school level education while incorporating the unique demands of being a high level student-athlete. However, since these schools revolve around sport, athletes who attend such schools likely endure training and competition that is more intense and more fierce than that seen in traditional high schools (i.e., high schools open to all students).

Some research has found that competing at an elite level during one's high school years, while also completing academic requirements, can have a negative impact on these athlete's mental well-being. They may be more likely to experience symptoms related to burnout, anxiety, and depression. In addition, these athletes may also develop unrealistic expectations around their current and future sport performance, and may place themselves at greater risk for injury or illness due to the high demands associated with their sport in conjunction with trying to literally make the grade in their required academic studies. Other research has found that athletes enrolled in these elite sport schools have the opposite experience and report lower levels of stress along with higher levels of overall well-being. Regardless of this apparent discrepancy, most researchers agree it is important for these elite-level high school athletes to have opportunities allowing them to explore interests and abilities outside of sport, thus facilitating a non-exclusive athletic identity (see Athletic Identity in the next section for more information) which is important for overall development and strong mental health.

With respect to mental health, specifically a group of researchers took an in-depth look at the experiences of eight athletes attending a sports high school. They found that the stigma around mental health (which tends to permeate sport culture), often stemming from the attitudes of coaches and peers, continues to be a barrier for these athletes in getting the support they need. They noted this was specifically the case for mental health concerns related to problematic eating and provided the overall conclusion that greater support is needed for elite-level high school athletes attending these specialized schools and who have ambitions to compete at a higher elite level. Given the pressures these athletes face regarding successfully completing their academic requirements, competing at a high level, and pressure to perform at a high level of competition after high school having mental health services readily available may need to be a top priority.

Athletic Identity

As noted elsewhere throughout this book, including within this chapter, identity development tends to be concentrated during the adolescent years which are traditionally associated with the middle school and high school years in the United States (e.g., approximately ages 10–19). Having a high degree of athletic identity means the person may reap the benefits of the various forms of capital associated with physical activity (see the section on Youth Sports in this chapter for more information on capital) and may see high levels of performance since someone with a high athletic identity is likely devoting as many resources as possible to their sport. Some researchers have found that a high commitment to sport may allow athletes to have better sources of social support, have positive experiences in sport and academics, and may increase their overall happiness. Others have noted specifically that when a high athletic identity is not exclusive (i.e., the athlete is aware of and identifies with other aspects of their life) an athlete is more likely to experience greater joy from participating in sport, have a more positive body image and higher level of self-confidence, and experience higher levels of motivation overall as well as a stronger sense of self-determination (i.e., the belief that one can make one's own choices based on their interests and values).

High levels of athletic identity that are exclusive (i.e., the athlete is not aware of and/or does not identify with other aspects of their life) can result in a lower likelihood of help-seeking when needed. This is believed to be due to a long-standing element of sport culture that reinforces being "tough" no matter what, and that seeking help can be perceived as a sign of weakness. In addition, athletes with a high athletic identity are more vulnerable to mental health challenges, including burnout, when they incur injury or illness that keeps them from their sport, or when they have to end their sport participation particularly when this is not by choice. In addition, they may experience mental health challenges associated with the loss of identity that comes with sport-related transitions (e.g., retirement from sport). Athletes are at greater risk for these vulnerabilities when their status as an athlete is tied to their self-worth. When their role as an athlete is threatened or comes to an end they may feel like they no longer have any worth as a human being which will inevitably result in mental health challenges.

James Marcia, a contemporary of psychologist Erik Erikson, expanded on Erikson's ideas surrounding identity development and noted that there are at least four outcomes of identity work during adolescence that are based on the degree to which a person engages in sufficient exploration of their interests, skills and values, and whether or not they have committed to an identity. One of these outcomes, foreclosure, has been examined in the context of athletic identity. Someone who has a "foreclosed" identity means that they have committed to an identity without engaging in exploration. This means they have not taken time to see what else is out there in terms of their interests, skills, abilities, values, etc. When an athlete prematurely commits to an athletic identity without this type of exploration, they may be at greater risk for negative outcomes including problems with substance use, burnout, and difficulty developing a career path or adjusting to a sport transition. Factors that can essentially promote athletic identity foreclosure may be psychological or social. For example, sport performance can impact an athlete especially when the approval from others such as parents and perhaps their local community is contingent on how well they perform. This much attention paid to an athlete's performance during their younger years can contribute to an overinvestment in the athlete role to the exclusion of exploring other interests, skills, and abilities.

Identify formation generally, and the formation of athletic identity specifically, can begin in earlier stages of life, and may extend beyond one's high school years. However, the high school years are a time when there is typically significant exploration and experimentation as adolescents work on figuring out who and what are important to them. During this time, athletes are likely determining their commitment to sport and whether or not they have the skills, abilities, and interest in competing during young adulthood as a collegiate, elite amateur, or professional athlete.

Collegiate Athletes

Collegiate student-athletes face unique challenges associated with being both a full-time student and an athlete. This is different in comparison to high school athletes at any level of competition since scheduling and time management are likely handled for them (e.g., practice time, time in class, time to study, etc. are determined for them). For college athletes, these challenges can include having to figure out how to budget their time effectively so they can do what is needed for their academics, social, and family lives while devoting hours each week to sport whether in workouts/practices, film sessions, or competitions. Most athletes also travel for competitions which take up a good deal of time in and of itself. As noted, part of the challenge of being a student-athlete is finding time for a social life. They can miss out on what their non-athlete counterparts are able to do (e.g., study sessions, informal socializing) leaving some feeling isolated and detached from their peers. In addition, not only are collegiate student-athletes held to their campus' athlete code of conduct which can include different expectations than a general student code of conduct, they are also held to the policies and requirements for eligibility set by governing bodies such as the *National Collegiate Athletic Association* (NCAA) or the *National Association of Intercollegiate Athletics* (NAIA).

The NCAA recently passed legislation mandating that mental health services are made available to student-athletes at member institutions. They specifically refer to the second edition of their document, published in 2024, entitled *Mental Health Best Practices: Understanding and Supporting Student-Athlete Mental Health.* On the cover page of the document there is a notation that mental health services made available to student-athletes must reflect the recommendations within the document.

The development of the NCAA's *Mental Health Best Practices* document involved an advisory group that included nineteen organizations external to the NCAA including the *National Alliance on Mental Illness*, *Society for Sport, Exercise, & Performance Psychology*, the *United States Olympic & Paralympic Committee*, *American Medical Society for Sports Medicine*, and *Association for Applied Sport Psychology*. In 2020 it was recognized that the previous version of the document did not adequately address the unique needs of "student-athletes of color, LGBTQ+ student-athletes, student-athletes with disabilities and international student-athletes" (p. 3). Discussions of the needs of these specific student populations have been incorporated into the second edition of the document (see also Chapter 6 for more information).

The NCAA's document describes the "spectrum" of mental health that includes "disrupted psychological functioning" and "wellness and thriving" (p. 4) along with several principles related to student-athlete mental health that can be used by colleges and universities to meet specific best practices. The principles include the fact that mental health is an important factor to consider in student-athlete functioning, emerging adulthood (i.e., the traditional ages of college students) is a time in life when mental health challenges are likely to surface, what puts someone at risk for and what may protect them from mental health challenges can change over time and circumstances, coaches play a pivotal role in student-athlete mental health, the mind and body connection is important to consider, issues related to "discrimination, maltreatment and psychosocial trauma" (p. 5) can have a deleterious effect on mental health, social media use can be a risk factor for mental health challenges, and ongoing collaboration between campus departments and offices along with an emphasis on striving to do better. Each principle is critical to adequately addressing student-athlete mental health, and is believed to help member institutions determine whether or not their efforts, related to the mental health of their athletes, reflect the NCAA's legislation and whether or not what they are doing is effective.

There are four specific "Mental Health Best Practices" outlined in the *Mental Health Best Practices* document. They are: "Create Healthy Environments That

Support Mental Health and Promote Well-Being," "Procedures for Identification of Student-Athletes with Mental Health Symptoms and Disorders, Including Mental Health Screening Tools," "Mental Health Action Plans That Outline Referral Pathways of Student-Athletes to Qualified Providers," and "Licensure of Providers Who Oversee and Manage Student-Athlete Mental Health Care." Each of these best practices includes several core components that instruct member institutions on what they need to do in order to meet each best practice item. Although the NCAA has provided guidance, and now legislation, on tending to student-athlete mental health, at least some athletes do not think their schools are doing enough. Overall student-athletes reported that regardless of the Division of the school (i.e., I, II, or III) those who were interviewed generally agreed that what their schools are doing is insufficient to support the mental health of their student-athletes.

The NCAA regularly collects data related to student-athlete mental health and provided a report in December of 2023 outlining the key findings which included a finding that although mental health has improved since 2020 (i.e., the Covid-19 era; see Chapter 10 for more information on the impact of Covid-19) rates of mental health challenges are still high among collegiate athletes. They also reported that the highest rates of mental health challenges were found among those who participate in women's sports (regardless of Division), BIPOC student-athletes, and LBGTQ+ student-athletes (see Chapter 6 for more information on Historically Disenfranchised Athlete Groups). Finally, the NCAA reported that the primary sources of stress for collegiate student-athletes were academics, planning for one's future, and finances. Additional sources of stress included the amount of playing time an athlete gets, concerns about their family, their relationship with their coach, and the team environment. According to this report only those who participated in men's sports saw a decrease of at least 5 percentage points on any of the metrics related to mental health from the previous data collected in the fall of 2021. Those who participated in women's sports reported either the same level of mental health-related concerns or a smaller decrease compared to those participating in men's sports. Although there is some improvement in mental health for some groups, in aggregate these findings may reflect student-athletes' concerns that not enough is being done to support their mental well-being.

Student-athletes were also asked about access to mental health support. On average most student-athletes (about 70%) knew where to go and who to talk to about their mental health. While nearly 70 percent of student-athletes noted that there is someone they trust, on campus, who could support them if needed, only about 50 percent of student-athletes say they would feel comfortable getting the support they need on campus. Student-athletes who compete in women's sports were more likely to express skepticism about whether or not mental health was supported or taken seriously by their coach and/or their athletics department. This seems to translate to these student-athletes also feeling much less comfortable than their men's teams counterparts when it comes to feeling comfortable talking with their coach about their mental health: only 40 percent of student-athletes competing on women's teams indicated they would feel comfortable doing so. A potentially contributing factor to this is a research finding that microaggressions related to mental health (e.g., an emphasis on "toughness," while having a mental health challenge is viewed as being "weak") were expressed by male-identifying coaches at a higher rate than female-identifying coaches, and mental health microaggressions were related to a lower level of mental health-related education for these coaches. Coach use of mental health microaggressions was also related to a reduced willingness to refer an athlete for mental health support. Since mental health microaggressions help to perpetuate mental health stigma, athletes who are around others expressing these microaggressions are less likely to seek mental health support when needed.

A recently evolving challenge for many collegiate athletes is related to travel. Although travel between states for competition is common for student-athletes, recent and proposed changes to collegiate athletic conferences (e.g., the Big Ten, and the Pac-12) may see more and more athletes traveling from one coast of the United States to the other. A group of scientists and physicians, led by Craig Heller, expressed concern for what this type of travel may do to athletes' sleep patterns and circadian rhythms (i.e., 24-hour cycle with predictable changes in the body). Abnormal circadian rhythms have been linked to myriad physical and mental health problems, including diabetes, seasonal affective disorder, and sleep disorders. This group offers suggestions to help others help student-athletes mitigate the impact of travel that takes them across multiple time zones.

Although college athletics, particularly at the Division I level, more and more closely approximates professional sports, the reality is very few college athletes will extend their athletic careers beyond graduation. Fewer than 2 percent of college athletes eventually play for professional teams. For some student-athletes transitioning out of sport is viewed as a change that provides an opportunity for personal growth, whereas others may see the end of their athletic careers as a loss that leaves them feeling uncertain about themselves and their lives. The degree to which an athlete is identified with this role (see the sections on

Athletic Identity earlier in this chapter, and Chapter 3 for more information on Athletic Identity) can influence these disparate reactions.

Elite Level/Professional Athletes

Most professional athletes will retire in their mid-late twenties or early thirties. Of course, there are exceptions such as Tom Brady who was forty-five when he retired from the NFL, and LeBron James who, in 2024 turned forty years old, and as of 2025 is still playing in the NBA. Even though being in one's forties is considered to be quite old for professional sports, retiring from a sport-related career in one's forties still means they are retiring decades earlier than the average adult in the United States when they retire from a more traditional career. The average professional athlete has three to four decades of work-related life remaining after retiring from sport, and this often results in the athlete needing to "recareer" (i.e., transition to another, different career).

Since retirement from professional sport with many productive work years remaining is the norm, a common recommendation for professional sport organizations is to provide a "comprehensive pre retirement plan addressing issues surrounding their transition out of athletic participation" (Chang et al., 2020, p. E80). This means having conversations and providing programming to professional athletes well prior to their actual retirement so there is time to contemplate "what's next." Relatedly, researchers agree that career-ending injuries for athletes can be accompanied by psychological effects that can last for quite some time. For professional athletes a career-ending injury means that they can no longer perform in the career that pays their bills and supports their family. Lest readers think most professional athletes are financially set for life because they earn so much money; according to the United States Bureau of Labor Statistics the median pay for a professional athlete in 2023 was just over $70,000. While this is a livable wage and for many quite a lot of money, this is not the kind of money that allows for saving and investing so the athlete never has to work again. Leaving one's sport can be challenging and it is estimated that when elite athletes leave their sport, as many as 20 percent struggle to manage the practical and psychological impact of no longer having sport in their life the way it has been. This is typically experienced as a significant loss and can be accompanied by a crisis of identity.

As is the case with athletes at any level of competition, there is typically a high degree of pressure to perform. Failure to perform may result in less playing time or being cut from a team altogether. This can be difficult to cope with when sport really matters to an athlete. However, when one's livelihood (professional athlete) or future livelihood (future professional athlete) is on the line the pressure can feel heavier. This kind of pressure can increase the athlete's risk for mental health challenges to include depression, anxiety, sleep problems, and problems with substance use. Of course dealing with diagnosable mental health challenges does not necessarily mean an elite athlete is unable to perform at all, or unable to perform exceptionally well. Michael Phelps, who has publicly talked about his struggles with his mental health, is an excellent example of an elite athlete who dealt with long-standing mental health challenges and who was exceptionally successful. It is, of course, unknown what his career may have looked like without experiencing mental health challenges.

A review of the literature, prepared by Andreas Küttel and Carsten Larsen, identified myriad factors that contribute positively or negatively to an elite athlete's mental health. These factors are characterized as "protective factors" or "risk factors," respectively, and can appear within the sports environment or in the athlete's personal life. Sport-related risk factors for elite athletes include experiencing a crisis when retiring from sport, inadequate support from teammates and coaches, and the sport-related stigma associated with seeking help for one's mental health. Personal risk factors also include inadequate social support from non-sport relationships (e.g., family), poor habits with respect to eating and sleeping, chronic stress in one's life (outside of sport), and problems with one's personality or identity. Protective factors, on the other hand, are believed to help prevent mental health challenges when present.

In the sport domain protective factors can include understanding mental health through mental health literacy, adjusting smoothly to retirement from sport, and positive sport-related relationships. In an athlete's personal life, protective factors can include good non-sport relationships, and having one's basic psychological needs met (i.e., self-determination theory's basic psychological needs of autonomy, competence, and relatedness), and actively engaging in behaviors that can help reduce the risk of mental health challenges such as learning healthy strategies for managing stress. It is interesting to note that in this review of the literature, fifteen total risk factors were identified compared to ten protective factors. This can reasonably be taken to mean that elite athletes may have more to contend with to maintain their mental health and may have to put in more effort to develop and ensure they have protective factors in their life.

Some research has shown that elite athletes may be at a similar level of risk for developing diagnosable mental health challenges compared to the general population. Some studies, when examining specific disorders in specific sports (e.g., eating disorders in lean sports), find that athletes are at greater risk. There is agreement, however, that elite-level athletes are at greater risk of experiencing a diagnosable mental health challenge when they experience an injury, are dealing with their upcoming or actual retirement, or are struggling to perform. In addition, given the expectations of performing at the highest levels, overtraining and burnout can occur which places an athlete at increased risk for mental health challenges. In addition, athletes at all levels, but perhaps specifically at the elite level, endure public and media-based scrutiny of not only their sport-based lives but also their personal lives. Overall the conclusion of researchers is that more needs to be done to ensure that elite-level and professional athletes have access to mental health resources at the same level of access they have to resources that support and heal their physical injuries.

Masters Athletes

Recent years have seen an increase in the number of "masters athletes" due to the aging of one of the largest generations: baby boomers. A master's athlete is usually defined as someone older than thirty-five since the body, in general, is likely to experience noticeable physical declines starting around that age. Some athletes become masters athletes when they continue to compete in sport following the end of their sport career (e.g., at the end of their collegiate career, or following retirement from professional sport), whereas others may return to sport after a lengthy period of time away from sport. Competitions for masters athletes can occur locally, nationally, and internationally.

The first *National Senior Games* in 1987 included around 2500 competitors all of whom were over the age of fifty. Since 2011, the number of competitors has remained in the neighborhood of 10,000 with the year 2019 having nearly 14,000 athletes all of whom were aged 50–100+. Senior athletes, of course, may reap the same rewards associated with sport at any age or level of competition, and may experience the downsides of sport participation to include injury and how that may intersect with athletic identity. The *International Masters Games Association* (IMGA) sponsors several different world competitions for masters athletes and notes that

> [e]verybody over the age of 30+ can participate (may vary for some sports) and register for the IMGA Masters Games events. There are no requirements on level or skills. Our events are open to anyone who wants be active, from professional levels to amateurs, from getting your PB to playing for fun. (International Masters Games Association, n.d., para. 2)

Thus, participating and competing in sport at the masters or senior level can be done by anyone at any time. No prior history with sport is necessary.

A Model of Successful Aging

Some have suggested that being a masters athlete means that such individuals can be held up as models for aging "successfully." The implication being if someone is still able to compete in sport at a relatively high level then they must be doing something right in terms of remaining healthy. Research examining the benefits of being a masters athlete has shown that such individuals are more likely to have lower levels of stress, depression, and anxiety compared to their non-athlete counterparts and are often determined to have aged more successfully in comparison to non-athletes. However, it is unclear if this is truly a unique benefit of being a masters athlete or simply an extension of the known benefits of engaging in physical activity at any point in life. In addition, there are significant variations in terms of genetics that impact one's ability to perform athletically at any age, which may also impact one's athletic longevity.

A recent study conducted by an international group of researchers led by Savannah Wooten from the University of Texas, Austin, hoped to extend what is known about the possible benefits of being a masters athlete by examining whether this status was connected to not only a reduction in negative emotional experiences such as anxiety and depression, but whether there were benefits in the other direction. That is, they wondered: Do masters athletes have greater positive emotional experiences and overall life satisfaction, and fewer sleep problems? These researchers surveyed masters athletes who competed at the *23rd World Athletics Masters Championships* and compared these results to the general population of the United States. Overall, they found that these masters athletes had higher levels of satisfaction with life and fewer sleep problems compared to the general population of the United States. There was no difference, however, between these athletes and the general population in terms of the level of positive affect (e.g., feelings of joy, excitement, and contentment).

One note of caution was identified by researchers examining masters athletes. When masters-aged adults, who are not physically active, compare themselves to master athletes, particularly those who compete at a high level, the inactive older adults may see masters athletes' achievements as unattainable which may ultimately discourage their own engagement in any amount of physical activity. Thus, while masters athletes may be seen as a source of inspiration, for some, masters athletes' achievements may be discouraging and viewed as out of reach.

Impact on Psychological and Social Factors

In some situations masters athletes experience both social and psychological benefits derived from their participation in competitive sport at the masters level whereas others seem to experience some drawbacks. Generally speaking, positive benefits of being a masters athlete can include better overall health and well-being due to the known benefits of physical activity to include having a sense of belonging and strong satisfaction with life. Drawbacks that may come with being a competitive masters athlete can include time away from family and friends particularly if they are not interested or invested in the athlete's sport participation. In addition, competitive masters athletes, like athletes in most age groups, may struggle with time management. It may be challenging, for example, to ensure they devote the time needed and desired not only to sport but to non-sport pursuits including time with family and friends.

A study conducted by researchers in Canada noted that there appears to be a threshold related to the level of participation prior to which masters athletes experience myriad benefits and after which they are likely to experience negative consequences, particularly with respect to their relationships. These researchers found that all participants, regardless of how involved they were with their sport, experienced benefits including lower levels of stress, higher levels of self confidence, and a sense of pride in their accomplishments. These athletes also reported experiencing benefits in their social relationships including things such as their children admiring what they have accomplished, and/or being able to engage in sport with children and grandchildren. The positive relationship effects were also found among fellow masters athletes with participants sharing that they felt a sense of camaraderie and mutual support. When masters athletes engage in their sport through training or competition at least five times a week they seem to have reached the threshold for when there is a negative impact on their relationships, particularly with friends and family. Participants engaged in sport more than five times per week stated that they were not only missing time with their family but also missing important family functions. Some participants described family as not understanding why sport was so important to them and therefore why they were willing to spend hours training when they could spend some or all of that time with family. In addition, their non-sport friends were noted as not understanding why their masters athlete friends devoted so much time and energy to sport which may contribute to a shift in one's circle of friends from those who don't "get it" to those who don't.

Conclusion

Athletes in any age group or competing at any level can face mental health challenges. Some elements that impact mental health-related experiences are unique to that particular group (e.g., retiring from sport, early sport specialization) and some factors are more universal (e.g., athletic identity, injury). Regardless of when or at what level an athlete participates in sport, it is clear that having sufficient mental health-related resources is important for the athlete's well-being and ability to continue to thrive in sport.

6

Historically Disenfranchised Athlete Groups

As is the case in society at large, historically disenfranchised groups in sport often contend with bias, prejudice, and discrimination. This chapter examines some of what is known with respect to the experiences of BIPOC athletes, athletes who identify with the LGBTQ+ community, athletes with disabilities, and athletes who are neurodivergent. Regretfully, there is not a lot of research conducted on the experiences of some of these groups of athletes, though the NCAA has regularly examined the experiences of BIPOC and LGBTQ+ athletes. It is hoped that readers will be challenged to reflect on their own experiences in sport (regardless of how one identifies), how those experiences may differ from those who do not identify in the same way, and what can be done to ensure all athletes have a space to compete in and enjoy sport.

Black, Indigenous, and People of Color (BIPOC) Athletes

In December of 2023 the NCAA published findings associated with the *NCAA Student-Athlete Health and Wellness Study* and reported that NCAA athletes reporting the most significant mental health-related challenges were those who identified as women, BIPOC, and LGBTQ+ student-athletes. Overall, rates of specific concerns decreased or remained about the same since the Covid-19 pandemic (see Chapter 10 for more information on the impact of Covid-19 on sport) but remain high. The NCAA reported statistics on student-athletes who identified as Black, Latinx, other, and white. When asked about specific elements that contributed to mental health challenges, at the top of the list were "planning for the future," "financial worries," and "academic worries." The percentage of white student-athletes impacted negatively by these and all other factors identified by the NCAA (e.g., family worries, playing time, coach relationship, etc.) was lower than all other groups on every factor. In terms of feeling negatively impacted by plans for the future 36, 37, and 38 percent of Black, Latinx, and other, respectively, felt negatively impacted compared to 29 percent of white student-athletes. For financial worries, those percentages were 35, 33, 30, and 19 percent, respectively, and for academic worries the percentages were 35, 42, 41, and 36 percent, respectively. No white students reported being impacted by "personal experiences of racism/racial trauma" whereas 10 percent of Black student-athletes, 6 percent of Latinx student-athletes, and 7 percent of student-athletes categorized as other were negatively impacted.

In a 2023 article addressing racism in the context of sport psychiatry, California-based sport psychiatrist Dan Begel detailed the long-standing history of racism in sport in the United States including efforts to exclude Black athletes from competing in sport, punishing Black athletes who refused to remain quiet about racism in sport, implementing intentional barriers (i.e., financial and academic) in an attempt to keep Black athletes out of sport, obstructions for hiring Black sport staff, and of course, harassment, ridicule, and violence against Black athletes. To be clear discriminatory actions like these also occur outside of sport; however, the focus here is on how BIPOC athletes are impacted within the context of sport.

Dr. Begel identified four different types of racism while acknowledging that categorizing racism in this way is meaningless when someone is on the receiving end of racist acts. Nonetheless, the four categories include violent racism (i.e., the purpose is to physical harm, kill, or terrorize), systemic or institutional racism (i.e., racism that is woven into a society's laws and systems), "sneaky" racism (e.g., racial profiling, discrimination), and "surprise" racism (e.g., microaggressions). These four categories of racism are not mutually exclusive and all forms of racism can and do occur at all ages and at all levels of competition.

The impact of racism on the physical and mental well-being of individuals is well-known at this point; however, very little attention has been paid to the impact of racism on BIPOC individuals specifically in the context of sport. There are, of course, numerous accounts of personal experiences with racism by sport personnel (e.g., coaches, owners of professional teams), fans, fellow teammates, and others. Much of what has been written about BIPOC student-athlete experiences focused on Black athletes. That is not terribly surprising; however, that can leave other BIPOC student-athletes feeling like their experiences are not as important. While the lack of data on other groups may reflect a lower rate of sport-participation the fact is that more research inquiring about the experiences of all BIPOC student-athletes is needed.

Dr. Begel concluded his publication by calling for providers who work with athletes in the mental health space to educate themselves on myths and misconceptions about race we may still hold, to bring up race and allow the athlete to decide if race is something worth talking about in this context, to acknowledge one's own racism and refrain from defensiveness when one's own racist comments or behaviors are identified, to appropriately stand up for athletes, not allow racist behavior, whether intentional or not, to occur without comment, to be prepared for resistance and hostility when you do identify racist behavior or comments by others, and refrain from taking a "color blind" position which results in ignoring an important aspect of the individual's identity.

LGBTQ+

Athletes on the "Queer-Spectrum" (i.e., non-straight sexual orientation) reported significantly higher rates of mental health concerns compared to their straight counterparts via the *NCAA Student-Athlete Health and Wellness Study*. For example, 55 percent of student-athletes on the queer-spectrum and 26 percent of student-athletes who identified as straight expressed feeling overwhelmed by all of their responsibilities and obligations as a student-athlete. Forty-seven percent and 22 percent of queer-spectrum and straight athletes, respectively, felt "mentally exhausted," and 39 percent compared to 16 percent, respectively, reported experiencing "overwhelming anxiety." With respect to gender identity on the same markers the percentage of those who identified as male struggling with these concerns was dramatically less compared to those who identified as female and even more so compared to those who identified as transgender or non-binary.

The *Human Rights Campaign* characterized 2021 as the "worst year for anti-LGBTQ+ legislation in recent history" (Human Rights Campaign, n.d., para. 1) noting that the trend seemed to be continuing into 2022. This organization also noted that "Transgender and non-binary people have been under attack for years—the pivot to sports is yet another front in this fight" (Human Rights Campaign, n.d., para 3). The majority of proposed and passed legislation by state governments is directed at transgender girls and women with the intent of preventing them from participating in sport on teams that reflect their gender identity (i.e., women's and girl's teams), and the NCAA has recently followed suite. In early February of 2025 the NCAA announced a change in policy that seems to reflect the legislation passed by many but not all states in the US. This legislation bans transgender females (i.e., those assigned male at birth) from competing on women's teams but will allow such athletes to practice with the teams. Similarly, an athlete who was "assigned female at birth who has begun hormone therapy (e.g., testosterone) may not compete on a women's team" (NCAA, 2025, Policy: NCAA Women's Team). As for men's teams, anyone assigned any sex at birth or who identifies with any gender can practice and compete on men's teams.

The 2024 Paris Olympics provided an opening ceremony that was somewhat controversial in part due to the decision to include sexual and gender diversity; however, these games also saw controversy with respect to transgender athletes, particularly transgender female athletes. At least one transgender woman was denied eligibility to compete in the Olympics in swimming. A female boxer was accused of being a transgender woman; however, she has reportedly always identified as female, has female on her passport, and has disclosed that she has a disorder of sexual development which can impact, among other things, genital development and hormones. She was allowed to compete as a female athlete, a decision that reflects the *International Olympic Committee's* eighteen-part mission statement, which states, in part: "to encourage and support the development of sport for all" (IOC, n.d., para 13).

As noted previously, concerns about transgender individuals competing in sport seem to center around transgender females. The thinking is that since these individuals were assigned male at birth, they would have an unfair advantage when competing against females who were assigned that sex at birth. The *Human Rights Campaign* noted that much of the proposed legislation designed to ban transgender athletes from participating in sport would impact children at the elementary, middle school, and high school levels (i.e., not at the highest levels of competition; however, the NCAA recently passed legislation that will impact transgender females who want to compete at the collegiate level). They also note that there has always been significant diversity among children and adolescents with respect to strength, height, and speed. Some cisgender females, for example, are exceptionally tall and will have a significant advantage over shorter cisgender females in some sports (e.g., basketball, volleyball). Similarly, some cisgender males have the ability to develop lean muscle mass quickly and extensively compared to other cisgender males, which decidedly gives them a greater advantage in sports that require a good deal of strength (e.g., certain contact, and combat sports).

Given the myriad benefits of participating in physical activity in sport (see Chapter 1 for more information), it has been argued that no individual should be kept from participating. Some may argue that they can participate but on teams that align with the sex they were assigned at birth; however, supporters of allowing transgender athletes to compete on teams that reflect their gender identity point to the significant mental health-related harms that come from effectively forcing a transgender person from living a life that aligns with who they are, including participating in sports that align with their gender identity. These significant mental health concerns can result in thoughts of suicide and death by suicide. Estimates, for example, are that among transgender individuals the rate of suicide attempts is between 32 and 50 percent worldwide. By way of comparison less than 1/2 a percent of people in the United States attempted suicide in 2022. The rate of suicide attempts among transgender individuals is believed to be so high due to what many readers might expect including things such as gender-based victimization to include discrimination and bullying, being rejected by those closest to them such as friends and family, enduring harassment by all manner of people including law enforcement and the general public, and so on.

A recent study conducted in 2024 asked nearly 300 transgender girls in high school why they chose or did not choose to participate in sport. Those who did participate in sport cited things such as physical and mental health benefits, the ability to have fun and connect with others socially, and the fact that participating affirmed their gender. Those who chose not to participate in sport endorsed reasons including the fact that they were disinterested in sport, the fact that teams were either "boys" or "girls" teams neither of which was a good fit, feeling uncomfortable around their peers when competing in sport, experiencing bullying or harassment, and physical or mental health-related limitations that made sport not appealing. The authors of this study concluded that inclusive sport environments are important along with education for coaches and others to help transgender athletes feel comfortable and confident participating in sport. In sum, transgender girls wanted to experience the same benefits that everyone who participates in sport experiences, but many seemed to feel unsafe or unwelcome doing so and elected not to participate.

Now more than ever adolescents and emerging adults have 24/7 access to what's going on in the world via social media and other internet-based outlets. Those identifying as a member of the LGBTQ+ community would, of course, have access to what others have to say about those who do not have a cisgender identity, and would likely be aware of legislation proposed and passed that limits their rights. For example, multiple states in the United States recently passed laws prohibiting classroom-based instruction on "controversial issues" such as gender identity and sexual orientation. Many of these laws were drafted following the 2022 "Don't Say Gay" bill passed in Florida. A settlement, in 2024, of the Florida law indicated that students and teachers can talk about gender identity and sexual orientation but cannot do so in the context of classroom instruction (i.e., students cannot be taught about these issues).

Although society currently seems focused on transgender athletes, the reality is homophobia in sport remains. One study, for example, found that over half of men's rugby and men's ice hockey players acknowledged using homophobic language on at least one occasion in the two weeks prior to being asked about their use of this type of language. The researchers found, however, that using this type of language was more related to the fact that using homophobic language was part of the culture rather than the actual attitudes or beliefs of those surveyed. The researchers advocated for interventions aimed at dismantling harmful norms such as the use of homophobic language.

The minority stress framework, conceptualized in the early 2000s by Ilan Meyer, has been used to explain the experiences of those who identify with "minority" (i.e., disenfranchised or historically marginalized) groups. The framework offers an explanation for how the experience of stigma and discrimination, related to how a person identifies, can be associated with higher levels of distress. This extends to the sport context. Historically gay and lesbian athletes have experienced and continue to experience discrimination and harassment. A study conducted in 2023 yielded results indicating that lesbian (L), gay (G), or bisexual (B) athletes who were "out" (i.e., they have revealed their sexual orientation to others) experienced greater mental health benefits compared to those who felt as though they had to continue to conceal their sexual identity. The researchers noted that those who were out still dealt with discrimination and harassment; however, they were able to be true to who they really were which seemed to outweigh the negatives for many LGB athletes.

Intersecting Identities

Those with intersecting identity face even more significant challenges. For example, those identifying with the LGBTQ+ community may endure harassment and violence related to their gender identity or sexual orientation, and when such individuals also identify as a person of color they may also experience racism and race-related oppression. Thus, those with historically minoritized intersecting identities can have even greater mental and physical health concerns. It has been found, for example, that individuals who identify as Black and LGBTQ+ have been found to report greater levels of discrimination, have poorer physical and mental health, and higher levels of substance use. Moreover, these negative outcomes have been found to be even greater in collegiate settings, particularly when individuals with these identities are also athletes.

Disability in Sport

As discussed in Chapter 1 of this book, there are myriad benefits for those who engage in physical activity in and outside of a sport context. These benefits can be found across the lifespan and across levels of competition. A group of researchers in Canada and the UK specifically examined the literature on health-related benefits of sport participation in individuals with a disability. The populations they examined included children, adolescents, adults, and elite-level athletes. Overall, they concluded that sport participation is beneficial for individuals with a disability that included benefits related to opportunities to interact with others, the experience of enjoyment while participating in sport, and through sport having the opportunity to challenge stereotypes often associated with individuals with disabilities.

The *Advocates for Life Skills & Opportunity* (ALSO) organization identified five common myths or misconceptions about individuals with disabilities. The first myth is that "Disability Means 'No Ability.'" Of course, individuals with a disability experience limitations that can make what they do look different in comparison to those without the same or similar disability; however, an activity done differently, of course, does not equate to an inability to engage in life-related activities to include activities of daily living and physical activity or sport. Another common myth is that "Physical Disability also Means 'Cognitive Impairment.'" While some individuals may have both a physical disability and a cognitive impairment, this is not always the case. Assuming that the two always go together can mean such individuals are unfairly treated and/or not allowed to engage in certain activities because they are inaccurately believed to not have the cognitive capacity to do so. A third myth identified by ALSO is that "People with Disabilities Cost Employers Too Much Money." ALSO noted that nearly half of all accommodations that are reasonable for an employee with a disability literally cost nothing and for another 40 percent or so the average cost of accommodations is about $300. This means that just over 10 percent of reasonable accommodations may have a high price tag. In comparison to $300 or less for nearly 90 percent of reasonable accommodations, it is not accurate to say that accommodating those with a disability is too expensive. Myth number 4 identified by ALSO is: "All Disabilities Can Be Seen." Unfortunately, those with non-visible or not obvious disabilities have likely encountered others who do not believe them when they say they are someone with a disability and may need accommodations. The *Centers for Disease Control and Prevention* (CDC) estimates that over 6 million individuals in the United States have an "invisible disability," and acknowledges that this number is likely an underestimate since many with an invisible disability may not identify with having a disability at all. ALSO noted that invisible disabilities can include mental health challenges including diagnoses on the Autism spectrum, concussion or traumatic brain injury (TBI), and learning disabilities. Finally, myth number 5 identified by ALSO is that "People Who Use Wheelchairs Can't Walk." Some individuals with disabilities such as multiple sclerosis and other medical conditions may not need a wheelchair all the time since the severity of their symptoms may wax and wane. Unfortunately, others may see this occasional use of a wheelchair as faking a disability or that they are simply looking for attention or sympathy from others.

Those who have ever watched the Paralympic Games that occur just after the Olympic Games will have noticed that some athletes have an "obvious" disability whereas others do not. The *International Paralympic Committee* (IPC) notes that to qualify for participation in the organized Paralympic sports the individual must have "an Underlying Health Condition that leads to a permanent Eligible Impairment" (International Paralympic Committee, n.d., para. 8). The IPC recognizes ten different types of impairment that are categorized into three groups: physical impairments, vision impairment, and intellectual impairment. The ten specific impairments include eight categorized as physical which are: impairments of muscle power, or passive range of movement, limb deficiency, leg length difference, short stature, hypertonia (muscle tension due to central nervous system [CNS] damage), ataxia (incoordination due to CNS damage), and athetosis (involuntary movements due to an underlying health condition). The remaining two specific impairments are their own category: vision impairment, and intellectual impairment.

The myriad types of disabilities recognized by the IPC reflect the notion that some people with a disability may appear to compete in a sport in the same manner as someone without a disability, and others may require special equipment or other accommodations so they are able to participate and compete in sport. Adapted sport is the term used to refer to sports that are modified in some way to accommodate athletes with a disability. These athletes may be referred to as "adaptive athletes." Adaptive sport refers to any sport that is modified in terms of equipment or rules in order to allow athletes who are disabled to compete. Adaptive sports can include wheelchair sports (e.g., basketball, tennis, rugby, motocross, lacrosse, hockey, archery, fencing, dance, etc.), and cycling and equestrian sports.

In 2021 the *American Academy of Pediatrics* published an article on promoting the involvement of children and adolescents in sport, recreation activities, and general physical activities. They identified benefits reflected in Chapter 1 of this book (e.g., wellness, strength, cardiorespiratory fitness, etc.), and included benefits that may be unique to those with disabilities including decrease morbidity due to things such as "pressure ulcers, and infections" (Carbone et al., 2021, p. 5). They also identified myriad barriers to children and adolescents, with a disability, participating in physical activity via sport or recreation. These barriers include false beliefs such as participation may be dangerous, there aren't any programs for those with disabilities, and sport-related rules are too complex or cannot be changed to accommodate those with disabilities. Additional barriers can include lack of transportation, and increased financial and time commitments. Things that may encourage or help facilitate participation in sport among those with disabilities include emphasizing fun and enjoyment instead of winning, including adaptations to sport such as longer periods of rest, more coaches, a lot of positive feedback, and ensuring the well-being of the athletes by watching out for fatigue or injury. Carbone and colleagues concluded that when healthcare providers take a thoughtful and informed approach to physical activity and sport participation there is no reason such activities should not be encouraged for those with disabilities in the same way and for the same reasons these activities would be encouraged for those without a disability.

Researchers in the UK who interviewed nearly two dozen elite-level athletes who compete in para-sports found that these athletes have identified several different concerns that require attention so that participation in para-sport can have the same benefits as it does for non-para-athletes. These athletes collectively called for a greater understanding of what contributes to the well-being of para-athletes with an emphasis on a holistic approach to each athlete whereby the athlete feels safe to communicate what they need so they can thrive in sport. They also called for support tailored specifically for para-athletes such as not requiring them to literally move closer to training facilities thereby leaving behind their social support systems and adapted household, and ensuring that sport-related support staff were well-educated on para-athletics and unique factors associated with competing in para-sport. The para-athletes interviewed also identified challenges related to having conflicting identities including "'athlete,' 'disabled,' 'role model,' and 'parent'" (Miller et al., 2024, p. 134) while being encouraged to maintain a high athletic identity. In addition, many of the interviewed athletes talked about having to repeatedly acknowledge their disability and justify why they required forms of support they were allowed to have and, in fact, were guaranteed because of their disability. Finally, while many of those interviewed noted that they appreciated the ability to compete in sport at a high level and stated that they were afforded opportunities that might not have otherwise been made available to them, they were also acutely aware of the disparity in any recognition or reward for their sport accomplishments in comparison to their non-para-athlete counterparts (e.g., Olympic compared to Paralympic athletes). In aggregate, these challenges were found to have negatively impacted the well-being of para-athletes.

Neurodiversity in Sport

The term "neurodiversity" was reportedly coined in 1998 by an Australian sociologist; however, recently, researchers have noted that the term "neurological diversity," which means the same thing as neurodiversity, was used a few years earlier than 1998. Regardless of when these terms were first used, neurological diversity or neurodiversity refers to how the brain develops in individuals and the fact that each human being's brain develops differently compared to all other people. Currently, neurodiversity is commonly used in reference to those whose brains develop significantly differently compared to most people. As a result, those identified as "neurodivergent" typically have a diagnosis of attention deficit/hyperactivity disorder (ADHD), an autism spectrum disorder (ASD), or a learning disability.

Estimates regarding the prevalence of these diagnoses range from less than 1 percent up to 11 percent. Less than 1 to 3 percent of those under the age of eighteen are believed to be diagnosed with an autism spectrum disorder. ADHD is believed to exist in approximately 5–11 percent of those under the age of eighteen, and anywhere between 3 and 10 percent of the world's population are diagnosed with a learning disability. It is suggested, however, that these prevalence rates may be lower than the actual number of folks who are neurodivergent. One of the most significant reasons for this underestimate is what researchers call "masking" or "camouflaging." This refers to when an individual masks or camouflages their neurodivergent-related characteristics by taking on neurotypical characteristics to adapt to or fit into environments that are prone to stigma or bullying. A significant proportion of those likely to mask or camouflage in this way are females. Although this strategy may help individuals avoid unwanted and harmful attention, the reality is these strategies themselves can result in higher levels of mental health-related symptoms to include stress, anxiety, depression, and fatigue. In short, masking requires an extraordinary amount of psychological and emotional resources so the individual can "fit in."

Recently researchers examined the literature to determine what benefits participating in physical activity and sport may have for children and adolescents who are diagnosed with an autism spectrum disorder (ASD). Overall, these researchers found several benefits for those diagnosed with ASD including assistance with developing social and emotional skills. They also found that physical activity helps in ways that are also seen in children and adolescents without an ASD diagnosis including improved sleep patterns, improved executive functioning (e.g., planning, understanding consequences), and support for metabolic health. What remains unknown is how much physical activity is optimal. Regardless of any optimal amount of physical activity, several studies noted that despite the known benefits for those diagnosed with ASD there is insufficient participation in physical activity and sport which may reflect inherent barriers to sport participation and engaging in physical activity for those who are neurodivergent.

In the context of elite-level sport, most of the research has been conducted with those diagnosed with ADHD. Researchers tended to focus on the association between ADHD and concussion such that ADHD has been identified as a specific risk factor for concussion (see Chapter 11 for more information on concussion). Although having ADHD may pose a challenge in this regard, additional research has found that being diagnosed with ADHD may be beneficial for high-level competition, with some studies noting that among elite-level athletes there appears to be a higher percentage of those diagnosed with ADHD compared to the general population.

Overall, research conducted in sport with those diagnosed with ADHD or ASD reported that these athletes called for greater understanding of the needs of neurodiverse athletes. One challenge associated with ADHD, specifically, is the prescription of effective medications that are classified as stimulants which are likely to be banned in sport competition. Depending on what is prescribed, taking a medically necessary medication (e.g., Ritalin) may violate anti-doping regulations which places athletes at risk for disqualification from competition. The alternative is for the athlete to not take their prescribed medication or taking approved but less-effective medication which will likely result in poor management of ADHD-related symptoms. It is possible for athletes to request a therapeutic use exemption or a TUE for the medication they are prescribed; however, there are specific rules and regulations that surround whether or not such an exemption may be granted. Educating coaches, fellow athletes, and other sport-related personnel can help combat stigma and misunderstanding that can impede inclusiveness, and training and competing in safe environments.

Overall, there is very little research in the experiences of neurodiverse athletes in sport. Most of the research has been conducted with collegiate athletes diagnosed with ADHD who compete in the United States. It has been noted that there are no studies that examined what sport organizations can do to best support neurodivergent athletes. Given the unique needs of neurodivergent individuals, education and training for coaches are important so that the uniqueness of such athletes can be supported, and their skills and abilities can be maximized in ways that neurotypical athletes are currently supported in traditional models of training and competition.

Conclusion

Historically disenfranchised groups who compete in sport tend not to have as much research or public attention paid to their struggles and their needs. As a result these athletes can encounter barriers that may prevent them from participating in sport at all, or may prove to require too many resources to manage resulting in an athlete leaving sport earlier than they might have otherwise. Not all athletes from these and other groups can or want to compete at the highest levels. They simply want to have equal access to sport and to feel safe in their sport participation.

Part II

Issues and Controversies

7

Athlete Risk of Death by Suicide

This chapter focuses on a difficult but important topic: suicidal thoughts, attempts to die by suicide, and death by suicide among athletes. Some issues related to suicide are not discussed here (e.g., substance use, mental health challenges, concussion) in part because these topics are discussed elsewhere in this book. In addition, these factors are known to put anyone at risk for suicidal thoughts and/or actions, not just athletes. The topics in this chapter are not exhaustive but address some common factors that may specifically put athletes at risk of suicidal thoughts or death by suicide.

Content related to suicide is, of course, difficult to read about. Those with a personal history of suicidal thoughts or attempts, or for those who know of someone important to them who died by suicide may find the content particularly difficult. It is recommended that all readers take care when wading through this material and stop reading if needed and/or engage in other methods of positive self-care (e.g., talk to someone you trust, take a break and do something you enjoy, spend time with a pet, etc.). Finally, if you or someone you know may be dealing with suicidal thoughts, do not hesitate to reach out for help.

Readers can call or text 988, or go to 988lifeline.org to chat to access the National Suicide Crisis Line. There are also options for those who use ASL (American Sign Language) or who use TTY (teletypewriter) devices to communicate. Callers who are veterans of the United States military can select option 1 to be transferred immediately to the Veterans Crisis Line (VCL).

Rates of Death by Suicide: General Population and Athlete Statistics

The Centers for Disease Control and Prevention (CDC) has tracked death by suicide since 1981. Death by suicide since then was at its lowest between 1991 and1995 as the sixth leading cause of death behind unintentional injury, malignant cancer, HIV, homicide, and heart disease. Between 1997 and 2007, death by suicide was the fourth leading cause of death after heart disease as the third leading cause of death, and between 2008 and 2011 it was the third leading cause of death following malignant cancer as the second leading cause of death. Since 2012 (through 2022) death by suicide has been *the second leading cause of death*, behind unintentional injury, among those aged 1–44 years old. Among those specifically in the 18–24 age range, death by suicide is the third leading cause of death after accidents and homicide. Overall, unintentional injury has remained the leading cause of death since 1981 by tens of thousands of deaths. As of 2022, the difference between deaths by suicide and death due to unintentional injury was just over 64,000 deaths. Regardless of this difference in incidence rates, the shift of suicide from the sixth leading cause of death to the second over the course of nearly twenty-five years is noteworthy.

Death by suicide can be shocking and profoundly life-changing for the loved ones left behind. It is no different when a death by suicide occurs in athletes. Some suggest death by suicide among athletes may have a greater impact on society itself since so many people see athletes as healthy in all ways and that they simply do not have problems like non-athletes do. This perception is changing given the highly publicized athlete deaths by suicide at the high school and collegiate levels, and in professional sports.

Among college students the rate of athlete death by suicide has increased over the past twenty years and is now the second leading cause of sudden death among athletes (the leading cause of sudden death among athletes is accidents) and has doubled within the last ten years compared to the first ten years of the study which examined data from 2002 to 2022. Every death, no matter the cause, is tragic; however, it is important to note that death by suicide is still relatively rare. This is clearly illustrated when considering the rate of death by suicide among athletes who competed on NCAA teams. As of 2022, there were over 520,000 NCAA athletes. The NCAA examined a variety of athlete-related deaths over a twenty-year period and found that there were just over 1100 athlete deaths in total, 128 of those being death by suicide. To be clear, this is 128 NCAA athlete deaths by suicide over the course twenty years. This is why athlete death by suicide is considered to be a rare occurrence. What is alarming is that the percentage of athlete deaths by suicide is increasing. During the first ten years of the study just over 7.5 percent of all athlete deaths were death by suicide and in the second ten years that percentage doubled to just over 15 percent. The NCAA study found that there were no significant differences in deaths by suicide by sex, race or ethnicity, or type of sport. It was, however, found that athlete death by suicide among Division I and Division II athletes was higher compared to Division III athletes. Even though the actual numbers are relatively small the fact that proportionally we're seeing more deaths by suicide among collegiate athletes than we ever have in the United States is concerning.

A recent examination of the literature on the rate of suicide among elite athletes, led by Eva-Maria Pichler, concluded that elite athletes are at reduced risk of thoughts of suicide, attempted death by suicide, and death by suicide compared to the general population. These elite-level athletes competed at the varsity level in college, were professional athletes, or were athletes who competed at the international or Olympic level. These researchers further concluded that those at greater risk for any suicide-related behavior included identifying as male, being non-white, and dealing with depression. There were not enough data to make a comparison between sports to identify any sport-specific risk factors.

Although participating in sport has been found to be a protective factor for athletes, including in the context of suicide, athletes are also highly likely to get injured which can increase the risk of death by suicide. One study examining suicide among high school athletes, for example, found that athletes did generally experience protection from suicide because they were athletes; however, they also found that injured athletes were at greater risk of attempting to die by suicide suggesting that injury may be an important factor when understanding why athletes may be at significant risk for suicide.

Injury

Those who participate in and/or watch sports know that injury is part of the game … literally. While many injuries may briefly (e.g., days or weeks) keep an athlete from practicing or competing some injuries may keep them out for much longer (e.g., months or a year or more), and in some cases are season-ending. Some injuries keep athletes out of sport permanently. These are typically referred to as career-ending injuries. The degree of the psychological or emotional impact of any injury will be experienced in part based on the severity of the injury and the recovery process, the amount of quality social support the athlete receives, and their level of athletic identity (see Chapter 3 for more information on Athletic Identity). An additional factor for elite level athletes is the threat to their livelihood either because their sport is their profession and they are paid sufficiently to live off of that income, or they do not get paid much for competing in sport but they have endorsement deals contingent on their sport participation.

Seeing a spike in psychological distress in athletes at the moment of and immediately following an injury is quite common. What is less common is significant psychological and emotional distress that continues for days or weeks (or longer) and may require formal support from a licensed mental health professional. Even less common are thoughts of suicide because of the injury, and acting on those thoughts. Nonetheless, when an athlete is injured they are automatically at higher risk of suicide compared to athletes who are not injured.

Musculoskeletal Injuries

Musculoskeletal injuries refer to injuries to the body's muscles and/or bones. The musculoskeletal system also involves tendons, joints, and ligaments all of can also be injured. Clearly many musculoskeletal injuries themselves are, of course, physically painful and rehabilitation and recovery from such injuries can be long and difficult. However, it is not the injury itself that leaves some athletes in a state of despair and desperation, but it is the impact of the injury on the athletes' sport career that can lead them to a desperate state of mind where death by suicide seems the only bearable solution.

Anita Baum, an Assistant Clinical Professor in the Department of Psychiatry and Behavioral Health at George Washington University, wrote about suicide in athletes, the factors that can contribute to this, and provided examples of athletes who experienced a musculoskeletal injury and who died by suicide. Related to musculoskeletal injuries Dr. Baum reported that in 2009 a professional golfer on the LPGA Tour had a back injury that resulted in her losing her "tour card." Earning a tour card is not easy to do and allows a golfer to compete in LPGA tour events that have millions of dollars in prize money. The following year this former professional golfer died by suicide and was said, by a family member, to have been depressed. In addition, a former NFL player, who previously had knee surgery, injured his knee leading to a second knee surgery within a year. For this football player, the injury was season ending. About a month prior to dying by suicide this player was quoted as saying that he "should just kill [himself]" (Baum, 2013, p. 80).

Concussion

Most of the research on injury in athletes and suicide is in the area of concussion and chronic traumatic encephalopathy (CTE). CTE became known to the average person when researchers at *Harvard University* started collecting the brain tissue of former professional athletes in high contact sports who had died. These athletes also had reported significant changes in personality, headaches, difficulty with sleep, and memory problems. Some of these athletes specifically requested that their brains be studied by researchers after their death, and some of these deaths were death by suicide.

There are many stories of professional athletes who competed in contact sports (e.g., American football, men's ice hockey) and who died by suicide after leaving their sport. Some specifically point to what they believe to be CTE (e.g., in suicide notes or in conversations leading up to their death by suicide) as the cause of their unbearable symptoms (e.g., headaches, insomnia, memory problems, increase in aggression, and depression). Some former NFL players specifically requested that their brains be given to universities conducting research in this area. Dave Duerson, who played for two different NFL teams, and Junior Seau who played for three different NFL teams both died by suicide and both shot themselves in the chest so that their brains could be preserved for study.

CTE can only be determined following death; however, researchers at *Massachusetts General Hospital* who collaborate with researchers at *Harvard University* on the *Football Players Health Study* reported that nearly one-quarter of former NFL players who believed they had CTE also stated that they frequently thought about suicide compared to only 5 percent of those who did not think they had CTE. One researcher from the *Harvard Medical School* reported that although there seems to be a connection between CTE and suicide, "the causes of suicide are complex, multifactorial and difficult to predict in individual cases" (Iverson, 2014, p. 162). This researcher suggested that additional information is needed to determine what role CTE may play in death by suicide among athletes.

Beyond professional athletes, a study conducted in 2023 examined the rate of death by suicide among high school athlete and non-athlete students. They specifically examined the degree to which these students experienced hopelessness and the degree to which they had thoughts of suicide after sustaining a concussion. Over 11,000 adolescents were part of the study and over 1700 sustained a concussion. Overall, male and female-identifying adolescents who sustained a concussion reported engaging in more violence (i.e., engaging in physical fighting) or were more prepared for violence (i.e., carrying a weapon), and reported feelings of hopelessness. All who were studied who had a history of a concussion were identified as experiencing feelings of hopelessness and were capable of suicide compared to those who did not sustain a concussion. Male-identifying adolescents who experienced a concussion were also more likely to report suicide attempts compared to male-identifying adolescents who did not experience a concussion. It is important to note, given the fact that this book is focused on athletes, that this study included anyone who experienced a concussion regardless of how it occurred or in what context (e.g., sport).

Among youth athletes, specifically, one study found that 10 percent of athletes who had a sport-related concussion and who had a post-concussion psychiatric outcome (e.g., were diagnosed with a mental health disorder following the concussion; See also Chapter 11 on Concussion for more information) also reported having suicidal thoughts. They also reported that one individual in the study died by suicide. This also illustrates what is already known about suicidal thoughts: they are far more common than we would like to believe; however, acting on those thoughts and dying by suicide is rare.

Overall, researchers examining sport-related concussion specifically concluded that more information is needed in order to determine what relationship, if any exists between concussion and suicide. Researchers have noted, for example, when examining NFL players overall, they were found to be at lower risk of death by suicide compared to the general population. However, when examining the impact of chronic traumatic encephalopathy (CTE) it has been found that these athletes are at increased risk for death by suicide which is still a rare outcome. As is the case with any highly publicized issues (in or outside of sport), cases that make national news can create a perception that an issue is more common than it actually is.

In addition to injury there are also other aspects of sport that may leave an athlete in such a state of despair that they feel like the only way to resolve the psychological and emotional pain is by death. These situations can include retirement from sport, pressure to win, and sport-related abuse.

Retirement from Sport

Retirement from sport can be a difficult process for many athletes, particularly those who are highly identified with the role of athlete (i.e., have a high athletic identity; see also Chapter 3 for more information on Athletic Identity) and who have not explored who they are and what value they have as a person outside of sport. Many who have not contemplated who they are and what they will do when competitive sport can no longer be part of their lives often experience significant psychological distress. This can lead to the development of depression and anxiety, among other diagnosable mental health challenges.

For some the loss of sport and identity is so devastating that suicide seems to be the viable only solution.

David Lester, who addressed the connection between retirement in sport and suicide in a book chapter published in 2013, noted that some former professional athletes transition from sport and stay connected to sport via a media job such as providing commentary on televised competitions. Some athletes, of course, do not have such opportunities and may be so heavily tied to their role as an athlete that they struggle to understand who they are and what they want outside of being an athlete. However, even when an athlete can remain connected to their team in some way that may still not be sufficient to fill the void of competing in sport, particularly if the athlete has to leave their sport before they are ready.

A professional rugby player, Dan Vickerman, who competed for nearly ten years at the highest level died by suicide and reportedly talked about how difficult it was for him to retire from sport. This example, however, also shows how devastating injury can be on an athlete's career ultimately forcing them to leave the sport before they are ready. Apparently, Vickerman suffered from recurrent stress fractures which forced him out of competition. He reportedly remained connected to the sport working for the *Rugby Union Players' Association* and had been working in real estate since he was forced into retirement due to injury. Following Vickerman's death by suicide, a representative of the *Australian Rugby Union* was quoted as saying "We as administrators need to continue to be ever vigilant. The transition from being a professional sportsman into the world after sport can be challenging … " (ABC News Australia, 2017, para 8 & 9).

Some professional organizations and national governing bodies (NGBs) have devoted resources to help athletes transition out of competitive sport. The United States Olympic and Paralympic Committee (USOPC), for example, offers a *Life After Sport* program involving one-on-one meetings to help athletes identify what non-sport skills and abilities they have, and the type of environments they typically thrive in to help them determine what types of career paths might be best suited for them. This type of effort can help an athlete expand their identity beyond sport and into other areas of interest that the athlete may have discovered for the first time, or uncovered following years devoted to sport.

Pressure to Win

It is not unusual for athletes, coaches, and others highly invested in sport to have a "win at all costs" mentality. Someone with this mindset places such importance on winning that they are willing to sacrifice anything to make that outcome happen. This can lead to doping (i.e., using performance-enhancing substances that are banned from competition), cheating, being overly aggressive in competition resulting in injury to one's self or another athlete, and sacrificing other interests or obligations so the athlete can devote all time, energy, and resources to winning. A group of researchers out of Israel led by Alex Krumer studied professional athletes and non-athletes in the context of the "time preference" of these two groups. Time preference refers to an individual's preference for when to receive their rewards: immediately or later. The researchers found that athletes who had the win-at-all-costs mentality tended to over-value the present. They wanted their reward now. As a result, these researchers concluded that college athletes, for example, may forgo pursuing or completing a college degree so that they can capitalize on the short period of time they have to compete at the highest level. This can further intensify the pressure to win since there is a limited period of time for competitive sport in one's life. One example of a former Olympic runner illustrates how devastating it can be for an athlete not to win.

Although an example from quite a while ago, Kokichi Tsuburaya, a Japanese Olympic athlete who was poised to win a silver medal in the marathon at the 1964 Olympics held in his home country of Japan, won a bronze medal when he was passed by another runner at the very end of the race. This was the first Olympic medal, ever, for Japan in a track and field event; however, Kokichi reportedly felt a deep sense of shame that he had let down his country because he allowed himself to be passed at the end of the race and therefore not winning the silver medal. He reportedly told a teammate that he had to make up for his "blunder" by winning gold at the next Olympics. Preparing for the next Olympic games significantly interfered with his personal life since those in charge of Kokichi's training reportedly refused to allow him to marry his fiancée because he needed to completely focus on his training for the next Olympics. His fiancée reportedly married someone else because her parents would not allow her to wait for Kokichi. In addition, the training regimen for the next Olympics was hard on his body and he suffered myriad injuries, at least one of which required surgery. He ultimately died by suicide at the age of twenty-seven in January of 1968—10 months prior to the start of the 1968 Olympics. Although Kokichi suffered both competitive loss and the loss of his fiancée, both of which may have contributed to his death by suicide, it appears as if his reported shame of not winning silver in the 1964 Olympics and his need to win gold at the next Olympics cost him his future wife and ultimately cost him his life.

Michael Phelps, the most decorated Olympian of all time, has become an outspoken advocate for the importance of athlete mental health sharing his own struggles including thoughts of suicide. He is quoted as saying "When I looked in the mirror, I saw a swimmer, not a human" (Dye, 2023, para 9), and pointed to feeling that "as a male athlete I could tell something was off … But I think I saw it as a sign of weakness and if I shared anything about it then it would give my competitors an edge" (Weisholtz, 2024, para 3 & 4). He apparently struggled with substance use as well, having been arrested for his second DUI two years before his final Olympics in 2016. He reportedly took part in group therapy that caused him to take a look at his life and contend with thoughts of suicide. In an interview he stated, "It was the lowest point that I have been to so far—I felt like I didn't want to be alive" (Pfeffer, 2022, para. 2). He has since stated that seeking treatment and going to therapy saved his life. Michael has become a spokesperson for the importance of tending to one's mental health. He noted an athlete can achieve greatness in sport while also taking care of one's overall well-being and mental health, suggesting that it is possible to win at some costs, but not all costs.

One athlete's whose life tragically ended in death by suicide was a collegiate runner who was a multi-sport athlete in high school, and who reportedly struggled with understanding who she was in and outside of sport. She was Madison Holleran who competed for the University of Pennsylvania. The author who wrote a book about Madison's life and death described the pressure Madison felt not only going about her daily life and the pressure to achieve academically, but also the pressure to achieve in sport. A part of that particular struggle involved the fact that like so many new collegiate athletes she was a star in high school, but was one of many excellent talents competing for a Division I program. She apparently had considered quitting the track team to take a break and figure out what was making her feel so badly but ultimately decided against it. Sitting with a friend and her friend's mom, Madison apparently had the thought that "If she quit, wasn't she just a failure?" (Fagan, 2015, para.67). There was certainly more going on for this talented young woman than pressure to perform in sport; however, that did seem to be among the more prominent themes that contributed to her death. Madison, of course, is not the only one to feel the enormous weight of competing at the collegiate level, and is not the only one to die by suicide. Many more suffer in ways that do not claim their lives, but suffer significantly. The pressure to achieve great things in sport can be unbearably overwhelming.

Sport-Related Abuse

Abuse can be physical, psychological, emotional, or sexual. Often abuse of any type occurs at the hands of someone known to the person being abused. The abuser is often in a position of power and is often trusted not only by the person being abused, but also by others around them who may disbelieve that such a person could be capable of abuse. This is unfortunately far too common in- and outside of sport.

The psychological and emotional consequences of sexual abuse in and out of sport are significant and potentially life-ending. These consequences can include weight loss or weight gain, low energy, acting out and causing harm to self or others, bullying, difficulty sleeping, hopelessness and helplessness, trauma-related symptoms (e.g., hypervigilance, nightmares), suicidal thoughts, attempts to die by suicide, and death by suicide. Many readers may be familiar with the scandal that rocked USA Gymnastics when the team physician who also worked and taught at the University of Michigan was found guilty of sexually abusing hundreds of female athletes including many competing at the highest amateur level in gymnastics: the Olympics. At least one athlete died by suicide due to her inability to cope with the aftermath of the abuse. She died prior to when others' claims of sexual abuse by this doctor were finally taken seriously.

A study published in 2021 examined the connection between having suicidal thoughts and having been physically or sexually abused among elite-level athletes who had retired from sport. Among those who participated in the study over 10 percent reported being sexually abused, and of those just over 2.5 percent reported that the sexual abuse took place in a sport setting. Nearly 11 percent stated that they endured physical abuse at some point during their lives and a small number of participants reported that they were physically abused by a coach. The researchers found that sport injury and retirement from sport among those who participated in the study did not account for having suicidal thoughts or making an attempt to die by suicide. They concluded that " … mental harm resulting from abuse and the athlete's psychological resources and behavioral traits, respectively, appeared to be the leading influences on susceptibility for suicidal thoughts and actions" (Timpka et al., 2021, p. 203).

Beyond elite-level sport, it is estimated that between 2 and 22 percent of amateur and high school athletes have been abused by a coach. In some states in the United States the chances of being abused by a teacher who is also a coach can be exponentially higher than being abused by a teacher who is not a coach. In the early 2000s a company that conducts background checks reportedly found that "15,000 convicted sexual offenders coach kids in out-of-school sports" (Tippin, 2003, as cited in Teasley & Gill, 2014, p. 4). This same company reported that "minority students" are more likely to be targeted for sexual abuse.

Abuse of any kind can occur in sport at any developmental age and at any level of competition. Athletes, and their families, put their trust in sport-connected personnel (e.g., coaches, trainers, sport medicine professionals) and believe that they will care for their athletes. In most cases, this is exactly what happens. Unfortunately, however, there are far too many people who take advantage of their position and status, and abuse those for whom they should be providing care and guidance. Those who experience abuse are also typically dealing with some mental health challenges and for some these challenges can result in suicidal thoughts or death by suicide.

Substance Use

Factors that generally place people at higher risk for death by suicide include biological males, military veterans and active service members, American Indians and Alaskan Natives, those who are part of the LGBTQ+ population, those who have a previous suicide attempt, and those who have a mental health or substance use disorder. In the United States, it is reported by the *Substance Abuse and Mental Health Services Administration (SAMHSA)* that opiates are found the in systems of 20 percent of those who die by suicide and alcohol intoxication is involved in approximately 22 percent of deaths by suicide. Chapter 2, *Describing Mental Health and Common Mental Health Challenges in Athletes,* describes rates of substance use among athletes, including collegiate athletes. Although there is not a lot written about substance use, athletes, and suicide, much can be extrapolated given what is known about the connection between substance use and suicide in the general population.

The book entitled *Suicide in Professional and Amateur Athletes: Incidence, Risk Factors, and Prevention,* noted that injured athletes, for example, may be more susceptible to abusing pain killers, and in some sports, such as rugby, alcohol consumption is part of the culture. While using these and other substances (e.g., performance enhancing substances) does not mean an athlete will have suicidal thoughts or attempt to die by suicide, substance use may place them at greater risk since at least 1/5 of the general population who die by suicide have some substance in their system at the time of their death.

Conclusion

There are myriad factors that may contribute to someone having thoughts of suicide and that contribute to someone acting on those thoughts. This chapter examined some of the factors that may contribute to why athletes die by suicide regardless of their level of competition or age. Sport-related transitions such as injury (whether career ending or not) and retiring from sport, feeling the enormous burden of winning or achieving no matter what, enduring abuse, and the use of substances in combination with other psychological and social factors can make some athletes feel like death is a better alternative than life.

8

Personal, Interpersonal, and Intergenerational Trauma

Readers sensitive to discussion of trauma, including descriptions of traumatic situations, are cautioned to take care when reviewing this chapter, and/or may want to skip this chapter until they feel ready to read it.

In this chapter, we will explore various traumas individuals can experience in and outside of sport, though the focus will be on sport. Some readers may be surprised to learn how common traumatic experiences are, and that even if someone did not experience the trauma personally they can still be impacted as if they did. An overview of sport-related trauma and how trauma in general can impact athletes is provided, as well as a discussion of the importance of developing a broader awareness of trauma in athletes to include implementing trauma-informed sport policies and programming.

Large T and Small t Trauma

In recent years researchers and practitioners have noted that trauma may be classified into two groups which are often referred to as "large T" trauma and "small t" trauma. Large T trauma typically refers to events that would be classified as traumatic by the *Diagnostic and Statistical Manual of Mental Disorders* (DSM) when, for example, describing criteria for posttraumatic stress disorder (PTSD). By definition, PTSD-related trauma requires that the traumatic event resulted in death or serious injury or nearly resulted in death or serious injury. The person diagnosed with PTSD may have been the one who was seriously injured or nearly died, they may have witnessed this in another person, or they may have learned about someone important to them who died or was seriously injured. These events can include serious accidents, interpersonal violence, sexual assault, natural disasters, war, and so on. It is important to note that experiencing the trauma in and of itself does not automatically mean someone has PTSD. There are myriad symptoms associated with this disorder and many people who experience this type of trauma do not develop PTSD.

Small t traumatic events, by contrast, do not threaten our physical lives or physical well-being but leave us struggling to adequately cope and may lead to disruption in parts of our lives. Such traumas can include divorce, legal trouble, working in a toxic environment, financial difficulty, and so on. These types of trauma can be overlooked by most people since they are relatively commonplace. Sometimes overlooking them and/or believing any distress associated with this type of trauma means the person is being overly dramatic which may indicate that they are (unconsciously) trying to minimize or avoid the impact of the event. It is not usually until someone has experienced an overaccumulation of these types of trauma and experience the full impact of the accumulated trauma that they will seek help. While a single large T trauma can in and of itself overwhelm our ability to cope and function, it may take several small t traumas to get us to the point where we notice impairment somewhere in our lives. Distinguishing between types of trauma in this way can be problematic in that it can lead people to think that some traumatic experiences are objectively "worse" than others. The reality is that the severity or the impact of a traumatic experience on someone depends on myriad factors including coping skills they have learned to help them manage other difficult experiences, and what they may have already experienced earlier in life.

Adverse Childhood Experiences

According to the *Centers for Disease Control and Prevention* (CDC, 2024), adverse childhood experiences (ACEs) can be described as "potentially traumatic events that occur in childhood (0–17 years)" (para. 3). Examples can include the child experiencing any form of violence to include abuse or violence in their home or surrounding community. ACEs can also include neglect and having someone close to them, such as a family member, die by suicide or who makes an attempt to die by suicide. ACEs also include experiencing things within the home that "undermine [the child's] sense of safety, stability, and bonding" (CDC, 2024, para 4) such as someone in the home with mental health or substance use challenges, separation or divorce of parental figures, when an important member of the household is incarcerated, being food insecure, housing insecure, or experiencing discrimination.

The prevalence of ACEs is quite high. Nearly 65 percent of adults in the United States reported experiencing at least one ACE, and just over 17 percent of adults reported they experienced four or more ACEs while growing up. A greater number of ACEs are often associated with inequalities associated with one's history (e.g., BIPOC, Jewish, LGBTQ+), gender, and socioeconomic status. Those who identify as female experience a higher number of ACEs along with those who are indigenous, and those who are unemployed.

ACEs are associated with myriad health conditions affecting the body and the mind including heart disease, and depression. Beyond the physical, psychological, social, and spiritual costs to the individual, the negative impact ACEs have on one's overall health and well-being is estimated to cost over $580 billion in Europe and nearly $750 billion in North America, annually. Researchers examining ACEs as it relates to monetary cost noted that reducing ACEs by 10 percent could reduce these costs (associated with things like cancer, diabetes, cardiovascular disease, anxiety, and depression) by over $100 billion.

ACEs and Sport

There has not been a great deal of scientific attention paid to the relationship between ACEs and sport; one study conducted in 2021 used data collected via the *National Survey of Children's Health* to determine if the experience of ACEs in children aged 10–17 years would impact sport participation. The number of ACEs experienced by children in this data set ranged from one to three or more. Results of this study showed decreased sport participation no matter how many ACEs were experienced; however, of those who reported experiencing 1 ACE, only those identifying as boys had an accompanying decrease in sport participation. Since participation in sport can have myriad benefits including developing resilience, these researchers recommended communities identify children who have experienced one or more ACE and find ways to encourage participation in sport. They also strongly suggest a trauma-informed approach for all who interact with youth athletes. Before exploring what it means to have a trauma-informed approach to sport, what follows are the ways in which various forms of trauma can show up in sport.

Sport-Related Trauma

When we think of sport-related trauma, it is likely that the first thing that comes to mind is a physical injury of some kind as a result of sport-related play and/or head trauma (i.e., concussion; see Chapter 11 on Concussion for more information). Other sport-related trauma can include interpersonal violence in the context of sport, vicarious trauma through sport, and intergenerational trauma that can impact one's performance in sport.

Injury-Related Trauma

Injuries of all kinds are common in sport. The *US Department of Health and Human Services* tracks sport-related injury data and notes that such injuries can be relatively minor (e.g., sprains) to more severe injuries (e.g., bone fractures and concussion). They also note that approximately 2 million adults, annually, end up in a hospital emergency department for a sport-related injury. With respect to sport-related injuries in youth Stanford Medicine estimates that of the approximately 30 million youth sport participants, over 3.5 million youth (fourteen years and younger) are injured every year to include approximately three-quarters of a million seeking care in a hospital emergency department.

Experiencing a single severe trauma, or multiple traumas in or out of sport impacts an athlete's sense of safety and control. There can be a posttraumatic response (that may or may not result in a formal diagnosis of posttraumatic stress disorder [PTSD]) that includes feeling intense fear and helplessness. Additional symptoms include re-experiencing the trauma by having memories of the trauma during one's day regardless of what else the person may be doing, having nightmares about the trauma, and possibly having flashbacks (i.e., reliving the trauma as if you are back there again). Individuals diagnosed with PTSD also try to avoid any reminders of the trauma, and may struggle with increased arousal which is often experienced by difficulty sleeping, high levels of anxiety, startling easily, and difficulty staying focused on things.

Whether someone experiences the injury-related trauma themselves (e.g., a compound leg fracture requiring surgery) or someone witnesses the injury-related trauma happen to someone else, the impact can be significant on one's ability to function as they usually do, and to feel psychologically okay. When someone witnesses a trauma happening to someone else, or they hear about it later, it is possible for that person to experience what is called vicarious traumatization. For some, the severity of their reaction can reflect symptoms of posttraumatic stress.

Vicarious Trauma in Sport

There is a great deal of research on vicarious traumatization among licensed mental health professionals who treat individuals who have experienced a trauma. In this context it is possible for treatment professionals, who listen to accounts of traumatic events, to develop posttraumatic stress-related symptoms. There has not, however, been a lot of research conducted on the impact of sport-related vicarious trauma. Vicarious trauma can be experienced by anyone including spectators, teammates, coaches, and other sport staff who witnessed a serious sport-related injury or life-threatening event in sport. What little research has been done in this area has confirmed what is found in the literature regarding vicarious traumatization of mental health professionals: those who witness a sport-related injury can be traumatized too.

Fans of American football may recall the horror that occurred during one of the last regular season games, on a Monday night, of the *National Football League's* (NFL) 2022 season between the Cincinnati Bengals and the Buffalo Bills (the game occurred early in January 2023). Bills player Damar Hamlin, 24 years old, suffered what is medically referred to as "commotio cordis" which is essentially a disruption of the normal heart rhythm caused by a blow to the chest right above the heart in the midst of a heartbeat. The result is cardiac arrest (i.e., the heart stops beating). Millions of spectators, collectively in the stadium and watching around the world, saw Damar stand up after what appeared to be a typical football tackle, then collapse. As quickly as possible athletic training staff ran onto the field and performed CPR because the athlete's heart had literally stopped beating and did not resume beating on its own. He survived.

In an interview with Michael Strahan a little over a month after this occurred, Damar was asked if he remembers standing up after he made the tackle. His response was "That's something I don't really want to get into deep into the details of" (ABC News, 2023, 0:59). He stated later in the interview that he did watch the film of his collapse "once or twice" while he was in the intensive care unit of the hospital adding that "I couldn't really watch it too much" (ABC News, 2023, 1:33) noting that he was still processing what happened and figuring out how to describe for himself what the event was like for him. And in the true form of a highly competitive athlete, when asked, he stated that the first thing he said after he was brought out of sedation was "Did we win?" (ABC News, 2023, 2:17). Importantly, the commissioner of the NFL allowed the Bills and Bengals to decide if they wanted to continue the game after his collapse and the decision was made not to complete the game. The good news is that Damar survived this traumatic event and returned to play for the 2023 NFL season. Clearly this was a traumatic experience for Damar; however, his near-death experience also impacted others in the league.

In the aftermath, some NFL players shared their thoughts and feelings via an article written by *The Athletic* NFL Staff (2023) about what happened including: "I can't even express the emotions. It's been a roller-coaster … I've got two kids at home who are expecting me to walk back in the door" (para. 6), "Calling my parents on Monday night and hearing their voices and hearing my dad ask questions that I'm not ready to talk about … And sometimes you got to find a way to compartmentalize it" (para. 13), "I'm sure every significant other of a player has said: 'This could have been you.' It touches really hard for us" (para. 19). In short, Darmar's on-the-filed trauma was not easy for fellow professional football players and their families to process, even though it did not happen to them.

Although research in the area of vicarious trauma in sport is scant at best, one study involved conducting in-depth interviews of two sport coaches about an injury they witnessed (they both witnessed the same event) which revealed vicarious traumatization. To be clear, the intent of this study was to understand the nature of vicarious trauma rather than to understand, in this case, what the injured athlete experienced. There is no suggestion here that the athlete's experience is unimportant or not traumatic. This particular study was focused on what happens when someone, in this case a coach, witnesses a gruesome injury.

There were myriad important themes revealed through interviews with the two coaches including the importance of making sense of trauma or giving some kind of meaning to it. For example, one coach noted that the injury they witnessed (involving a compound leg fracture which means there was a lot of visible blood, bone, and tissue) could have been much worse than it was adding that the athlete did not lose their leg and would be able to walk again. Both coaches interviewed experienced "flashbacks" and what are called "intrusive thoughts." Flashbacks refer to reliving the trauma such that it feels like you are experiencing the trauma all over again—as if you are there. Intrusive thoughts refer to having memories of the event whether you want to or not. Both coaches talked about things in their daily lives that would trigger such memories or a flashback (e.g., seeing an ambulance, watching TV, and seeing someone with a similar injury). One coach noted that their coaching was impacted two years later in that they made decisions about athlete recovery noting that " … I suppose in a way I'm probably holding people back because I'm not as confident coaching as before it all happened" (Day et al., 2013, p. 7). Both coaches talked about avoidance related to the trauma by not wanting to talk about it with anyone, but did try to seek social support in an effort to accept what happened. The authors of this study noted that even though there were similarities in how both coaches responded, they did not respond in the same ways revealing different coping strategies some of which were healthy and others less so. The authors emphasized the fact that when dealing with trauma in any capacity it is important to understand the individual's experience rather than trying to impose expectations on how someone is likely to respond.

Another study on vicarious trauma in sport examined the impact of witnessing a serious injury of a fellow athlete that resulted in hospitalization and an inability to re-engage with sport for at least three months. Injuries witnessed included various bone fractures and tissue tears (e.g., ACL or tendon tear). The non-injured athletes were asked to describe the injury they witnessed in as much detail as possible and what their subsequent reactions were. The authors identified three categories of responses including athletes' immediate responses to the injury that included fear and anxiety, shock, and physical symptoms such as nausea and shaking. Athletes also expressed a range of emotions in response to the injury including relief that it wasn't them who was injured, sadness for the athlete who was injured, and disappointment for losing a valued team member. Finally, study participants expressed various ways they identified with the injured athlete including knowing how painful an injury can be, how difficult it can be to rehab and recover from an injury, and remembering their own injury experiences. These athletes also described symptoms related to posttraumatic stress including intrusive thoughts about the injury (i.e., they kept thinking about it and/or had difficulty concentrating), an acute awareness of how easy it is to get injured (i.e., feeling helpless), avoidance of reminders of the event such as not practicing at all or not practicing specific skills, and not watching athletes complete specific skills or removing specific equipment from the gym. Athletes did attempt to cope with the aftermath of witnessing the injury by seeking support from others, thinking about the fact that injury is simply part of the sport, and adjusting how they trained or how they talked to themselves about the injury so they could "move on." The authors reported that despite difficulty coping with the immediate aftermath of witnessing a fellow athlete's injury these athletes were able to gradually reengage with their sport.

The research that has been conducted in the area of sport-related vicarious trauma has been done with a very small number of participants which means there is little that can be assumed in terms of how the experiences reported by these study participants reflect what others would experience if they witnessed someone else get seriously injured via sport. This means that there is a great deal more to be understood in terms of what is universal about the impact of witnessing an injury (i.e., everyone experiences the same thing), how witnessing an injury may impact different groups (e.g., coaches and athletes, spectators, sex, different age ranges), and how reactions may be unique to each person (i.e., not everyone may be able to re-engage with their sport for reasons unique to them).

Interpersonal Violence in Sport

Another type of issue in sport that can contribute to a trauma response (e.g., PTSD-related symptoms) is interpersonal violence. Violence, in general, is defined by the *World Health Organization's World Report on Violence and Health* as

> the intentional use of physical force or power, threatened or actual, against oneself, another person, or against a group or community, that either results in or has a high likelihood of resulting in injury, death, psychological harm, maldevelopment, or deprivation. (Krug et al., 2002, p. 5)

Interpersonal violence, specifically, "refers to violence between individuals, and is subdivided into *family and intimate partner violence* and *community violence*" (Violence Prevention Alliance, n.d., para. 5). Interpersonal violence can include physical or sexual violence, psychological violence that is also referred to as emotional violence, and neglect or deprivation of some kind. In the context of sport, the *International Olympic Committee* refers to interpersonal violence in sport as "non-accidental violence in sport" (Edwards et al., 2023, p. 1).

Perhaps the most well-known, contemporary, case of interpersonal violence in sport involved *USA Gymnastics* and the *Michigan State University* (MSU) doctor they used to treat their female-identifying athletes. Complaints about this doctor were reportedly made to MSU as far back as 1998. In 2014 a formal Title IX complaint was made, and in 2015 the FBI got involved. Over the years since 1998 athletes, including at least one athlete under the age of thirteen, reported their concerns but since the perpetrator was revered as a sport doctor and as a person, those who lodged their complaints were reportedly not listened to, or their claims were dismissed by others who knew him as "not possible." Over 150 victim impact statements were made at his trial in 2017 that included several high-profile members of the *US Olympic Women's Gymnastics Team* including Aly Raisman, McKayla Maroney, and Simone Biles. A lawsuit against the FBI claiming significant failures in how they handled the case was recently settled by the Justice Department based on 139 claims, for nearly $140 million. In addition these and other world-class gymnasts called for the US Olympic Board of Directors to be disbanded given their gross mishandling of sexual abuse allegations made over the course of many years. The convicted physician was sentenced to 40–175 years in jail. The impact on these athletes' lives is significant and in many ways immeasurable.

In an *International Olympic Committee* (IOC) consensus statement published in the *British Journal of Sports Medicine* authors noted that non-accidental, or interpersonal violence in sport is a "blind spot for many sport organisations through fear of reputational damage, ignorance, silence or collusion" (Mountjoy et al., 2016, p. 1019). The authors identified myriad groups who may be at higher risk of non-accidental violence due to power dynamics related to "Sex, Gender, Sexual orientation, Race, Ethnicity, Indigeneity, (Dis)ability, Age, Athletic Ability, Athletic longevity, Faith, Socio-economic/Financial status … or a combination of these" (p. 1020). They identified the impact violence inflicted on any athlete can have to the sport organization in which the violence occurred; however, they also specifically note the lasting impact interpersonal violence can have on the athlete. Not surprisingly, all aspects of an athlete's life can be negatively affected by this type of violence. As a result of this type of violence, athletes can struggle financially, have problems in their relationships, struggle with mental health concerns, engage in problematic behaviors, have difficulty managing emotions, have negative thought patterns that can, among other things, impact self-esteem, and athletes can experience physical problems that can include being ill, getting injured, experiencing a decline in performance, engaging in self-harm behaviors, and engaging in problematic eating behaviors.

Mountjoy and colleagues, via the IOC consensus statement, identified abuse and harassment as "the gateway to non-accidental violence" (p. 1020). They noted that when the sport world (to include fans) sees abusive coaching strategies as just part of the game, the result is that those who witness such behaviors will not report them. Furthermore, the athletes themselves are not likely to report abusive coaching behaviors and therefore are also not likely to seek help for what they are going through. The types of harassment and abuse identified in the IOC's statement include "sexual harassment and abuse," "physical abuse and forced physical exertion," and "neglect." The authors noted that sexual harassment and abuse typically occur in the context of someone abusing their position of power, and, unfortunately, these types of violence occur in every sport and at every level of competition. They note that those at the highest risk for this type of abuse are athletes who are part of the LGBTQ+ community and/or who are disabled. They also note that peers rather than coaches are the ones most likely to engage in this type of violence. Overall, perpetrators tend to target those who are vulnerable and look for opportunities where there are not many, if any, other people around.

With respect to physical abuse and forced physical exertion, and neglect, Mountjoy and colleagues noted there is little research in these areas in the context of sport and much of what is known is based on what has been publicly reported. Physical forms of abuse in sport are believed to be perpetrated by nearly anyone associated with sport in any way including family and fans. The authors note that the importance of winning at any cost, and the ways in which we idolize athletes can contribute to an acceptance of many forms of violence in sport as simply part of the game. In essence, the message sent is that when athletes are exposed to physical forms of violence, they should simply accept it as part of being an athlete.

Violence in the form of neglect refers to situations in which a policy was not in place or something was not done that could have prevented an athlete from getting ill, getting injured, or dying. As an example, many readers may be familiar with publicized stories of athletes who were denied proper hydration, or were forced to continue to physically exert themselves beyond what their body could tolerate. The most widely publicized stories of incidents like this resulted in the athlete's death. The authors of the IOC consensus statement note that what often contributes to these forms of neglect is seeing athletes as assets or tools that are used rather than as human beings who have rights.

The authors conclude their article by noting that the evidence of non-accidental violence in sport supports the critical importance for all involved in sport to not only be aware of these forms of violence but also to identify and implement solutions so violence against athletes does not occur. They offer specific recommendations related to prevention and/or reporting behaviors for sport organizations, athletes themselves, sport-related healthcare providers, and those who engage in research related to sport.

Intergenerational Trauma

Intergenerational trauma refers to trauma that was experienced by one or more people and that is psychologically passed along to later generations. Historical trauma is a type of intergenerational trauma that impacts individuals who are part of a specific group such as a specific cultural, racial, or ethnic group. Examples of historical or intergenerational trauma include domestic violence, poverty, genocide, oppression, colonization, racism, and so on. Intergenerational trauma was initially identified in the late 1980s as part of a study that revealed survivors of the Holocaust had disproportionately higher use of psychological services compared to others. The study found that this group was overrepresented by 300 percent. Recent empirical investigations of others impacted by intergenerational trauma include Indigenous people in the United States forced to attend residential schools, African American and Black people who have generational experiences of slavery, forced segregation, and systemic racism, and those who are part of families that have a history of being refugees. Experiencing intergenerational or historical trauma can put individuals at greater risk for substance use problems, thoughts of suicide, common mental health diagnoses such as depression and anxiety, and difficulty managing one's emotions which may be expressed through anger and violence.

Intergenerational trauma means that not everyone in a particular family directly experienced the traumatic events themselves (although they may have) and that younger generations inherit the trauma by how they are parented and through "epigenetics." Epigenetics refers to changes in DNA with respect to which genes are activated and which ones are not. It is known that factors outside of trauma such as eating habits, exercise habits, and degree of stress can impact the turning off or turning on of specific genes. Research has demonstrated that these types of genetic changes can be passed down from one generation to the next. When these genetic changes occur in the context of intergenerational trauma, genetic relatives may be at greater risk of both physical and mental health challenges. Research examining pull-one's-self-up-by-one's-bootstraps intergenerational trauma noted that when working with children in a mental health capacity it is important to screen parents for adverse childhood events (ACEs) since their own trauma may be, epigenetically and/or through their parenting style, passed along to their children.

To date, there are no studies of how intergenerational trauma may impact those who participate in sport; however, some athletes have come forward to discuss how intergenerational trauma impacted them. An article published in the online version of *The Dallas Morning News* had the headline "A surprising number of elite athletes faced childhood trauma." Those familiar with the pervasiveness of trauma, particularly ACEs, would not be surprised to know that elite athletes would be no more immune to early childhood trauma than non-elite athletes. The article also mentions an examination of Olympic medalists compared to Olympians who did not medal that found the medalists were disproportionately exposed to trauma at a rate of 4:1. This can make it appear as if trauma produces excellence in sport; however, subsequent research found that it was not the trauma that led to excellence but the athlete's ability to understand, cope with, and learn from the traumatic experiences that mattered. This, of course, is much easier said than done.

Joe Williams was a professional rugby player in Australia and a member of the Wiradjuri people who are Indigenous to Australia. He talked about how he was hazed by older players (e.g., late hits, hits to the head) resulting at least once in a significant concussion. He stated that the result of the concussion impacted his ability to trust himself and to trust others. He described feeling paranoid and frequently feeling confused or disoriented. In order to cope with the incessant "noise" in his head questioning every decision he made and everything he did, he used alcohol and drugs to escape the noise and described his drug use as "enough drugs to kill a small elephant" (Hepburn, 2022, para. 4).

Like many athletes, Williams did not share his struggles with anyone in part due to the stigma surrounding mental health challenges in sport and not wanting to be seen as a problem by the league which in many other ways provided positive experiences. He also noted, however, that his decision to remain silent about his struggles was fueled by being Wiradjuri who have a pull-one's-self'-up-by-one's-bootstraps mentality. He described the devastating impact colonization had on his and other Indigenous peoples. He stated that during this time members of the Australian government forced indigenous families to fit into and be part of non-Indigenous Australian culture by taking from their families tens of thousands of Indigenous children (similar to what happened to Indigenous children and families in the United States). These children are referred to as the "stolen generations." Williams attempted to die by suicide feeling like he had failed everyone in his life including his children. He described a mix of emotions when he "woke up" the following day.

In the article written about Williams, it is reported that the suicide rate of Indegenous Australians is nearly two-and-a-half times higher than non-Indigenous Australians. Indeed, mental illness, substance use problems, and death by suicide are exponentially higher among Indigenous populations compared to those who are members of the colonizing culture. It is reasonable to conclude that Williams along with other contemporary Wiradjuri people have experienced intergenerational trauma. With regard to the Wiradjuri people, Williams talked about how "Indigenous Australians are constantly navigating two worlds … one of which has been historically unsafe for them" (Hepburn, 2022, para. 19). He noted that prior to children being taken from homes as part of forced assimilation, the Wiradjuri people were a strong community of people who looked out for one another. As of 2022 Williams is a "First Nations" advocate for mental health and has since learned the Wiradjuri language, dances, and stories that connect him to his cultural heritage which is grounded in mutual and community-based support. He reportedly travels Australia speaking to people about the impact of trauma and the importance of mental health awareness.

Indigenous Canadian track and field Olympic hopeful, Rilee ManyBears, described not having to work twice as hard as others to reach the Olympics, but "three times as hard" because of living a "First Nations life." He noted that the barriers to make it to such sporting heights are numerous and included racism, and growing up in a household where drugs and alcohol use was commonplace. Another Indigenous Canadian athlete noted that as the years progressed during school age years fewer and fewer Indigenous athletes remained in sport. Overall, professional athletes who are also a member of an Indigenous peoples point to the additional barriers of poverty, forced residential schooling, and lack of opportunity as preventing many Indigenous athletes from competing in, let alone believing it is possible to compete in sport at the Olympic level.

There are myriad stories about athletes who have experienced and are experiencing intergenerational trauma, some of them fully understand the impact of this whereas many do not.

Intergenerational trauma may still seem strange or unlikely to some; however, if one thinks about this in terms of survival it can explain how and why intergenerational trauma exists. In essence, trauma experienced by those in the past leaves a significant impact on them and they learn how to survive such experiences. Later generations are beneficiaries (for better and for worse) of that prior learning that may propel them to ensure such a thing never happens to them and/or are crippled by something they cannot put their finger on—because they didn't directly experience it. What we know now through extensive research is that intergenerational trauma can be passed down, genetically, just like one's eye color, or how tall one is.

Understanding that traumatic experiences are far more common than one might think, and that a trauma response can occur via vicarious traumatization or intergenerational transmission of trauma can help others be appropriately sensitive to how athletes may "show up" when they are practicing or competing in sport. This type of sensitivity can encompass having a trauma-informed approach.

Trauma-Informed Sport

The Substance Abuse and Mental Health Services Administration (SAMHSA) outlines "six key principles of a trauma-informed approach: safety, trustworthiness and transparency, peer support, collaboration and mutuality, empowerment, voice and choice, and cultural, historical and gender issues" (SAMHSA, 2014, p. 10). SAMHSA notes that a trauma-informed approach can be implemented in a multitude of settings. They also suggested that implementing such an approach typically means an organization or group has to change so their policies and procedures reflect the six principles of a trauma-informed approach. Implementing a trauma-informed approach in sport settings is entirely possible and highly encouraged, and the *Center for Healing and Justice Through Sport* (CHJS) strongly recommends such an approach with youth athletes.

The CHJS created a document, also known as a "white paper," that begins with "Childhood trauma is a pervasive public health issue in the United States with significant lifelong impacts" (CHJS, n.d., p. 2). In this document, the organization highlights the neurological effects of traumatic experiences that include "dysregulation" because an overload of stress can cause certain areas of the brain to shut down or work less effectively. The result can be a child or adolescent (or adult for that matter) who dissociates (e.g., daydreaming, or disconnecting from reality), or who becomes hyper-aroused. Being hyper-aroused means a person is exceptionally sensitive and responsive to stimuli which can in turn result in an exaggerated startle response, difficulty staying focused, irritability, difficulty sleeping, and being hypervigilant. These are also symptoms associated with posttraumatic stress.

CHJS cites numerous studies throughout their white paper on the topic of trauma-informed sport and notes that because of the known benefits of physical activity for the brain, body, and mind participating in sport may be the only time someone with a trauma history feels mentally and physically good. They identify the importance of "consistent and caring relationships" as well as "consistency and predictability" as being key components of interacting with those who have trauma in their histories or who are currently experiencing trauma. Relationships that foster a sense of safety (i.e., are consistent and caring) help to calm the internal physiological reaction (aka, fight or flight response) that leads to hyperarousal or dissociation. This frees the brain to devote resources to important aspects of sport and life: skill acquisition, learning, and growth. Having a predictable structure to sport can also be exceptionally beneficial for those who have experienced trauma. Predictability helps with a sense of safety since athletes know what's about to happen and what comes next. Otherwise, athletes with a trauma history are left with the uncertainty of not knowing what may happen after a scrimmage or a particular drill which can, in turn, activate the fight or flight response. Similar to what sport psychologists recommend for any high-performing athlete executing a specific skill, CHJS recommends a routine at the start of practice that is the same from one practice to the next (e.g., a specific pattern of exercises to warm up the mind and body). If a plan changes from one day to the next or needs to change in the moment, then providing this information to athletes ahead of time helps athletes with a trauma history understand what is going on and what they should expect.

A group of researchers out of New York provided recommendations and techniques for implementing a sound trauma-informed sport-related program. The article is packed with practical advice and strategies and is called *Creating Trauma-Informed Sports Programming for Traumatized Youth: Core Principles for an Adjunctive Therapeutic Approach.* They specifically identify "ten trauma-sensitive skills for youth players." Among these ten skills includes "showing up." The authors indicate that it may take a great deal of effort for some kids to literally show up to and participate in a sport program. They may have had to navigate substantial barriers just to physically get there. These researchers state that remembering and acknowledging this are important even when such kids may "act out" in ways that are disruptive. The remaining nine trauma-sensitive skills include mindfulness, focusing skills (i.e., helping kids manage triggers associated with trauma), checking yourself (i.e., help kids learn to identify and manage their emotions), speaking your truth (also related to understanding their emotional experiences), understanding the difference between good and bad stress, play to their strengths (i.e., going out of your way to help a child identify and maximize what they are good at), reframe (e.g., mistakes or failure can be viewed as an opportunity to learn), be a friend (this is intended to address social isolation that often occurs with those who have experienced trauma), and making community contributions (i.e., help them focus less on individual accomplishments and more on how they can help their team or community). There are numerous other practical recommendations offered including those who interact with youth athletes to use a "C.L.E.A.R." method of communicating. C = using a calm tone of voice, L = active listening, E = explain what you're doing and why, A = ask questions that encourage the athlete, and R = reduce the noise which refers to minimizing distractions that occur during communication (e.g., literal noise around you, and being distracted while talking or listening).

Conclusion

There are myriad types of trauma that people at any age can experience. Some people are impacted more than others which may depend in part on the type of trauma experienced, the number of traumatic events experienced, their degree of quality social support, and their ability to employ effective coping strategies. Even with effective coping and strong social support individuals, including athletes, can still feel the negative effects of trauma long after the traumatic experiences occurred. Taking a trauma-informed approach when working with athletes can help them more fully engage with sport. Moreover, implementing as many recommendations as possible associated with trauma-informed sport can help athletes with a trauma history more fully benefit from and enjoy sport. Although much that is written about trauma-informed sport discusses this approach in the context of youth sports, the reality is many if not most of these recommendations and strategies can also be implemented or considered in the context of adolescent and adult athletes.

9

Esports

Although esports have yet to be recognized as a sport by many spectators, competitors, and athletes in traditional sports, there are some who have suggested all sports can be placed on a continuum whereby sports relying heavily on physicality are on one end and sports requiring a higher degree of cognitive effort, such as chess and esports, are on the other end. Regardless of whether esports are considered to be a sport like traditional sports there is a great deal of overlap between the two in terms of pressures experienced, and challenges associated with training and competing. In addition those who compete in traditional or esports can face mental health challenges that impact well-being and performance, and competitors in both can benefit from mental skills training (aka, performance enhancement skills). This brief chapter will explore the ways in which esports and traditional sports are similar and the ways in which esports are unique.

What Are Esports?

Esports is a relatively new form of competition that stands for electronic sports and can be defined as a multiplayer video game played competitively for spectators. Esports can be played individually or in teams and involve head-to-head competition via single-player, first-person shooter games, multiplayer online battle arenas (MOBAs), and video versions of physical sports such as basketball, soccer, or hockey. While there is some controversy as to whether or not esports can or should be referred to as a sport, according to a four-part online article series on esports published in 2020 by the *Harvard International Review*, esports have been incredibly popular and can rival the viewership seen by traditional sports.

Although the first recorded esport event occurred at Stanford University in 1972, the reality is that esports' true origins coincide with the advent of the "World Wide Web" now known, of course, as the Internet. Since the early 1990s, people's interest in esports has grown exponentially. Among those who participated in a recent survey 6 percent stated that they started playing esports in the 1980s and about 25 percent started playing prior to 2000. Today, esports are global and competitions are broadcast via live-streaming platforms while others can be viewed in person. As of 2024, the global market value of esports was over $1.5 billion with just over $1 billion specifically accounted for by the US esports market. The games that have the largest payouts at $30 million and $25 million, respectively, are Defense of the Ancients 2 (DOTA 2) and Fortnite. Top-earning individual players have won upwards of $7 million. One of the top esports teams in the world, TSM, has been valued at over $500 million and in 2020, opened a multi-million dollar training facility that "will contain content studios for creators and a wellness center for physical and mental health" (Cullen, 2019, para. 1). This suggests that at least some esports teams have the earnings and infrastructure to support players similar to traditional sports.

Esports clearly have many components similar to traditional sports including millions of dollars in earnings, corporate sponsorships, and market shares; however, they also deal with similar inequity issues seen in traditional sports such as gender inequity. The esports world is dominated by males and the top-earning female esports player earned sixteen times less ($450 thousand) than the top earning male player ($7 million) as of 2024. In addition, as has been illustrated throughout this book, athletes in traditional sports encounter issues that can compromise their physical and mental well-being. As we'll see in this chapter, players in esports encounter similar issues as well as some that are unique to esports.

Similarities and Differences Between Traditional Sports and Esports

There are myriad similarities between traditional sports and esports including the fact that both are forms of entertainment that typically have an audience. They both require skill, the ability to follow rules, and are competitive in nature. Just like with traditional sports, esports have players and managers, students can earn scholarships to compete at the collegiate level, and high-profile/elite esport players and teams can get endorsement deals. Similar to traditional sports, esports have benefits such as engaging in fair play and teamwork, developing necessary skills to engage effectively in digital environments, and promoting prosocial behaviors that may include things such as altruism and cooperation.

Researchers examining the experiences of elite-level esports players have found that they experience a great deal of pressure not dissimilar to those in traditional sports. Contributors to stress include performing in front of an audience and problems with communication among team members. In addition, both traditional sports and esports can involve "negative" aspects of competitive sport including fixing competitions, use of performance-enhancing substances, and gender-related issues. Although many people may never see esports as "real" sports, the reality is the same issues that occur in traditional sports also occur in esports. Some may simply look a bit different given the venues in which players train and compete. Despite these similarities, research in the area of esports is minimal and therefore not much is known about the impact competing in esports has on players.

Scientists who do study esports have noted that one of the things inhibiting adequate research is how to define what esports are as well as how to define those who compete in esports (i.e., should they be called "athletes"). What to call those who engage in esports has yielded myriad terms including esports players, gamers, esports competitors, esports athletes, professional gamers, and so on. Researches in the UK suggest the most appropriate term is esports athlete abbreviated as e'athlete. They suggest that this term should be used in the way that the term "athlete" is used in traditional sports. Use of this term can also help distinguish between those who play Internet-based games in a non-competitive way (i.e., not an e'athlete) and those who do (i.e., an e'athlete).

Those trying to incorporate esports into the lexicon of sport have suggested that sports overall should be considered in terms of a continuum with those that are more physical in nature (e.g., football) on one end and on the other end those that require more cognitive skill or brain power (e.g., chess). There are organized teams and competition for every sport on the continuum; however, it is the medium used to engage with the sport that differs. Traditional sports involve physical exertion whereas esports require an electronic system through which an esport player, or e'athlete, controls a character or avatar. As such, esports would likely fall closer to the "cognitive skill" side of a hypothetical sport continuum. Because esports do require a strong mind/body connection to effectively manipulate the controls required to play the game there is still some physicality involved. And, similar to traditional sports, in order to excel in esports e'athletes must dedicate hours of their time training to refine their skills.

It has been well documented that physical activity can have myriad benefits for a person that extend beyond benefits for the body (see Chapter 1 for more information). Physical activity has been shown to improve overall well-being and can decrease symptoms of depression and anxiety. This is one way in which esports significantly differs from traditional sports. Researchers have demonstrated that playing video games for long periods of time may contribute to depression, academic problems, substance use problems, and behavior problems. Among adolescents identified as having internet gaming disorder (see the Internet Gaming Disorder section later in this chapter) those who identify as boys had higher rates of anxiety, depression, and lower emotional intelligence, whereas those who identify as girls with this disorder showed higher levels of depression. Thus, just as traditional athletes are susceptible to mental health challenges related to sport participation, the same is true for e'athletes.

Pressure to perform at a high level, performance-based expectations to live up to, cognitive and emotional regulation during game play, and coping with competitive losses are all experiences e'athletes contend with. Esport teams are also no different from traditional sport teams in terms of issues that can arise with problematic communication, interpersonal conflicts, and toxic behaviors. When e'athletes compete in front of audiences (live streaming or in person) they are subject to scrutiny and criticism from fans and the media, and female e'athletes have been shown to endure gender discrimination, and online harassment. All of these elements can contribute to mental health challenges that may impact an e'athletes overall well-being and level of performance.

The National Collegiate Athletic Association (NCAA) recently established a policy that NCAA institutions (particularly Division I institutions) must provide mental health support for athletes due to the high rate of mental health challenges among athletes and due to the fact that athletes overall tend to underutilize mental health services. This does not, however, help esports e'athletes, even those competing at the collegiate level, since the NCAA does not include esports among the sports they oversee. Researchers have, therefore, called for those who support esports to establish mental health support systems for e'athletes. They advocate for providing education around how the culture of esports (e.g., maladaptive sleep patterns) impacts well-being as well as education and training programs designed to teach e'athletes skills that help them cope with the stressors and environment of being an e'athlete. Finally, those interested in understanding and supporting esports also advocate for mental health literacy programs for e'athletes. Research conducted in the area of mental health among traditional athletes indicates these types of programs and interventions help with recognizing the signs and symptoms of mental health, reduce stigma associated with mental health, and bolster help-seeking among athletes. At this time, there is no reason to believe similar programs developed for and implemented with e'athletes would not have similar results.

Esport-Specific Factors That Impact Mental Health

Overtraining, or "grinding," in esports can lead to a dysfunctional work-life balance and an overall decline in well-being. The nature of internet-based gaming can also negatively impact sleep patterns due to screen exposure during nighttime and problematic beliefs about sleep hygiene (e.g., beliefs about whether or not a regular sleep-wake schedule is necessary).

Very little research has been conducted, to date, on how the stress associated with esports can contribute to the development of diagnosable mental health challenges among e'athletes. One study found that common stressors associated with esports (e.g., pressure experienced during game competition, low quality of sleep, game uncertainty) were linked to the presence of symptoms associated with depression and anxiety. This study also noted that not only is more research needed in general for esports but that researchers should examine how pressures such as which game is being played, specific player's status as an e'athlete, and where the e'athlete is in their career may impact mental health. The nature of esports performance-related concerns experienced by e'athletes who can benefit from developing strong mental skills is similar to what is seen in traditional sports and can include struggles with confidence, difficulty coping with distress or adversity, performance anxiety, challenges with team dynamics, and so on. Improvement in esports play requires strong mental preparation and the "right" state of mind, and limited research has shown that as much as 50 percent of a player's improvement may be accounted for by mental skills preparation.

A study conducted by the cybersecurity company, Kaspersky, found that over 75 percent of e'athletes who regularly compete in esports noted that good mental health is essential for performing well under pressure. When e'athletes were asked about what is required for being able to perform at a high level, at the top was having a computer with adequate processing power (i.e., good equipment). Next was practicing or playing as much as possible (i.e., training). Fourth from the top was having a good mental well-being. Nearly 65 percent of e'athletes surveyed agreed with the notion that if they are not mentally prepared, and do not take care of their mental well-being, their performance will suffer. Specifically, in this same survey, e'athletes identified getting enough sleep, mental preparation, taking breaks and moving around, staying hydrated, staying physically fit, and good nutrition as important for performing at one's best.

Due to the performance-related pressures associated with esports competitions, many teams have hired sport psychologists to help manage the mental demands of being an e'athlete as well as the mental health challenges that come with high-level performance. In 2016, one of the most successful teams that competed in *Counter-Strike: Global Offensive* (CSGO) tournaments was unable to win a major tournament due to their difficulty managing stress associated with a high-pressure competition. After hiring a sport psychologist and finally winning a major tournament, members of the team noted that their success was due to having learned how to maintain their composure (i.e., emotional regulation). Generally, e'athletes have reported benefitting from applying sport psychology strategies often used by traditional athletes including learning how to adjust one's focus or concentration, using positive self-talk, and using strategies to regulate their emotions.

A study conducted in 2022 by the University of Winchester in England and led by Matthew Smith found factors such as stress, ongoing sleep problems, burnout, and social anxiety (i.e., anxiety related to the possibility of being scrutinized by others) are common among e'athletes and further noted that mental health challenges found among e'athletes are similar to those found in athletes competing in traditional sports. They identified unique demands placed on e'athletes such as there not being an official "off season" for esports, and that e'athletes must "use skilled fine motor co-ordination while facing a high cognitive workload that includes, attention, information-processing and visuo-spatial skills" (Smith et al., 2022, p. 2). This is another way of saying that the cognitive load required for competing in esports is quite high and quite different from that which is required in traditional sports.

The results of the study conducted out of the University of Winchester identified fifty-one specific stressors e'athletes experience. These stressors represented internal (i.e., team or individual issues) and external (i.e., scrutiny and criticism, event issues) stressors, and included general themes such as a lack of shared goals on the team, difficulty managing esport and life balance, dealing with comments made on social media about specific players, communication issues, and dealing with what happens when the team loses. Overall, team issues were the predominant stressor category including things such as communication between e'athletes during competition, criticism by others on the team with the concern that e'athletes might be dropped from their team, and overall lack of confidence. These e'athletes were also asked about their coping strategies to help manage these stressors. Strategies included emotion-focused coping (i.e., managing emotions felt as a result of a stressor), problem-focused coping (i.e., in the moment strategies to deal with a stressor), avoidance coping (i.e., strategies to distance themselves from stressors), approach coping (i.e., directly confronting the stressor), and appraisal-focused coping (i.e., reframing or re-evaluating what occurred during competition). Researchers have noted that during gameplay e'athletes relied too heavily on avoidance strategies and struggled to implement emotion- and problem-focused strategies during gameplay which are preferred and effective strategies.

Notably this study was only conducted with male-identifying e'athletes due to far fewer female-identifying e'athletes competing at the professional level despite the fact that gaming activities are nearly equally split between the two genders during adolescence. Skill level does not seem to be the determining factor as to why there are fewer female-identifying e'athletes since, with equal training time they perform at the same level compared to their male-identifying counterparts. Despite this, female-identifying e'athletes are not considered to be "hard core" gamers, and as noted previously do not earn at the same level as male-identifying e'athletes. In addition, research has found that female-identifying e'athletes are subject to sexual harassment in ways male-identifying e'athletes are not. This, of course, can contribute to declines in participation and declines in mental health.

Research overall has shown that higher levels of internet-based gaming can negatively impact e'athletes' overall well-being. Specific mental health challenges that have been associated with internet-based gaming include depression and anxiety, social phobia, internet gaming disorder, and interpersonal sensitivity.

Common Physical Problems Associated with Esports and Well-being

Researchers who study the impact of competing in esports have found multiple biological markers of stress among e'athletes including an increase in cortisol levels. Cortisol has been identified by medical professionals as the primary stress hormone that can be activated during the fight or flight response (i.e., the body's response when a threat is detected). When cortisol levels increase, there are changes in our body's ability to fight off illness. In addition, higher levels of cortisol have been linked to a suppression of the reproductive system, and the normal growth process. This hormone is also implicated in changes in mood, motivation, and fear.

Other physical symptoms associated with long periods of internet-based gaming include pain in the neck, back, wrists, and hands. Gamers can also experience computer vision syndrome that according to the *American Optometric Association* is also known as "digital eye strain" and can be characterized by eyestrain, headaches, blurred vision, dry eyes, and neck and shoulder pain. Some of these symptoms can be reduced with better lighting, ensuring the distance from the person to the screen is optimal, ensuring good posture while seated, and correcting vision problems that have not yet been corrected (e.g., the person is not using corrective lenses like glasses or contacts). Given the known mind-body connection and the fact that physical problems such as those identified here can lead to mental health challenges, and vice versa, it can be argued that in this way e'athletes deal with similar challenges as traditional athletes. Although an e'athlete will not have traditional sport-related injuries such as concussion or a broken bone that may impact a traditional athletes' well-being and ability to compete, e'athletes may experience unique esport-related injuries, such as computer vision syndrome, that can impact their mental well-being and ability to perform at their very best.

Internet Gaming Disorder

A unique mental health challenge that can occur for e'athletes directly related to what they do is internet gaming disorder. With each new edition of the *Diagnostic and Statistical Manual of Mental Disorders* (DSM), there is a section entitled "conditions for future study." The current version of the DSM includes a potential future diagnosis of "internet gaming disorder." If it is formally included in future editions of the DSM, it is likely to be classified along with substance use disorders and gambling disorder; all of which have an element of addiction. In fact, the Chinese government has classified internet gaming disorder as a form of addiction, and South Korea has established prevention and treatment programs for problematic internet gaming, labeling it a threat to public well-being.

According to the DSM, internet gaming disorder generally involves a persistent use of the internet to play games that leads to distress or impairment in the person's life. Specific symptoms include being preoccupied with internet games such that thinking about and planning for playing internet games takes up a significant amount of the person's time and energy. Those with this disorder may experience withdrawal symptoms when they do not have access to internet gaming, tolerance for gaming such that the person needs to spend even more time engaged in internet gaming, unsuccessfully trying to stop or control their gaming activities, loss of interest in other activities, not being fully honest with important others (including treatment providers) about how much time they spend on internet gaming, and so on. The DSM makes specific note that internet gaming disorder is different from internet gambling which would be diagnosed as gambling disorder (see the following section and Chapter 2 for more information on Gambling Disorder).

The primary feature of internet gaming disorder, excessive time spent playing on the internet or playing video games, is what is required of esports players, particularly those for whom esports is their profession and who therefore may play games for more than twenty-two hours per week. Comparatively, about one-third of teenagers who are interested in esports may play internet or video games for five hours or more each day. That volume of play outpaces the hours spent by professional esports players. Though this amount of game play does not mean such individuals have internet gaming disorder, the fact that the primary symptom of the disorder is essentially required to be an e'athlete the high amount of game play can put them at higher risk.

Gambling Disorder

Gambling disorder is a condition that can be formally diagnosed and treated by a licensed mental health professional. Generally speaking, for someone to be considered to have a clinical challenge with gambling they engage in recurrent gambling that causes significant distress or impairment in the person's life. Distress or impairment can refer to things such as needing to gamble with larger sums of money in order to get the feeling they are after, feeling a high degree of discomfort if they try to stop or cut back on their gambling, being preoccupied with gambling (e.g., most of the person's thoughts are about past or future gambling including how to get money to gamble with), losing one's job or an important relationship due to their gambling behavior, and so on. Gambling disorder is classified along with substance use disorders in the DSM due to the fact that symptoms of the disorder reflect addiction as do the symptoms associated with substance use disorders.

Esports betting has increased at a rate similar to the popularity of esports themselves. Research in this area initially attempted to compare esports gamblers to those who gamble on traditional sports, engage in online betting, etc. These studies, however, demonstrated that the people who gamble on esports are very different from those who gamble on traditional sports. For example, those who bet on esports tend to be younger than those who bet on traditional sports, and esports bettors seem to have more gambling-related problems. In addition, those who bet on esports believe much more knowledge and skill are required for esports betting compared to betting on traditional sports, though this has not been found to be true.

There is still a lot that is unknown about gambling or betting in esports. The legality and regulation of esports betting are different from one state to the next including whether or not e'athletes can place bets. This is similar to betting on traditional sports. A unique element of betting in esports is "skin betting." A "skin" in a video game refers to items that can change the appearance of a character in a video game. Since skins do not improve the performance of the character, they are only aesthetic in nature. Generally, skins can be purchased or earned within a game itself; however, some skins can be quite rare and therefore are highly desired by players. Skin betting would, of course, occur by the players themselves and the legality of this type of betting is uncertain since actual money is not involved until a player exchanges a skin for money on secondary markets for pennies on the dollar, thousands of dollars, and in some cases tens of thousands of dollars. Given the involvement of this type of money, there is no reason not to suspect that e'athletes engaging in skin betting could develop symptoms associated with gambling disorder.

Conclusion

Although esports require unique skills and have unique challenges associated with being an e'athlete, there are many similarities between this type of competition and traditional sports. E'athletes and traditional athletes have to perform under pressure and may benefit from developing mental skills to improve and enhance their performance. Moreover, both traditional athletes and e'athletes may contend with aspects of their respective competitive arenas that can contribute to the development of mental health challenges requiring specialized treatment. Nonetheless, there are aspects of esports that diverge from traditional sports making at least some of their experiences unique in comparison, and worthy of researchers' time and attention.

10

Covid-19 and Athlete Mental Health

Although the global pandemic is officially over, Covid-19 still exists and continues to impact people negatively, including athletes. This chapter will address the impact of Covid-19 on the mental health of individuals as well as the mental health systems in place in the United States. Then we will explore the impact of Covid-19 specifically on athletes who experienced abbreviated or canceled seasons, the inability to easily connect with their team, and the impact long Covid has had on some athletes' sports careers. Finally, we'll briefly take a look at some of the inequities that remain in sport highlighted by the Covid-19 pandemic.

Impact of COVID-19 on Mental Health in General

As most readers know, Covid-19 first appeared late in 2019 in China and made its way to the United States in January of 2020. By March of 2020 the *World Health Organization* declared Covid-19 to be a global pandemic. Lives were disrupted in myriad ways and many people struggled to cope with the upheaval they experienced even if they did not contract the disease themselves or knew someone who was severely, medically affected by the virus, or who died because of the virus.

Significant mental health challenges among adults in the United States rose exponentially with one study reporting that by the end of 2020 the rates of anxiety and depression were four times higher than they were in early 2019 (i.e., pre-pandemic). Adults were taking more prescription medications for mental health, using mental health counseling services at a higher rate, and many were unable to get the mental health care they needed. Because of Covid-19-related restrictions, many mental health practices had to shift to providing telehealth services (i.e., virtual services) in a large-scale way or exclusively in order to follow federal or state guidelines requiring physical distancing which further disrupted mental health services. Some have characterized the rise in mental health diagnoses and the accompanying skyrocketing need for mental health services as the second pandemic. Even as the impact of the Coivd-19 pandemic has waned, the impact of the pandemic on mental health and mental health care has continued.

The American Psychological Association reported in late 2022 that 60 percent of providers surveyed could not take on new patients and almost 50 percent reported that they could not keep up with the demand for services. The largest increase seen for services was from thirteen- to seventeen-year-olds. Waiting lists for services from practitioners reported an average wait time of three or more months. Services from a specialist (e.g., eating disorders, neuropsychology) have been reported to be much longer and can be a year or more. In 2024, the *American Psychological Association* published the document *Barriers to Care in a Changing Practice Environment: 2024 Practitioner Pulse Survey*, which reported that while more psychologists have openings in their practices for those who need mental health care, over half of psychologists surveyed indicated they still did not have openings for new patients.

Impact of Covid-19 on Athlete Mental Health

The impact of Covid-19 was significant for athletes, and some could argue, for sports fans as well. The year 2020 saw the unprecedented cancellation of major sporting events including the remainder of the *National Basketball Association's* (NBA) season, *NCAA March Madness*, the *Summer Olympics* (delayed until the following calendar year), and the *Major League Baseball* (MLB) season. These leagues and sport organizations, with significant fan-based revenue on the line, found ways to resume competitive seasons within health and safety guidelines. Fans of the *National Basketball Association* (NBA) and the *Women's National Basketball Association* (WNBA) may recall watching competitions in "the bubble." However, the *National Women's Soccer League* (NWSL) was the first to move their competitions to a bubble (i.e., a dome where sports can be played indoors). Despite this type of creativity, sport-related revenue was significantly impacted. Prior to the pandemic the sports industry was projected to bring in over $135 billion. After the pandemic, that revenue was projected to be just over $73.5 billion; a loss of nearly half of what the industry would have generated in ticket sales, TV revenue, tourism, and fans buying sport gear and memorabilia.

What this meant, though, was that professional athletes were still competing and sports teams and organizations were still bringing in revenue.

When the country was on lock-down, competitive athletes at all levels were not permitted to participate in organized sports since "social distancing" required people to generally stay away from one another. In most cases student-athletes lost at least one entire competitive season. As previously noted, professional athletes also saw interruptions to competitive seasons; however, in many cases these athletes were still allowed to continue to practice and compete pending negative Covid-19 test results. When allowed, these competitions either did not have fans in attendance at all or in very limited capacity.

Among collegiate athletes, mental health concerns during the Covid-19 pandemic increased as they did among the general population. A specific stressor reported by student-athletes during this time was limited access to their sport. For many athletes sport is important for their social and emotional well-being. Sport-related practices and competitions are times to connect with friends, display their talents, receive guidance from trusted leaders (e.g., coaches and captains), and have a sense of belonging. Although efforts were made to keep athletes connected to one another through virtual practices and socially distanced or virtual social gatherings, the loss of regular in-person connection was significant.

Interestingly, some research found student-athletes experiencing low overall well-being and lower quality of life during the pandemic were not tied to being quarantined due to a positive Covid-19 test, or knowing someone who was seriously medically impacted by contracting Covid-19. Instead, what researchers found that contributed to student-athletes generally feeling unwell including symptoms related to depression, anxiety, and the inability to get good restorative rest, was the lack of access to facilities, teammates, etc. Research conducted outside of the context of Covid-19 supports this notion. Prior to the pandemic, student-athletes were vulnerable to feelings of depression and anxiety when their access to training facilities and support services was limited. The advent of the pandemic magnified what was already a problem for many athletes.

Among children and adolescents, participation in physical activity and sport decreased significantly shortly after the onset of the pandemic. This is, of course, accounted for in large part due to the health and safety guidelines requiring social distancing. Following the onset of the pandemic nearly 70 percent of adolescents (athletes and non-athletes) reported having high levels of distress; whereas high levels of distress pre-pandemic were found in about 30 percent of adolescents. Adolescents who had lower levels of distress reported having strong attachments to their parental figures and peers. Moreover, adolescents who had participated in sport prior to the pandemic and who were able to remain physically active or who found a way to continue to participate in their sport were less depressed.

Loss of sport for many athletes for any reason, even if only temporary, can leave them feeling lost and unsure of not only what to do with themselves but feeling lost about who they are. Indeed, for those who participate in competitive sport, being an athlete is a significant part of their identity (see Chapters 3 and 5 for more information on Athletic Identity). Research in the area of identity consistently shows that when an important aspect of our identity is threatened or lost, we often experience emotional distress that can lead to mental health challenges. The impact of the loss of a specific identity, such as being an athlete, is even more pronounced for those who have a limited number of identities. If an athlete, for example, has a high degree of athletic identity, most of their friends are probably athletes, most of their activities likely revolve around athletics, and they are likely to define themselves as an athlete and not much else. Ideally, any of us can point to any number of roles we have that help make up our identity. Having a variety of aspects of our identity such as being a friend, pet parent, a volunteer, a teammate, and a family member helps soften the blow of temporarily or permanently losing another aspect of our identity. When one part is lost, we have others that can fill in the void. Nonetheless, if the lost identity is really important to us, more so than any other part of our identity, then we will feel that loss much more strongly than if it were an identity that had roughly the same level of importance as our other identities. Since the impact of the Covid-19 pandemic resulted in the loss of sport for millions of athletes, many of these athletes endured a significant loss that may have resulted in mental health challenges they might not have otherwise experienced. At its most tragic, the loss of the ability to participate in sport resulted in death by suicide in some young athletes. One father of a high school student noted that his son, a high school football player who died by suicide at the end of 2020, had difficulty adapting to the impact Covid-19 had on daily life.

Research conducted examining Covid-19's impact on the mental health of student-athletes found that a greater number of those identifying as female experienced anxiety compared to those identifying as male, and the impact was found to be even worse for those living in poverty-stricken areas. Athletes who had to be quarantined experienced more anger and low mood, whereas athletes who had a teammate quarantined reported higher levels of anxiety. Athletes participating in spring sports felt less anger compared to their non-spring sport counterparts since spring sports, generally, did not require as many restrictions because most could be played outdoors making social distancing requirements much easier to follow while engaged in sport. Student-athletes directly impacted by Covid-19 had more anxiety, lower mood, and more anger. In more significant cases when an athlete contracted Covid-19 they may have experienced significant declines in aerobic performance. And in cases where an athlete developed "long Covid" they may have had to leave their sport (long Covid refers to symptoms associated with the virus that last three months or longer). Researchers specifically examining how student-athletes fared when they were able to continue to participate in sport found that these athletes experienced less anxiety and depression compared to those who saw their seasons significantly impacted. As a result of these findings, researchers have advocated that everything possible should be done, within any future health and safety protocols, to allow athletes to participate in sport to preserve their psychological well-being.

Elite-level athletes, too, experienced disruption in their athletic lives. A study examining the impact of this disruption on mood, mental health, and overall life satisfaction found that each of these decreased when athletes were required to remain isolated from others (i.e., home confinement). By contrast, each of these factors improved when athletes were slowly allowed to re-engage with sport including during the "semi-lockdown" stage which allowed professional athletes to practice and compete under strict circumstances. For non-professional athletes, however, those who followed social distancing protocols and wanted to practice or train on their own faced closed gyms, pools, weight rooms, and so on as a result of social distancing requirements.

Given the impact on overall well-being among student-athletes and elite-level athletes, some have suggested that the language we use around staying physically safe should be examined carefully. For example, some have suggested that the term "social distancing" should have been replaced by "physical distancing." Even though most people, in theory, understood they needed to physically stay away from other people, using the term "physical distancing" would reinforce the notion that it is only physical distance that is important, not completely cutting off contact with important others.

Impact of Long Covid on Athletes

Most people who contract Covid-19 recover within about a month of being infected and some may take up to twelve weeks. Long Covid, however, involves experiencing new or recurring symptoms after the initial onset of Covid symptoms resolve, and can involve one or more organ systems. For athletes, long Covid can mean their sporting careers have to be put on hold or ended altogether.

Reports of long Covid in athletes surfaced not long after the pandemic hit. It was believed that young, healthy people would fare well and recover quickly from Covid-19. In the vast majority of instances, this was true. However, for some young, healthy individuals long Covid has dramatically altered if not devastated their lives. For athletes, this has left them dealing with the question "what now?" A Division I (Division I is largely considered to be elite-level sport) American football player, age twenty-two, developed long Covid leaving him short of breath even when shopping in a grocery store. In 2021, after having to sit out an entire season, he announced that he had to leave sport to protect his health. One WNBA player, who had long Covid, felt progress when they were simply able to engage in long conversations with loved ones without becoming overwhelmed with exhaustion. And in a story posted to *YouTube*® in 2023 by *Sky Sports*, two athletes with long Covid were interviewed: an Olympic rower, and a highly nationally ranked tennis player. Each reported that they had to be housebound for long periods of time and for the tennis player, had to be in a wheelchair. The rower was able to recover and start training again for the highest levels of competition. It was noted that she was among very few athletes in the world to recover from the devastating impact of long Covid and return to high-level competition; however, upon returning to elite-level training with her country she had to stop training abruptly due to the resurgence of a long Covid symptom that left her unwell for months. She reportedly made the decision that her body could no longer handle this level of training and had to quit her sport. At the time the story was reported, the tennis player still required a wheelchair.

Many athletes impacted by long Covid that ended their careers have made peace with the fact that they are no longer competitive athletes and for others the "itch" is still there making time away from sport difficult at best. Since the loss of something as important as sport to an athlete can be difficult and complicated, recovery from the psychological and emotional impact of that loss can take time.

Ongoing Impact of Covid-19 with "Normal" Return to Play

Although the pandemic has officially ended according to the *World Health Organization*, concerns about the spread of Covid-19 linger. Athletes participating in major sporting events still test for Covid-19 and depending on the health and safety guidelines at the time, may or may not be able to participate if they test positive for the virus. Since being outdoors is still considered to be the "safest" place in terms of the spread of Covid-19, many sports are considered to be safe for athletes, sport personnel, and fans.

The largest and most popular bike race in the world, the *Tour de France* saw two favorites during the 2024 *Tour* unable to compete due to testing positive for Covid-19 before the race even began. Despite this, it was not until well into the 21-day race that *Tour* organizers started requesting that journalists wear masks when interviewing the athletes, and many athletes themselves elected to wear a mask under these circumstances. The delay in this type of requirement was reportedly due to the fact that the race organizers did not have any protocols in place to manage a flare-up of Covid-19. In addition, officials overseeing the 2024 *Summer Olympic Games* in Paris did not express concern over the possibility of a Covid-19 outbreak despite welcoming thousands of athletes from across the globe and over 15 million visitors from around the world. Some *Olympic* athletes tested positive for Covid-19 very early in the games leaving some wondering about the potential for an outbreak at the event. This lack of planning for Covid-related issues for two major, global sporting events suggests that there is a lack of concern for any serious impact of Covid-19 on large groups or individuals.

For most people, athlete or not, contracting Covid-19 may go unnoticed if the person is not testing for it, or may experience mild symptoms that may or may not be attributed to Covid-19. However, some people remain at high risk of a severe form of the illness including older adults, infants, and those of any age with certain underlying medical concerns. For some athletes at the 2024 *Summer Olympics* even feeling a little bit "under the weather" can jeopardize their ability to compete at all or at a high level. For example, one story reported that several members of the Australian women's water polo team tested positive while in Paris and had to pause their training due to not feeling well. At one point most of the affected teammates were able to return to training and competition and one teammate was still unable to. Although their lives were not in danger, their *Olympic* hopes were.

Covid-19 and Gender Inequity in Sport

The impact of Covid-19 on sport brought to bear more attention to the issues that have continued to plague sport over the decades including inequalities for those who play women's sports, inequalities for indigenous athletes, and a resistance to social justice movements since sport is a highly commercialized money-making machine. An article published in 2024 stated that "[t]he unblinking drive toward global sport gigantism, commercialism, and capitalism was upended by the Covid-19 pandemic, leaving in its wake many questions about the purpose, impact, and meaning of sport" (Zipp & Nauright, 2024, p. 185). While it is highly unlikely that competitive sports as we know them are not going away or changing any time soon, the pandemic allowed some of these issues to receive much more attention and there was more time and energy available to fight for equality in sport.

Athletes who play for women's sports have continued to face inequalities compared to those who play for men's sport despite the fact that Title IX was supposed to level the playing field. Covid-19, however, seemed to spark a significant growth in support, including financial support, for those who play for elite women's sport teams. It was predicted that in 2024 there would be a 300 percent increase in revenue compared to revenue generated in 2020. This projection put women's sports revenue over $1 billion for the first time in history. In addition, women's sport in 2020 accounted for about 4 percent of media coverage and it is projected to see an increase to 15 percent in 2024. This is still a small percentage compared to media coverage of men's sports; however, the jump is meaningful.

The pandemic also revealed additional ongoing gender inequities for athletes who compete for women's or girls' sports and for Indigenous athletes. In terms of gender, many teams for female-identifying athletes were discontinued leaving many with no opportunities to play or compete. What seems to account for this is the fact that the loss of so much business in and outside of sport meant that there was a drop in expected revenue and decisions about what costs could be cut were made. In terms of sport, the result was that a disproportionate number of girls' or women's teams were discontinued. This, as noted previously, can be a devastating loss for athletes. With respect to Indigenous athletes, more and more are competing on the world stage and therefore have been invited more and more into Western sports. What has not occurred, however, is an increase in attention given to sports that are unique to Indigenous cultures. Indigenous sports do not yet exist in mainstream world competitions despite the addition of other sports such as flag-football (the 2028 Summer Olympics), and break dancing (2024 Olympics).

Conclusion

Overall, the Covid-19 pandemic was devastating for the mental well-being of most people who lived through it. For athletes the disruptions as a result of health and safety protocols around social distancing meant that they had to give up a significant part of who they are. Even though temporary, at the time we did not know when or if things would go back to "normal." Some athletes have contracted long Covid which has severely impacted their ability to continue in sport, which in turn negatively impacted their mental well-being. One potentially positive outcome of the pandemic was the fact that it highlighted ongoing inequities in sport that still need to be addressed and that are receiving increasing attention.

11

Concussion

In recent years there has been an increase in attention paid to concussion, particularly in the context of sport. As a result, our collective understanding of how serious a single concussion or repeated concussions can be has grown. More is understood with respect to the interaction between concussion and mental health, and researchers who devote their careers to understanding concussion have updated treatment protocols for concussion to ensure the best recovery possible.

How a Concussion Occurs

The human brain weighs approximately three pounds and is believed to be fully developed by around age twenty-five. As powerful as the brain is (processing all information coming in through our senses and controlling everything in the body), it is extremely fragile in comparison to the bone that encases it. The brain is suspended, floating in the skull, in a bath of cerebrospinal fluid which is consistently produced by the body and replaced every few hours. The fluid helps to buffer against regular contact with the skull in order to prevent damage to the brain itself since the skull, of course, is much harder than the soft tissue that makes up the brain.

A concussion can occur when the brain decelerates rapidly due to contact with an object of some kind (to include a person, the floor, goal post, etc.). Since the brain has the consistency of soft tofu or soft gelatin, in a collision with the skull which requires about 1100 pounds of pressure for it to break, the brain will lose and will be damaged. As a result of concussion, there are neurochemical changes in the brain that impact how the brain functions. Researchers acknowledge there is still not a lot known about what happens in the brain; however, there is evidence to suggest that when a concussion occurs membranes of neurons getting stretched resulting in defects in these membranes. The defects impact how potassium and calcium enter and leave neurons. Since the amount of potassium and calcium needed by a neuron to function properly is fairly precise, the disruption of this process can cause significant problems in brain functioning. In order to restore the proper functioning of neurons, the brain consumes more glucose (i.e., blood sugar). However, as will be discussed in the following section, the brain has been found to use less glucose following a concussion which would impede recovery.

Symptoms Associated with Concussion

The symptoms of concussion can vary widely and can impact any number of the body's symptoms. One common myth associated with concussion symptoms is that you have to experience a lack of consciousness (i.e., getting "knocked out") in order to have a concussion. *Nationwide Children's Hospital* reports that approximately 90 percent of all concussions do not result in a loss of consciousness. In addition, they noted that concussion symptoms do not always show up immediately and can take a couple of days to emerge.

Having a concussion results in symptoms that can impact your ability to think and process information, as well as impair your body's ability to do what it needs to do or you want it to do. Symptoms of a concussion can vary from one person to the next; however, symptoms tend to be experienced physically, cognitively, emotionally, and can impact one's sleep. When someone sustains a concussion, it is not uncommon for them to not know where they are, what their name is, and to have difficulty standing or walking in a straight line. Those who watch enough sports have likely witnessed an athlete who sustained a hit to the head, get up, and either fall back down due to dizziness or struggle to walk in a straight line and might appear to be drunk. All of these symptoms are the result of damage to brain tissue (i.e., neurons) which ultimately interferes with the brain's ability to effectively control itself and the body.

Physical symptoms of concussion include having headaches, feeling dizzy including problems with balance, vision problems including sensitivity to light, sensitivity to noise, and feeling nauseous or vomiting. Cognitive symptoms include difficulties with memory, feeling confused, problems with focus and concentration, feeling like your processing speed is slow, having the sense of being "foggy" (i.e., brain fog), and difficulty thinking clearly. Sleep can be impacted in a variety of ways including sleeping more or less than you typically do, and having difficulty falling asleep. Emotional symptoms include feeling nervous or anxious, feeling irritable, or feeling sad and generally more "emotional" overall. The good news is that about 90 percent of those who have a concussion see their symptoms go away within a week or week and a half. In extreme cases, concussion symptoms can linger for a year or longer.

Children and adolescents who have sustained such a concussion have been found to be more likely to have academic problems and a decline in their overall quality of life. Some researchers have found that following a concussion in laboratory studies with rats the brain uses less glucose. Glucose is blood sugar which is critically important for adequate brain functioning and therefore a drop in glucose consumption by the brain indicates that there is a problem. These same researchers found that when a second concussion is sustained within twenty-four hours the brain's consumption of glucose drops even further. This significant disruption in the brain's ability to use necessary fuel can help explain why concussion symptoms can impact nearly every facet of our experiences (i.e., emotions, thoughts, and behaviors). Since the brain is at high risk for sustaining another concussion within one-and-a-half weeks of the initial concussion, ensuring the concussed person receives adequate treatment to reduce the risk of another concussion shortly after sustaining the first one is critically important so the brain can revert back to using the resources it needs to heal and function adequately.

Impact of Concussion Based on Age

Researchers have reported that concussion, also referred to as mild traumatic brain injury (mTBI), is a public health concern (see also *A brief history of concussion as a public health issue* by the Concussion Alliance for more information) that has grown over the years. Moreover, concussion is identified as a "common injury" sustained by children and adolescents. The swiftness of recovery from a concussion is impacted by age in ways that tend not to favor the young. Adults often see their concussion-related symptoms dissipate by a week to a week and a half whereas children and adolescents can see a longer recovery process.

According to researchers who are part of the *Children's Hospital of Philadelphia* network, over 70 percent of the concussions seen in children (i.e., under the age of eighteen) were sustained in the context of sport. The remaining concussions were most likely due to either injury as a result of a fall or a result of being struck by an object including being struck by a person, motor vehicle accident, assault, or bicycle. Overall, these researchers concluded that the majority of sport-related concussions were sustained by children six years of age or older. They reported that 18 percent of concussions in children ages 0–4 were sport-related compared to 67, 77, and 73 percent of concussions that were sport-related in ages 5–11, 12–14, and 15–17, respectively. These age ranges predominantly cover the adolescent years.

As noted previously, concussion results in problems related to one's physical and cognitive functioning, and mental health. Research has shown that when concussion occurs during the adolescent years the risk of long-term impact of this type of injury increases because the brain is developing and changing rapidly. Readers who are students of psychology or neurology may be familiar with a concept called "plasticity" in the brain. The idea is that when the brain is injured it is remarkably capable of repairing itself, and, if needed, reorganizing its cells (i.e., neurons) to pick up the functioning that may no longer be possible by the damaged part(s) of the brain. Brain plasticity is at its most effective during childhood. Adolescents are, of course, developmentally between childhood and adulthood. An adolescent brain is more well developed than a child's brain; however, there is still a great deal of development and organizing that occurs during this developmental period and extends on average, into a person's mid-twenties.

Although an adolescent brain is arguably more "plastic" than an adult brain, adolescents are at increased vulnerability to disruption that may occur during this time. For example, researchers have found that the brain's ability to change the strength of the connection between neurons (i.e., synaptic plasticity), specifically during adolescence, leaves a person much more vulnerable to problems when this process is disrupted such as through brain injury. Noticeable problems can include difficulty controlling one's emotions, difficulty with processing information logically, and difficulty controlling one's impulsive behaviors. In addition, an adolescent's brain seems to react more strongly to stress which in turn makes adolescents more vulnerable to depression.

With respect to high school students and suicide specifically, researchers have found that having a concussion put students at greater risk for engaging in a physical fight or carrying a weapon which the authors characterized as behaviors that reflected suicide capability. Male-identifying students who sustained a concussion were more likely to feel hopeless and report a suicide attempt compared to male-identifying students who did not sustain a concussion. For both male and female-identifying students the more concussions sustained over a twelve-month period the more likely they were to report a suicide attempt, feelings of hopelessness, engaging in fighting, and having been involved in a sport. An additional study found similar results specifically noting that not only were high school students who sustained a concussion in the context of sport or physical activity more likely to report depression-related symptoms and thoughts of suicide, they were also more likely to have a plan for suicide and have a suicide attempt.

Sex, Race/Ethnicity, and Socioeconomic Status (SES)

Researchers examining concussion also reported some differences between certain demographics including sex and race/ethnicity. In terms of sex, researchers only reported data related to those identifying as male or female (i.e., non-binary was not included) and found that for those identifying as females 66 percent of concussions were sport-related and for those identifying as male just over 74 percent were sport-related. Sports that pose the highest risk for concussion in those identifying as male are American football and ice hockey. For those identifying as female the sports placing them at higher risk are soccer and basketball.

In terms of race/ethnicity, categories included by researchers were non-Hispanic white, non-Hispanic Black, Hispanic, non-Hispanic other/multiple races, and Unknown. The percentage of concussions based on race/ethnicity that were sport-related included nearly 76 percent, nearly 50 percent, just over 65 percent, nearly 62 percent, and just over 75 percent, respectively. There are no conclusions that can be drawn on what these differing rates of concussion may mean. Similarly, when examining differences between those of different socioeconomic status, it is difficult to draw meaningful conclusions based on what has been found. Researchers used the type of health insurance payor their patients had as a proxy for socioeconomic status (i.e., access to resources, prestige, and power). They noted that individuals who had Medicaid (federal- and state-based health insurance for those who have limited income and resources) or who were self-pay saw sport-related concussions at a rate of nearly 46 percent, compared to those who had private insurance (e.g., Blue Cross/Blue Shield, Harvard Pilgrim) at just over 76 percent of concussions that were sport-related. They noted that not much can be construed from these results and suggest that there may be other factors at play that explain the significant differences between type of health insurance and race-ethnicity. Such factors could include access to care, whether or not parents could take time off from work for doctor's appointments, and the fact that some schools have healthcare providers who may provide treatment on the sidelines when the injury initially occurs.

Prevalence of Concussion in Sport

Some reports indicate that as many as 1.6 to 3.8 million sport-related concussions occur each year in the United States. Statistics on the rate of concussion among high school students includes the fact that in 2020 around 2.5 million students had a concussion as a result of participating in sport or being engaged in some other form of physical activity. Researchers examining this population studied data collected from over 11,500 high school students. From this sample, they found that nearly 2000 students experienced a single concussion in the previous year, over 350 experienced two concussions, just over 160 had three concussions, and over 185 had four or more concussion in the previous year. These numbers suggest that around 6 percent of high school student athletes who sustain one concussion will sustain at least one more. Regardless of age, those who have had one concussion are at greater risk for another with the highest risk for a subsequent concussion within ten days of the initial concussion. This suggests that full recovery from the initial concussion is important.

In terms of the overall prevalence of concussion, it is likely that the numbers are lower than what athletes are actually experiencing. It is not uncommon, for example, for individuals to fail to recognize they have had a concussion and therefore would not be included in this data. In addition, some athletes may intentionally attempt to hide their concussion-related symptoms. One study, for example, found that of those surveyed over 40 percent of college athletes "knowingly hidden symptoms of a concussion to stay in the game" (Torres et al., 2013, p. 279) and another 22 percent said they would probably not report concussion-related symptoms to their coach or sport medicine staff (e.g., athletic trainer). Although well-trained sport staff may recognize symptoms of concussion in an athlete who attempts to hide their symptoms, it is certainly possible that staff with concussion-specific training may overlook more subtle symptoms that are not as obvious and/or that the athlete is working hard to mask.

Sport Type

Perhaps not surprisingly, sports where there is a good deal of contact (i.e., "contact sports") have among the highest rates of concussion. Of those who have been studied and who had a sport-related concussion 16 percent were football players, nearly 15 percent were soccer players, nearly 10 percent were basketball players, and nearly 5.5 percent were ice hockey players. Sports in which there is contact, limited contact, or no contact and represented fewer than 5 percent but greater than 1 percent of those studied included lacrosse, wrestling, field hockey, rugby, cheerleading, baseball, volleyball, bike riding, softball, gymnastics, and snowboarding. All other sports registered some measure of concussion but the rate was less than 1 percent of those studied. Researchers also noted that children experience concussion in a wide range of activities outside of organized sport and include things such as playing, recess, and gym class. They noted that this non-sport activity grouping in which concussion occurs had the fourth highest rate of reported concussion after football, soccer, and basketball. This suggests that simply doing what children do is a significant risk factor for concussion.

How Concussion Has Historically Been Handled in Sport

The history of concussion in the context of sport is fraught. Athletes, coaches, teammates, and even sport journalists have referred to someone sustaining a concussion, likely a significant one, as "getting their bell rung" and in the context of boxing being "punch drunk." Every now and then, concussion is still referred to in these ways. Using such euphemisms surely contributed to the thinking that concussion is not that serious. Historically, a term used with professional athletes, "goldbricking," referred to someone who was avoiding their work but continuing to collect pay. The example used via the *Concussion Alliance* involved Jim Brown (an NFL player in the 1950s and 1960s) who noted that he sustained a concussion during a football game and elected to sit out following this injury but was accused of goldbricking since he could not prove that he was injured.

In the current day and age, there is much more attention paid to concussion and concern for the short- and long-term impact of concussion especially if it goes untreated. However, since most competitive athletes want to compete, many work very hard to mask any symptoms of a concussion because they are at risk of being pulled from practice or competition for a single play, an entire game, or depending on the severity of the concussion, for many weeks. This tendency of athletes and some coaches to want players to play, no matter what, in combination with the findings associated with CTE led the National Football League (NFL) to have independent neurologists or neurosurgeons assess whether or not a player has sustained a concussion and if it is safe for them to return to play. Other sport associations such as the National Hockey League (NHL), the National Basketball Association (NBA), and the NCAA have professionals examining concussion and intervening when needed. Some have questioned the effectiveness of these policies pointing to the experience of Miami Dophins' quarterback Tua Tagovailoa who sustained three significant concussions in a relatively short period of time. Following his third concussion he was ultimately cleared to play and the decision about whether or not he should return to a sport which proved dangerous to him was given to Tagovailoa. He elected to return to play and was quoted as saying "I love this game, and I love it to the death of me" (Merrill, 2024, para 9).

Policies and laws related to concussion historically involved legislation that focused on prevention and how employees can be compensated. According to the *Concussion Alliance*, it was not until 1996 when the *Traumatic Brain Injury Act* was signed into law by President Bill Clinton that the focus shifted toward reducing the rate of concussion and supporting both research and treatment of concussion. In 2009 the *Lystedt Law* was passed in the state of Washington, three years following the injury sustained to the law's namesake, Zack Lystedt. He was thirteen years old when he sustained a concussion just prior to halftime during a middle school American football game, and was allowed back on the field at the start of the third quarter. Unfortunately, Zack eventually collapsed on the field and underwent emergency surgery in an effort to provide more space for his swelling brain. Eventually, after multiple strokes, being on a ventilator, and being in a coma he did awake but was permanently disabled. It took close to a year before he could speak, over a year before he could move any limbs, and three years before he could stand, with assistance. The Lystedt Law requires concussion-based education for those closely involved with athletes including the athletes themselves, their coaches, and their parents. Other states eventually passed similar laws.

It has taken some time for this and other countries to recognize that someone who got their "bell rung" actually sustained a brain injury. How concussion is handled on the sidelines, and the nature of treatment and prevention protocols has changed over the years; however, the research that is consistently conducted with those who sustain a concussion in any circumstance (i.e., sport or non-sport) helps to inform these protocols and ensure all who sustain a concussion receive the best possible care and recovery.

Concussion and Mental Health

The connection between mental health and concussion is no longer in dispute. In their chapter entitled *Psychological Consequences of Concussion*, physician Mary

Daley and colleagues noted that when someone has mental health symptoms following a concussion there is a high probability that the person experienced mental health symptoms prior to the concussion itself.

As medical and mental health professionals have developed a greater understanding of what happens as a result of concussion, there is more awareness of the interplay between concussion and mental health. Researchers have found that nearly 30 percent of athletes who experience a sport-related concussion will report one or more psychological symptoms following the concussion. This translates to about 1.1 million athletes, annually, who will report psychological symptoms following a sport-related concussion. The most commonly occurring mental health-related symptoms following a sport-related concussion are problems with sleep at nearly 35 percent and irritability at nearly 30 percent. Anxiety symptoms, feeling more emotional, and feeling sad are reported at rates of 18 percent, 17 percent, and 16 percent, respectively. The overlap between symptoms associated with concussion and diagnosable mental health challenges related to depression and anxiety is significant.

Post-concussion mental health symptoms can be observed among those who do not have a history of a recent head injury or no head injury at all. Those who already have a diagnosis of attention-deficit/hyperactivity disorder (ADHD) or who have symptoms associated with high anxiety and who had a concussion six months prior or longer (i.e., "not recent") endorsed symptoms consistent with having a recent concussion. Similarly, those without a history of a concussion endorsed concussion-like symptoms if they experienced symptoms related to clinical depression or if they did not have sufficient sleep prior to testing. Researchers examining a possible link between "persistent post-concussion symptoms" and mental health noted the consensus among experts is that concussion symptoms should abate by about three months following the concussion. Symptoms that persist are likely associated with something else going on such as a preexisting mental health-related diagnosis. Overall, these researchers found that individuals who scored high on screenings for depression and anxiety also scored higher on post-concussion symptoms that impact their cognitive abilities as well as their physical and emotional well-being in comparison to "healthy controls" and those who had a history of a sport-related concussion but no history of mental health challenges prior to their concussion. They also found that the group with a sport-related concussion and a mental health diagnosis such as depression or anxiety scored similarly on a measure of post-concussion symptoms compared to those who screened high on depression or anxiety but who did not have a sport-related concussion. These findings suggest that an existing or prior history of mental health challenges will result in post-concussion symptoms that are more severe compared to those who do not have such a history. In aggregate, these findings suggest that the intersection between certain mental health-related symptoms and concussion-related symptoms can mimic one another and may or may not indicate the current or historical presence of a head injury.

In their 2018 book entitled *Concussion: A Clinical Profile Approach to Assessment and Treatment*, Drs. Anthony Kontos and Michael Collins noted that while there are specific symptoms related to depression and anxiety that are unique in comparison to concussion there are many symptoms that overlap. For example, with respect to depression, they noted that depression-related signs and symptoms that also occur with concussion include feeling sad or irritable, having memory difficulties, experiencing problems with sleep, feeling fatigued, difficulty with concentration, and feeling confused. In terms of anxiety, shared signs and symptoms with concussion include feeling nervous, having headaches, feeling nauseous, feeling fatigued, feeling dizzy, and dealing with numbness or tingling. Athletes who experience concussion have been found to report changes in anxiety and mood up to two weeks following a concussion. Although these changes are considered to be "subclinical" (i.e., not to the level of being diagnosable) up to 13 percent of those with a concussion will report anxiety-related symptoms that can be diagnosed, and 6 percent report depression-related symptoms that can be diagnosed. In addition, when an individual has mental health challenges prior to experiencing a concussion they are an increased risk for these mental health symptoms to persist following a concussion.

Suicidal thoughts and actions among those who experienced a concussion have gotten a good deal of publicity in recent years due in large part to high-profile professional athletes who had a history of multiple concussions and experienced severe changes in mood, behavior, and personality characteristics. Prior to their deaths some athletes specifically requested that their brains be studied for chronic traumatic encephalopathy (CTE), and family members of others made this request to understand why their loved one's behaviors and personalities changed so dramatically. Individuals (athletes or non-athletes) with a concussion history are at two times greater risk of suicide compared to those without a concussion history. Although sustaining a concussion as a result of a contact sport (e.g., American football) does not, in and of itself, place someone at greater risk for suicide, severe concussion which is more likely to be sustained in contact sports, is linked to a higher risk of suicidal thoughts. The more severe the concussion, the greater the risk for suicidality. What can complicate our understanding of concussion as well as when treatment and what kind are indicated, is the fact that concussion-related symptoms do not always present themselves immediately following the concussion itself.

A review of the literature, conducted by Gary Senecal and colleagues, on psychosocial factors impacted in the context of head trauma in sport, concluded that symptoms associated with CTE (specifically found among those who participated in contact sports) do not appear in many athletes until years following their departure from their sport. CTE specifically has been linked to significant disorders such as "depression, suicidal behavior, bipolar, apathy, poor impulse control, aggressiveness, parkinsonism, sleep apnea, and eventually, dementia" (Senecal et al., 2017, p. 5). CTE is a type of "tauopathy" which refers to a group of neurological disorders, including Alzheimer's and Parkinson's disease, that involve problems with the tau protein. This protein is important for the proper functioning of neurons, therefore when there are problems with this protein there will be problems with neuronal functioning in the brain. Confirmation of CTE can only occur post-mortem (i.e., after the individual has died) when pathologists can determine the way in which tau protein abnormalities are distributed in the brain. There are efforts to refine brain imaging technologies such as PET (positive emission tomography) scans to identify CTE among those who are living; however, results are in their infancy and are not conclusive. Thus, a definitive CTE diagnosis can still only occur if the concussed brain is autopsied.

Regardless of when CTE is suspected or ultimately diagnosed, Gary Senecal and his colleagues found that athletes who undergo a sport transition, including retirement from sport, can exhibit psychosocial symptoms that are similar to those who were diagnosed with CTE. They noted that factors that can impact how smoothly a sport-related transition goes, such as athletic identity and social support, can "contribute to and/or exacerbate a similar range of symptoms that has been associated with CTE" (Senecal et al., 2017, p. 3). As such, these authors call for neuroscientists to focus on sport career transitions to develop a much fuller understanding of CTE-related symptoms including when they manifest. It is only when those who study and treat brain injury take a biopsychosocial approach (see Chapter 3 for more information on the biopsychosocial approach) to understanding the effects of a head injury will we be able to develop sufficient protocols for prevention and treatment.

Concussion Protocols

Over the years the protocol for treating concussion has changed in large part because there is greater understanding of this "invisible" injury and how devastating the impact can be in the short- and long-term health and well-being of the individual. As noted in a previous section, "catchy" phrases such as being "punch drunk" or having your "bell rung" were euphemisms used in the context of a blow to the head and experiencing symptoms like disorientation/confusion, and balance problems. Using such phrases detracted from how serious head injuries can be. Early on after concussion was understood more fully, the most effective treatment was believed to be complete rest in a dark room with little noise. Essentially it was believed that the brain needed full rest (i.e., it should not be used, voluntarily, at all). Currently, however, researchers and practitioners have recognized, through formal research and treating patients, that a brain injury is most effectively treated like any other injury to the body. Some rest is needed, and in some cases that may include things like wearing sunglasses and not being exposed to a lot of noise; however, just like any other injury to the body, the injured body part will recover most effectively when it is gradually used under the direction of specialists.

Current protocols involve gradually having the concussed individual using their brain more and more. In fact, some researchers found that for adolescents who sustained a concussion even some screen time is recommended for recovery. In terms of mental health, the restrictive protocols (e.g., removal from routines, temporary withdrawal from school and/or sport) resulted in an increase in mental health struggles related to mood. Research indicated that, of course, people benefit from routines and activity, and in many cases the social isolation resulting from being removed from one's daily routine and activities (including screen time) contributed to a decline in mental health. Additionally, when the primary instructions for recovery for concussion involved complete rest, researchers found an increase in anxiety and mood-related symptoms.

As more is learned about the nuances of concussion from one person to the next, the severity of the concussion, and the extent to which someone has sustained repeated concussions it is likely that treatment and recovery protocols will change again. Ultimately, this ensures that the best possible care is available to those who need it.

Conclusion

Concussion is a brain injury that can vary in severity. Symptoms of a concussion can show up immediately or take weeks or months or longer before they surface. Regardless of when symptoms surface, an individual is at risk for sustaining another concussion within ten days of the initial concussion indicating that proper recovery time is imperative to properly heal the brain. Mental health and its relationship to concussion has received greater attention. Findings indicate that some indicators of mental health challenges, among those without a concussion, can be similar to what is found in those post-concussion. In addition, researchers have reported that symptoms related to mental health challenges post-concussion often mean the person had been struggling with their mental health prior to sustaining a concussion. As we continue to learn more about concussion, treatment protocols have changed making recovery from a concussion much more effective.

12

Name, Image, and Likeness (NIL)

One of the most significant changes to college athletics since the early 1900s, when the National Collegiate Athletic Association (NCAA) was founded, is athlete compensation via NIL (i.e., name, image, and likeness) deals. NIL has allowed athletes to earn money based on who they are and how they perform in their respective sports. Prior to NIL collegiate athletes were forbidden to accept money or gifts related to attending a school or competing for a particular athletics department. Although NIL legislation now allows student-athletes to make money, the NIL landscape is currently fairly unregulated and can leave some student-athletes vulnerable to predatory practices by sport agents hoping to capitalize on the athlete's name, image and likeness, and by groups attempting to get athletes to compete at their school. All of this can have an impact on an athlete's overall well-being.

What Is NIL and Why Is It Important?

In 2009 a former men's collegiate basketball player successfully sued the NCAA for using his likeness (the "L" in NIL) in a popular sport video game, and a later petition to the Supreme Court by the NCAA opposing the earlier court's decision was unsuccessful (the court did not hear the case). This ruling has been identified as the impetus for the heated debate about whether or not student-athletes should be compensated for others' use of the athlete's name, image, and likeness. As of 2024, thirty-two states have NIL laws on the books and have largely modeled their legislation on the original Fair Pay to Play Act passed in California in 2019 and put into effect on January 1, 2023.

"NIL" stands for name, image, and likeness and specifically refers to who "owns" an athlete's name, image, and likeness and therefore who can profit from it. As discussed in more detail below, collegiate athletics is big business.

Schools and organizations that rank highest in terms of revenue use high-achieving and/or well-known athletes on marketing materials to boost ticket sales, sell merchandise, recruit high school prospects, and so on. Prior to NIL legislation colleges and universities, including the NCAA, would use athletes' names, images, and likenesses for their own benefit while disallowing athletes themselves from benefiting financially or via non-monetary gifts.

Since its inception in 1906, the NCAA was designed to regulate amateur intercollegiate sport with the intent of making a clear distinction between professional and college sports. They specifically noted that collegiate athletes should be focused on academics first and foremost giving rise to the moniker "student-athlete" (note that "student" is first, by design). The NCAA hoped to preserve the amateur nature of sport by protecting "student-athletes from exploitation by professional and commercial enterprises" (NCAA, 2011, p. 5). Additional rules and policies were implemented by the NCAA for the purpose of protecting athletes from exploitation including rules around financial aid and scholarships. Overall, the NCAA's policies and its intent to keep collegiate sports at the amateur level were initially designed to protect athletes. The collegiate sport landscape, however, has changed dramatically since 1906.

Collegiate sports are big business. The most lucrative collegiate sport in the United States is football and since the late 1800s "football financed not just every other sport, but the growth of schools themselves" (Kirshner, 2020, para. 5). In the 1920s, for example, the University of California's athletes brought in over $186,000 nearly 95 percent of which came from football alone. Scrolling forward to the twenty-first century, the dollar amounts are in the tens to hundreds of millions for "blue chip" athletic programs. For example, in 2018, Louisiana State University (LSU) athletics brought in $145 million, 60 percent of which was from football alone.

Coaches' salaries have also seen tremendous growth. In 1904, John Heisman (the namesake of college football's Heisman trophy) made $2550 in salary plus a percentage of game ticket sales. It is estimated that as of 2024 that would translate to about $88,000 which is a fraction of what many Division I university coaches make in the current era. In 2019, for example, the head football coach of Clemson University signed a deal that would earn him nearly $10 million, per year, for ten years. At some colleges and universities other sports and their coaches earn more than football. Regardless, coaches' multi-million-dollar salaries, college's and university's multi-million-dollar sport facilities, and so on are funded through ticket sales, merchandise, and, of course, television deals. As of 2023, it was estimated that the Big Ten schools would bring in over $70 million, each, from football and basketball deals with mainstream television stations. Lucrative deals in the hundreds of millions or billions of dollars have been signed with media stations to televise, for example, the college football playoffs. Recently, a twelve-year deal was made with ESPN for over $5.5 billion, and the NCAA itself is reported to have recently signed a deal with ESPN to broadcast various men's and women's NCAA championship games for $920 million.

College athletics, collectively, generates an estimated $13.6 billion dollars in revenue (annually as of 2022) out earning Major League Baseball (MLB), the National Basketball Association (NBA), and the National Hockey League (NHL). Despite generating revenue that out earns their professional counterparts, college athletes, prior to NIL, were not allowed to capitalize on their athletic fame and prowess. By contrast, professional athletes, through collective bargaining agreements made between owners of professional teams in the United States and their respective players' associations, receive 50–60 percent of the billions in revenue generated in their sports.

As the dollars earned through college sports have increased, student-athletes and their advocates have asked how colleges and coaches can financially benefit from a product produced by non-paid student-athletes who are often referred to as "unpaid laborers." One argument against collegiate athletes getting paid is that student-athletes are "paid" by getting a college education, in some cases at a reduced rate (i.e., a partial scholarship) or for "free" (i.e., a full scholarship); however, research has confirmed what many have known for a long time: student-athletes do not always have what they need even with a full scholarship. A study conducted in 2022, for example, found that 60 percent of college athletes were food insecure (37% of whom were categorized as "very low" on a measure of food insecurity) compared to 42 percent of the general college population. These researchers also found those who were at greater risk of food insecurity were football players and track and field athletes. These athletes reported concerns such as not getting enough to eat, worry related to there not being enough food to eat (i.e., the food will run out), and worry regarding food running out before they had the money to purchase more. Over half of the athletes surveyed stated that they ate "less often than they felt they should because there was not access to enough food" (Reader et al., 2022, p. 5), and nearly three-fourths of athletes reported that "they did not eat for an entire day because of a lack of access to enough food" (Reader et al., 2022, p. 5).

Factors contributing to food insecurity among college athletes include factors such as whether or not they live on campus (living off campus was identified as a risk factor), high nutritional requirements leaving many athletes without enough food because they did not have the money to buy what they needed (either through school meal plans or on their own), and being a member of a historically disenfranchised racial/ethnic group such as Black/African American or Native Hawaiian/Pacific Islander all of whom were more likely to be food insecure. Given the importance of fueling for sport and overall well-being, food insecurity is exceptionally problematic. Not having access to enough food is particularly problematic given the billions of dollars in revenue generated for schools and athletic departments as a result of the high-performing athletes who require substantial fueling to perform as expected. NIL deals may help some athletes afford additional food not covered by college meal plans; however, the size of NIL deals varies dramatically from one athlete to the next.

Disparities in NIL

Although not fully studied or understood, there may be elements of unfairness (real or perceived) in the NIL landscape. Student-athletes, for example, may elect to enter the transfer portal to enroll schools with a larger market assuming (accurately or not) that NIL deal opportunities may be better than where they were prior to entering the portal. An additional source of unfairness that, unfortunately, permeates sport at all levels of competition is gender inequality. In the context of NIL, athletes who compete for men's sports account for just over 67 percent of all NIL deals whereas athletes who compete for women's sports account for just over 32 percent of deals. In addition, the vast majority of top earners via NIL are males. As of 2024 only six of the top fifty NIL earners competed in women's sports. The savvy use of social media has allowed some female athletes to transcend this disparity in being a top earner (e.g., Livvy Dunne, LSU Gymnastics, with over 5 million followers on Instagram). Athletes participating in football account for nearly 50 percent of NIL deals and tend to fill the top spots for NIL earnings. As of 2024, thirty-four of the top fifty NIL earners are football players. In addition to the earning disparity between those who participate in men's compared to women's sports, and the disparity between types of sport, international athletes who compete for a school in the United States are likely prohibited from signing NIL deals given the limitations of the visa (i.e., the official document that allows someone to travel or live in another country) that allows them to be in the United States.

NIL and "Collectives"

An additional concern related to NIL is something called "collectives." Typically, NIL involves deals between individual companies and an athlete, and more than likely that is what most people had in mind when considering establishing NIL as a method of compensation for athletes. Not long after NIL was put in place, however, collectives started forming.

A collective is not formally affiliated with a college or university in any capacity; however, collectives' founders and members tend to be alumni of a particular college or university. Their purpose is to raise money that can be used to pay athletes for their NIL. In theory this means that members of the collective who own businesses can offer more money collectively, rather than individually. The concern is that collectives tend to function like "boosters" which have very specific, strict rules in terms of what they can and cannot do with respect to how their money is used in athletics. Boosters are those affiliated with a college or university who raise money and provide services to support their school's athletics department as a whole or a specific sport. According to the NCAA boosters are specifically not allowed to "encourage a prospect's participation in university athletics or provide benefits to prospects that were not previously provided" (NCAA, n.d., para. 7). Essentially, boosters cannot have contact with a prospective student-athlete which includes being prohibited from providing gifts of any kind to a prospective student-athletes' relatives. Boosters are also restricted in their contact with student-athletes who are already enrolled in the college or university.

At one point in the NIL process, the NCAA specifically stated that boosters can offer NIL deals to athletes as long as they are not officially affiliated with the college or university and its athletic department. Boosters are still not allowed to entice athletes to sign with their school's program; however, various booster groups have given tens of thousands of dollars to scholarship athletes and in one instance paid the tuition of walk-on players for the football team. Although this may technically not break NCAA rules (though that can be debated), how many teenagers and their parents would turn down the kind of money that can be offered via NIL deals? As of 2022 a survey of athletic directors found that at least 90 percent expressed concern that collectives offering NIL deals to athletes may be breaking the spirit of NCAA rules related to "improper recruiting inducements." Those who are negatively impacted the most when NCAA deems these rules are broken are typically the athletes themselves, many of whom do not know that any rules were broken.

What do the rules about boosters have to do with collectives? Some have suggested that collectives are a way around the booster rules in that collectives are known to entice prospective student-athletes with very large NIL deals that likely impact their decision to sign with one school over another. In this context it is important to recognize who prospective college and university athletes are: they are high school students who typically lack adequate decision-making skills to sign deals that are in their best interests. Early in 2023, ESPN reported on a significant NIL deal worth $13 million offered to a top football prospect (i.e., he was still in high school). He is reported to have committed to the school, apparently in large part due to the NIL deal, then asked to be released from this commitment because the NIL deal offered by a collective fell through. This may seem simple enough; however, there are rules about signing a commitment letter. Even when an athlete can be released from such a commitment there is a good chance any other programs interested in the prospect already filled their rosters by the time the commitment was voided and therefore cannot sign additional athletes. This potentially leaves the athlete with very limited choices. When high school student-athletes (and by extension, their families) are offered large sums of money (sometimes in the millions of dollars) for their NIL this can be difficult to walk away from. Even if an athlete takes their time to consider all possible consequences and outcomes of signing such a deal, it may be impossible to anticipate which deals may fall through. Having a good sports agent can be one way to manage NIL deals and to ensure the deal is truly in the athlete's best interest; however, there is also no guarantee that a sports agent will have the athlete's best interest in mind.

There are, of course, highly reputable sports agents; however, finding one may not be as easy as it seems. Although there are state and federal laws regulating sport agencies, there are many who try to take advantage of collegiate athletes and sign them to deals that violate NCAA rules and state or federal laws. Some athletes have successfully sued predatory sport agents to have their contracts voided; however there are also stories of some athletes being threatened by disreputable sport agents who signed them to inappropriate if not illegal contracts. The lure of the possibility of big money through NIL deals can leave student-athletes vulnerable to predatory practices by those hoping to take advantage of and profit off of student-athletes navigating a still new and not fully regulated financial opportunity. This means that not only may an NIL deal offered by a collective or through another source be predatory, the agent hired to represent the athlete in these deals may also try to take advantage of the athlete to get as much of the NIL money themselves as possible. This type of situation, without any doubt, would be stressful for anyone, let alone a teenager trying to navigate a world operated by adults who typically have very specific agendas.

Implications of NIL for Mental Health

NIL has been referred to as the "wild west" because initially protocols, rules, and laws surrounding NIL did not exist or were unclear. State laws have since been passed to help regulate this largely unregulated effort but vary widely from one state to the next. As of mid-2024, the United States Congress has several pieces of legislation before them that are intended to make NIL policies and rules uniform across the country. Regardless of what future state laws may be passed or federal legislation implemented, NIL is controversial in that many see this as an important milestone toward compensating student-athletes at all, whereas others have noted that student-athletes should be compensated based on the revenue they help generate (similar to professional athletes). All of this still leaves young adults vulnerable to consequences of signing NIL deals they may not have considered.

Harris et al. (2021) identified psychosocial stressors associated with NIL that are not beneficial for student-athletes and have been referred to as "hidden consequences" of NIL. These so-called hidden consequences refer to things such as "role engulfment," athletes needing to be a "brand manager," and finding an appropriate sport agent to help the athlete negotiate NIL deals. Overall, however, because NIL is still relatively new there is not enough known about the impact of NIL on the well-being and mental health of student-athletes and whether or not NIL truly benefits athletes.

Role engulfment refers to having an identity (i.e., athlete) that dominates any other identity. In many cases when asked who they are, an athlete is likely to say "athlete" or mention their specific sport (e.g., "field hockey player") as their primary and possibly only identity (see also the "Athletic Identity" section in Chapter 3 for more information). Maintaining such a singular identity is encouraged when athletes are told they must devote all or nearly all of their time and energy to their sport and perhaps to view themselves as "athlete-students" rather than the other way around. Role engulfment as an athlete has been suggested to exacerbate issues student-athletes already experience on college and university campuses including social isolation, and difficulty coping with all of the demands on their time and energy; both of which can negatively impact mental health. Having an NIL deal might further exacerbate these concerns since it is one more aspect of their lives that revolves around being an athlete and requires an athlete's time and energy. Related to this is the amount of time and energy require to manage one's "brand" as an athlete.

A "brand manager" is defined as a professional role devoted to managing a company's brand-related marketing to include the company's products and services. Brand managers can make anywhere between $80,000 and $162,000 annually when hired in this role for a company and typically require education at least at the bachelor's level. In short, being an effective brand manager is a profession for which people get specific education and training. Student-athletes who have or who are considering an NIL deal must learn how to be an effective brand manager without the education and training of those who do this professionally. The higher profile an athlete is, the more likely it is they must see themselves as a "brand."

Consumers of any sport-related product have positive thoughts and feelings about some brands and not-so-positive thoughts and feelings about others. These thoughts and feelings are evoked via advertising campaigns, having their brand associated with certain sports, specific teams, or specific athletes. This means, of course, brands of any kind must be careful about what is presented to the public, what is said or printed that may be shared by others, and that nothing negative is associated with the brand. For example, high-profile professional athletes who have lost major endorsement deals due to perceived unacceptable or controversial behavior include Lance Armstrong, Michael Vick, Michael Phelps, Tiger Woods, and Maria Sharapova. The same can occur for student-athletes with an NIL deal who are unable to effectively manage themselves from the perspective of brand management.

Promoting a brand of any kind means, in part, that people have heard of the brand and know what it is. A significant medium for promoting one's brand is through social media, and creating brand awareness requires a great deal of exposure. It is estimated that nearly 75 percent of NIL-related activity promoting an athlete's brand occurs on social media. This content is categorized under "influencers, content creation, and brand promotion." Since student-athletes are likely their own brand managers, they are the ones frequently posting content which, of course, requires time and energy they may or may not realistically have. A solution, of course, would be to hire an actual brand manager; however, for most athletes this is not financially feasible since the average NIL deal is believed to be between $1000 and $2000. There are some athletes who make exponentially more than that (i.e., $1,000,000+ in NIL deals) but these athletes are typically part of large Division I schools and have hundreds of thousands to millions of social media followers.

As noted, having and maintaining an NIL deal requires posting media content (usually social media) consistently. Many high-performing athletes already have a love-hate relationship with the media since many athletes have media requirements (e.g., half-time interviews, post-game interviews), and, of course, many athletes often have stories written about them via various media outlets often extolling the greatness of their athletic skills or scrutinizing their mistakes. NIL is viewed as placing greater pressure on athletes to engage with the media and generate attention for their brand. Moreover, athletes must navigate this very fickle terrain often without much if any media-related training.

Since NIL is so new, there is very little known about the actual impact of NIL, and all that comes with it, on athlete mental health. Peter Economou and Alexander Gamble recently published an article discussing NIL and presented a case study wherein the student-athlete presented for help related to sleep problems, anxiety, and stress all of which were reportedly related to the athlete's struggle to make a decision about whether or not to enter the transfer portal because of multiple NIL deals offered to him by other institutions. In addition, it was reported that the student-athlete felt pressure from his family to pursue the most lucrative offer. A significant part of the struggle was the tension between wanting to be loyal to the institution that originally recruited him and loyalty to his family's wishes. Overall, these authors noted that sport psychology practitioners are in a unique position to help a student-athlete navigate this type of stressful scenario and note that such practitioners should ensure they are adequately educated on NCAA rules and regulations surrounding NIL, the transfer portal, and NIL-related legislation that may impact athletes navigating this rugged and unforgiving terrain.

Since NIL is viewed as something that may add pressure to student-athletes already feeling the pressure to perform in their sport and in the classroom, there is concern that the NIL landscape may exacerbate serious mental health challenges. In recent years, there has been an uncharacteristically high rate of athlete death by suicide (see also Chapter 7 for more information). Death by suicide among NCAA participating athletes doubled from the twenty-year period of 2002–22, and is the second leading cause of death among NCAA athletes after accidents. Although death by suicide is still a rare event, the increase in numbers is alarming and many of the stories associated with these athletes point to the pressures of being a collegiate athlete particularly with respect to performing in the classroom, in their sport, and fitting in. There is currently no direct connection between death by suicide and NIL; however, the speculation is that adding one more fairly complex thing to an athlete's already full plate will not help. [Those struggling with suicidal thoughts can access the National Suicide and Crisis Lifeline in the United States by calling or texting 988 or by visiting 988lifeline.org]

Even when NIL deals, of any size, are brokered in good faith and honored, those who have shelled out the money expect to get a return on their investment. They expect the athlete to make money for them by representing their product or service through athletic achievement. Opponents of NIL are concerned that not only do student-athletes have to worry about performing well enough to keep their spot on the team and, perhaps, more importantly, to keep their scholarship to the school, now they also have to worry about whether or not they are performing well enough to keep the NIL deal they have and attract new ones. Whenever money is involved, the situation immediately becomes a business transaction and businesses want results. There is no doubt this can contribute to the stress level of anyone, including high school and collegiate athletes.

Conclusion

Collegiate student-athletes are already at higher risk for some mental health challenges (e.g., depression and anxiety, eating disorders, substance use; see Chapter 2 for more information). Some have suggested that the added pressure of NIL deals, whether they are made with the best interest of the athlete in mind or not, places greater stress on athletes making them even more vulnerable to developing new mental health challenges or making existing mental health challenges worse. Moreover, because NIL is still relatively unregulated some athletes have already been prey to those looking to capitalize on the athletes' name, image, and likeness.

Part III

Scenarios

Case 1

Malik Has a Career-Ending Injury

Malik has been playing football since he was in elementary school. He is currently in his junior year of high school and is getting scouted by Division I and Division II colleges and universities. His plan has been to play for a blue-chip Division I program with the hope of getting drafted by the NFL. He has had injuries throughout his playing career including a couple injuries that required him to rehab for weeks or months prior to being able to return to play. He found the process of rehabilitating his injury, and not being allowed to practice or compete, frustrating, at best, and sometimes pushed his recovery too much which resulted in re-injury and added recovery time until he was cleared to play.

Malik has "lived and breathed" football for as long as he can remember. Growing up he had posters of his favorite NFL players hung on the walls of his room, and still has his role model for football excellence hung near his desk in his room so he can always see it. He has inspirational quotes from his favorite football players and a few from the best players in other sports. He watches football every chance he can get. This includes purchasing a "season pass" for streaming professional and DI games, and he watches his own film looking for ways to improve his game. Although he has some friends who compete in other sports at his school, he nearly exclusively hangs out with members of his team and looks forward to team meetings and practices.

Malik is currently dating one of the cheerleaders for the team and they have been together since his sophomore year in high school. Together, they are able to talk about Malik's games and she offers her opinion about how she thinks he did that particular game. He appreciates that she knows enough about the game that they can have conversations about the sport without him having to explain too much of the typical football lingo.

Malik's father played high-level football in college and was drafted in a late round to play in the NFL. He was a decent player but bounced around between teams ultimately playing in the NFL for only three years. He was not picked up by another team after being let go mid-season by the last team he played for and therefore had to figure out "what's next" since he had not planned for such an early retirement from football. Malik's father has worked with his son on improving his football IQ and abilities ever since his Pop Warner football years. Malik watches film with his father regularly, and looks forward to this time as one of the only ways he and his father bond and connect. Although his mom does not know football very well, she has attended every game he has ever played and is his "biggest fan." His younger brother sees Malik as a role model and tries to do whatever he does so he can also play high-level football. Occasionally, his brother is "allowed" to watch film with Malik and his father. Maliks' father has said that he is preparing Malik for the NFL.

Malik plays on the offensive line for his high school team and often ends up on the bottom of a pile of players particularly when they run a play designed for a short yardage gain for a first down. In the middle of the season their team ran a quarterback sneak and he felt someone land hard on his leg, heard a "snap," and screamed in excruciating pain. After players from both teams got up from the pile, they all frantically waved the athletic training staff over. Malik looked at his leg and noticed something pushing against his compression pants and noticed a growing blood stain surrounding that area. Malik's leg was stabilized and wrapped, and he was carted off the field and loaded into an ambulance. He was ultimately diagnosed with a severe compound fracture of the lower leg which required surgery that was unsuccessful. Ultimately there was enough damage from the injury and unsuccessful surgery that doctors had to remove Malik's leg below the knee thereby ending his football career and his hopes for playing at the DI level and ultimately for the NFL.

Since his injury, Malik has pulled away from his friends and canceled his streaming subscriptions to watch professional and collegiate football. He is at the point where he can begin his rehab through physical therapy but has cancelled all appointments set up for him. When asked why he won't go he usually says "why bother?" When his friends come over to his house to visit, he refuses to see them and declines all invitations to come to team practices and team-related social events. Whenever anyone brings up getting fitted for a prosthetic, he gets angry and lashes out. He has started consuming alcohol to numb his emotional pain and has been overusing his prescribed pain medication for the same reason.

Analysis

Malik clearly has a high athletic identity, specifically, a strong identity as a football player. Most of his time had been spent on football-related activities (e.g., training, watching film, streaming games), and nearly everyone in his life is connected to football in some way either through the team (e.g., most of his friends are teammates) or through him (e.g., his girlfriend and parents), and his goals have nearly all been related to continuing his football career.

Having a high athlete identity served him well while he was still able to play since all of his efforts were devoted to becoming the best player he could be. Now, however, he appears to be unable to see a future for himself outside of football since he feels like there is no reason to rehabilitate after his surgery and has rejected any efforts by others to talk about a prosthetic. He is abusing both alcohol and pain medications (likely opioids) and is at risk for becoming addicted if he is not already.

Malik would benefit from talking with a licensed mental health professional who is also knowledgeable about sport and substance use. It would initially be important to determine if Malik has a substance use issue that requires treatment. There are mental health professionals who specialize in this type of treatment and a referral to such a professional may be indicated. In addition, focusing on helping Malik find motivation to rehab following his injury will be important to ensure the injured leg can function as well as possible so he can tolerate a prosthetic one day, should he decide to pursue using one. Overall, Malik will likely need to go through a grieving process related not only to the loss of his lower leg, but also his plans to be a collegiate and ultimately a professional football player. Helping Malik explore who he is outside of football while empathizing with the fact that the plans he had for his future career are no longer viable will be important.

Case 2

Chris Is Bullied for Being Non-Binary

Chris currently uses the pronouns they/them; however, prior to alternative pronouns being used broadly in society they felt highly uncomfortable with being identified by the pronouns associated with their assigned sex at birth, which was male. Although Chris has consistently participated in sport throughout their life and had the coordination and skills to compete effectively on boys' teams, they never truly felt like they fit in or could be true to who they are. They also did not feel like they would fit in competing on girl's teams.

Chris has been a two-sport athlete since middle school participating in soccer during the fall then track and field during the indoor (winter) and outdoor (spring) seasons. They earned a starting role on their soccer team during their sophomore year as a right winger and kept this status through their senior year. During their track seasons they were a sprinter and middle-distance runner. They had the most success in the 200- and 400-meter events, consistently making it to regional competitions and during their senior year making it to nationals with their team's 4 x 400 relay.

Chris has established friendships in and outside of sport but has felt the most comfortable with their non-sport friends. Chris felt confident there were at least a few teammates on their soccer or track teams that might accept them if they knew Chris' gender identity. After getting to know one of these teammates a bit more and spending time with them outside of sport and school, Chris, at a recent social gathering, decided to let this particular teammate know that they have struggled to feel fully comfortable in sport and confided that they prefer the pronouns they/them and that they have never truly felt like they fit in with boys' or girls' teams. The teammate seemed to listen without judgment, nodding and asking questions but never really reassured Chris that they were okay with Chris' non-binary status. As the conversation was winding down Chris became more nervous that they may have made a mistake outing themselves to this teammate.

Chris asked their teammate "Please keep this between us, okay?" The teammate nodded and said "Sure"; however, Chris did not feel reassured by their teammate's response, suspecting that the teammate was now uncomfortable around them. Chris' fears seemed confirmed when they saw the teammate talking with some of the other teammates who gestured toward Chris with looks of shock and horror on their faces. Chris quickly found other non-sport friends at the gathering, who knew about Chris' gender identity, to try to take back a sense of safety. Unfortunately, any safety they felt was short-lived when Chris' teammates walked over to them and one of them jabbed their shoulder.

"Hey. Are you serious? Are you one of *those* people who refuses to use the right pronouns?"

Chris felt shocked and froze not knowing what to say or how to respond. They felt their non-sport friends move slightly away from them but not completely walk away, though they did not say anything either. Chris stood there as various teammates barraged them with questions about their sexual orientation, their gender identity, and started criticizing nearly everything about them including how they spoke, clothing they wore, and so on. Chris left the gathering earlier than planned and refused to interact with anyone (in person or virtually) the rest of the weekend. When classes resumed on Monday, they felt all eyes on them in the hallways and in the classrooms.

Walking down the hallway to their next class, groups of girls giggled as they walked past and Chris felt something hit the back of their head. They turned around to see the teammate they confided in laughing at them. Practice was no better. Typically, Chris was an integral part of practices and scrimmages as teammates often passed them the ball and seemed to work with them on the field. At this practice, however, no one passed them the ball and the coach yelled at Chris to get their act together. There seemed to be an uptick in gender-based slurs and at least one teammate intentionally bumped into them on purpose saying, "Watch it fa#got!"

The next day Chris convinced their parents to let them have a sick day and not go into school. Their mood had declined significantly and they even avoided interacting with their family and skipped most meals. Chris returned to school the next day and things were the same or worse depending on the class and who was in it. Their non-sport friends seemed to want to support them but didn't know how so they felt more and more isolated. Chris struggled to keep up with their school work, unable to stop thinking about the looks, the slurs, and the overt aggression on the soccer pitch. They felt hopeless and not sure what to do. Chris knew their parents and sister loved them but it wasn't the same. They felt like an outcast for the first time in their life. They are looking forward to heading off to college in the fall and "starting over" with new people.

Analysis

Chris seems to know who they are in the context of gender identity and while they have some support from family and some friends, they do not have the support they want and likely need from their peers. Although not covered in this scenario, it also appears that Chris' coach has not intervened in any way to quash bullying behavior.

Chris' decline in mood, decline in academic performance, and the presence of "hopelessness" are reasons for concern. Their optimism about college and their support from family are positive forces in their life right now. Even so, Chris would benefit from a referral to a licensed mental health professional, ideally one who specializes in concerns related to gender identity. If that professional is also familiar with sport, that would be even better. Although Chris is not struggling with their gender identity, per se, they are struggling with how to cope with not only a lack of sufficient support but also outright bullying.

Chris may, indeed, be able to start over in college and feel a greater sense of acceptance. In the meantime, however, seeking support from a licensed professional who has helped others navigate non-binary identities can provide an opportunity for Chris to explore their options for internal coping strategies (e.g., managing their thoughts and feelings about how others have responded) and external coping strategies (e.g., determining if talking to the "friend" who outed them, or to the coach to have them establish a more accepting team culture is something they would want to pursue). Chris' counselor would also be able to help them plan for ways to ensure, as much as possible, how to find people in college who will accept them as they are, and to develop strategies for dealing with others who do not accept them.

Case 3

Brenda's Coach Triggers Her Trauma

Brenda is starting her junior year of college and has been a starter on the college's field hockey team since her sophomore year. At the end of last year, the coach announced she was leaving to take another coaching job at another institution. Brenda was sad to see her go because she felt like the coach seemed genuinely interested in the well-being of her athletes and supported not only their growth in sport but also in life. There were a couple of times during her first two years on the team that Brenda felt like she needed some time to focus on school work or focus on her overall well-being. Brenda was able to talk with her coach to identify a plan that would not only benefit Brenda but also not leave the team in a difficult position. Before the coach left for her new job she met with the team and let them know she had heard of her replacement but did not know the new coach personally. She added, however, that the new coach was "an excellent coach with an impressive win/loss record."

During preseason all of the returning players and new recruits met with the new coach as a group. She introduced herself and her coaching history. She ended by saying that she planned to bring this team to nationals and that every single player was on the "chopping block" with a final message to members of last year's starting roster: "Don't get complacent. You're not safe either."

Although Brenda felt a bit shaken by this change in tone and atmosphere, she felt more determined than scared to work hard and prove that she not only deserved a spot on the team but that she deserved to retain her starting role. At their first full practice, there were new faces in addition to the new recruits. Coach notified the team that there are a few new players who went through the transfer portal to compete with this team and the coach approved them to join. She implied that their spots were already secure.

As the team started warming up as they typically did the coach started yelling that they weren't running fast enough and that their drills were "for sh*t." When they started scrimmaging, she consistently yelled at specific players, including Brenda, letting them know they were probably going to get cut. After practice,

Brenda asked to meet with the coach privately. She felt very nervous but chalked that up to meeting with a new coach and asking for more clear feedback.

They went to the coach's office where Brenda asked if the coach was willing to give her more specific feedback about her skills and effort that the coach did not like. The Coach, sitting behind her desk, got up from her chair and stood over Brenda who was sitting on the other side of the desk and said sternly "If you don't know, you don't deserve to be on my team." Brenda started to speak but did not have a chance as the coach continued raising her voice slightly,

> My teams are successful because I know how to get them prepared. But they also know what is expected of them. If you do not know what I expect, then you have a problem. From what I could tell, you don't know what you're doing. I have no idea how you made it this far in this sport. It's not looking good for you. Anything else?

Brenda shook her head no and walked out of the coach's office.

As she left, Brenda felt like she could not catch her breath and felt her hands shaking. She closed her eyes tight trying to not see childhood images replaying in her mind that felt like were happening right then and there. She could see her father standing over her berating her. She saw herself shake and cry as he continued to yell at her and tell her she was not good at anything. She could hear him say all those years ago: "If you don't know what you did wrong, you're not good enough to be my kid." She felt the pain on her face as he backhanded her leaving her cheek bruised and her nose bloodied.

The following day at practice Brenda could feel the coach's eyes on her and heard her yelling at most players, including Brenda, except her hand-picked recruits from the transfer portal. As they were scrimmaging, the coach yelled at Brenda specifically to "get it together or get off the pitch." Brenda felt her face flush, her grip on her stick tighten, and her breathing become more rapid. She charged at one of the transfer portal recruits who was dribbling the ball and looking to score. Brenda pulled her stick back, and hit the other player in the shin, hard. Brenda took possession of the ball, dribbled toward the opposing goal, and did not hear the screams of the teammate she hit nor the shrill sound of the whistle calling for play to stop. One of her friends on the team ran toward her and got several feet in front of her holding her hands up and urging Brenda to stop.

Brenda collapsed onto the ground crying, hyperventilating, and turned her head to see nearly everyone surrounding the teammate she hit and the athletic trainer tending to her injury. She saw the coach march over to her. The coach said: "You're done," and walked away.

A few of Brenda's close teammates looked at her bewildered but also knew her well enough to know something was wrong. This was not like her at all. A few provided reassuring comments about the other player, that she was okay but would have a nasty bruise and might have to sit out of practice for a bit. Another teammate tried to reassure Brenda by saying something about the coach being a "bi*ch" and she was completely out of line threatening Brenda's spot on the team like that. Several asked Brenda if she was okay.

Analysis

Although an extreme example, Brenda's past traumatic experiences were clearly triggered by the coach's approach to coaching and way of interacting with her athletes. It is, of course, not the coach's fault that Brenda has a history of verbal, emotional, and physical abuse by her father growing up; however, a scenario like this is not terribly uncommon and it is the coach's responsibility to consider that some athletes may have a trauma history.

The coach would benefit from learning about trauma, how common it is, and likely interactions that can lead to the types of reactions Brenda had. Learning about trauma and ways to minimize the possibility of retraumatizing an athlete with such a history is referred to as "trauma-informed coaching."

Brenda appeared to have a panic attack after meeting with the coach in her office, and acted out in a dangerous way the following day as a result of not having fully processed what happened the day before, and likely having not fully processed her original traumatic experiences in childhood. Not everyone will have as strong a reaction as Brenda's. Differences in reactions can be explained by the presence or absence of trauma, having already learned how to manage trauma responses and/or responses to stress, and how the coach handled the situation specifically with respect to whether or not the coach responded in a trauma informed way.

Although Brenda had friends offer support and acknowledge how damaging the coach's response seemed to be it is clear that Brenda also needs formal support, by a licensed mental health professional specifically trained in working with those who have a trauma history, to help her work through her past trauma and learn how to identify her own trauma-based reactions so she has the opportunity to prevent responding in ways that may get her in trouble or hurting someone else. It would be reasonable for her friends/teammates to encourage her to get support from the college counseling center which could result in a referral to a trauma-specialist if the counseling center does not have someone with this training on staff.

Case 4

Samantha Has an Eating Disorder

Samantha has been a distance runner since middle school. She tried a few other sports before she found running. Although she was a decent athlete and could pick up other sport-specific related skills relatively quickly, she realized she loved running. She had an excellent coach in middle school who was supportive and encouraging of all athletes on the team regardless of their performance level. Samantha lived in a large suburb of a major city in the United States that had several different middle schools. At the end of the year, they all competed in a "city championship" and Samantha won that race in her final year of middle school. She received a letter from the cross-country coach at the high school she would be attending the following year congratulating her on her accomplishment and providing kind words about having Samantha on the team.

Samantha remained highly competitive in high school and was a member of the varsity team her first year of high school. Samantha was consistently among the top three runners of her team each meet and consistently placed in the top 10 at meets with multiple schools. Samantha was proud of her abilities and received ongoing support from her coach, teammates, and family. She wanted to continue to make them and herself proud, and felt like the last thing she could do to become even more competitive was to eat healthier.

Samantha's mother cooked dinner for the family every night and created well-balanced meals; however, they were not always low in fat content. Samantha started asking her mom to prepare more grilled instead of fried chicken, to not put butter or sauces on the vegetables, and started declining a small dessert after dinner. She used to grab toaster pastries for breakfast when she left for school each morning but switched to grabbing a banana and an apple. She usually brought her lunch from home and, again, made requests of her mom (who also packed Samantha's lunches) to limit high fat and/or high sugar foods from her lunch. She decided instead of having her mom not pack a bag of chips with her sandwich that she'd simply give the chips away to her friends.

Samantha's change in diet (note: in this context "diet" refers to what she consumes and not that she "went on a diet") helped her feel "light" and more energized, and that her clothes were fitting a bit looser. She also noticed a decrease in her practice and race times (i.e., she was running faster) that from week to week often bumped her up to the number 2 varsity runner on the team. She also received praise from her coach for working so hard at practices which was "clearly paying off." She proudly told him that she was also eating healthier and felt so much better. He also supported her efforts with her food intake as well.

Samantha continued to notice small gains in time over the next two weeks. Following that she started to feel more tired and achy. Her coach also asked her how she was feeling because her times started to slip a bit. She replied that she just felt tired and a little "under the weather" but that she'd be sure to get a good rest and get back to her old self. Samantha remembered the burst of energy she felt, how light she felt, and how her times improved when she started eating healthier. She decided to make more of an effort to cut out all "bad" foods. She did not allow herself to eat carbs (e.g., no more bread or pasta), and was paying closer attention to the number of calories she ate with the goal of continuing to lower her overall caloric intake. She became more vigilant about what was in other foods she ate and stopped eating dinners with the team when they were at a teammate's home because she didn't know how the food was prepared and what "unhealthy" ingredients would be in the food. Her teammates would ask why she wasn't eating and she'd simply say that she wasn't hungry or that she had already eaten; both of which were not true. She started feeling terrified of gaining weight and loved hearing the compliments she got from both boys and girls at her school for losing weight.

Samantha assumed she lost a little bit of weight when she first started paying attention to what she was eating and started weighing herself to be sure the number on the scale kept decreasing. She started weighing herself several times a day and made a determination about whether she could eat anything else based on what the number on the scale was each time she weighed herself. She lost more weight and began to look noticeably unhealthy. When she was getting ready for practice after school, she felt weak but convinced herself to ignore the feeling. She sat with her teammates listening to the coach talk about the plan for the day's practice. When she stood up with her teammates to go down to the track for a workout, Samantha fainted and fell into her teammates. She woke up immediately looking up at concerned faces and everyone asking if she was okay.

The coach sent everyone down to the track to do a warm-up run while he stayed behind with Samantha.

He asked if she was okay and she said "Yeah, coach. Sorry about that. I'm okay. Give me a second … I'll get down to the track with the girls … " The coach cut her off and said:

> No. That's not going to happen. We're going to call your parents and you are either going to your doctors or the ER if your doctor can't fit you in right now. Also, I'm going to give your parents the name and number of a psychologist. She knows sport really well and she knows about eating problems. You've lost a lot of weight; Samantha and I can see by your reaction (Samantha looked scared and started to protest) that something more than just a fainting spell is going on. Promise you'll meet with her at least once just to see what she has to say. Okay?

Samantha nodded with tears rolling down her face.

Samantha met with the psychologist who was licensed to diagnose and treat mental health illnesses with a specialty in treating eating disorders, and was also a sport psychologist. The psychologist told her and her parents that she was diagnosed with an eating disorder. Given how low her weight had gotten, having had fainting episodes (Samantha "confessed" that she had felt dizzy a lot and had fainted several other times when no one else was around), and Samantha's very strong fear of gaining weight including saying that she still had more to lose, the psychologist indicated that she should take brief break from her sport to be sure her mind and body were healthy enough to sustain her body in and outside of sport.

Analysis

Samantha was lucky that she never got injured from one of her fainting spells. Feeling dizzy and fainting can be an indicator that someone has not had enough to eat or is dehydrated. The psychologist knew this and asked Samantha some very specific questions about how much she ate, how she felt about certain types of food, what her reaction would be if she were told she needed to gain weight to be healthy, and so on. The psychologist diagnosed her with anorexia nervosa. Although this can be an exceptionally dangerous disorder (it has one of these highest mortality rates for psychiatric disorders), Samantha had a number of things in her favor that could make her recovery relatively quick. Although she did meet full criteria for an eating disorder, it was identified within two to three months of the start of it. The quicker a mental health disorder is identified and treated, the much quicker the recovery time. She also had a coach who paid attention to how she was doing and who listened to his gut when he thought something serious was going on and that it was not just medical. We can also presume at this point that she has supportive parents since they brought Samantha to the psychologist as soon as it was recommended.

With the appropriate permissions, Samantha's psychologist made sure her primary care provider was aware of what was going on and what the psychologist recommended for frequency of check ins for weight and vitals. She also made sure the weights would be "blind weights" (i.e., Samantha would not see or be told the number on the scale) at least at the start, and referred Samantha to a registered sport dietitian who also had education and training for eating disorders.

Although Samantha did not fully return to her sport before the end of the outdoor track season, she was cleared to start limited training with the team. She continued to meet with her psychologist to talk about what it was like to be training again and how she was feeling about food and her weight. Before the summer ended, she had been fully cleared to return to her fall cross country season without any restrictions. She continued to meet with her psychologist regularly and had far fewer medical check ins, and was checking in with her dietitian every two to three months. It would also be recommended that even if the eating disorder is in remission that Samantha continue to be assessed for relative energy deficiency in sport (REDs) by her dietitian to be sure she was still able to adequately fuel herself based on the demands of her practice, workout, and competition schedule.

Case 5

Lamar Is Struggling to Fit in and Builds His Confidence through Sport

Lamar is a sophomore in college who always felt "out of place." He had a few friends in high school and hung out a lot with them, but never really felt like they fully accepted him or even that they really knew him. Lamar knew he generally felt a disconnection from his friends but couldn't really figure out why. Overall he felt "lost."

During his middle school and high school years, he almost exclusively focused on academics with the goal of becoming either a surgeon or a lawyer. He knew both could make a lot of money and came with a good amount of prestige. His family had a lot of members working as high-level professionals. Some were medical doctors or lawyers, and some were CEOs of billion-dollar companies. Some of his other family members had less prestigious jobs like being a teacher, an office manager, a mechanic, and so on. He noticed that overall, these family members seemed happier than his other family members. But he really liked the fact that his other family members had really nice houses, cars and clothes, and were able to go on expensive vacations.

When he got closer and closer to college, he realized he felt more and more confused about what he wanted to do with his life. He didn't talk with anyone about how he was feeling and kept saying that his plan was still to be a doctor or a lawyer and that he was leaning toward becoming a lawyer. Family slapped him on the back, and told him that he'd make his family proud; that it was a fine profession. He was glad that they were all proud of him but he felt even more alienated because they didn't know that he wasn't sure at all what he wanted to do.

By the time he got to college he decided not to declare a major of any kind which made him feel like an outcast again since everyone else seemed to know what they wanted to do with their lives, or at least what they wanted to study in college. His school, however, had small meeting groups with all of the undeclared students and he realized he wasn't the only one who didn't know what they wanted to do. Some were trying to decide between more than one specific major before declaring but many more said what Lamar was thinking: "I have no idea what I want to do." Everyone was encouraged to explore as much as possible in terms of courses they took, clubs on campus, club or varsity sports, and so on. Lamar took the advice to heart and started attending meetings of a few different clubs. He realized he didn't like any of them. The people were nice enough, he just wasn't interested in the focus of the clubs. The faculty leading the meetings for the undeclared students reminded them that determining what they didn't like was just as important as identifying what they did like. Lamar kept exploring and when he was trying to go to sleep, he would allow his mind to wander to what he liked to do when he was a kid.

He saw himself reading a lot but also playing outside with his friends. He remembered they would play made-up games, or formal games like hide and seek when he was younger, and play basketball in someone's driveway when he was a bit older. He decided he would explore the club sports his college had since he knew he wasn't interested in competing at the varsity level. He found that some of the club sports teams were just as competitive as varsity sports and steered clear of them. Unfortunately, one of those highly competitive club sports was basketball. Lamar was hoping he would feel comfortable there since he enjoyed playing it for fun as a kid; however, after attending the initial informational meeting it became clear that the coaches and returning athletes were pretty "intense." He ultimately found the club tennis team and remembered that he used to hit the ball back and forth with his mom or dad at the city's tennis courts. They never really "played" tennis but he learned how to hit the ball over the net and how to keep it in bounds. And he remembered that it was fun for him. The school also did not have a varsity tennis team and those who were competing for the team seemed to be there to improve their skills, but mostly to have fun. Lamar formally joined the club and started attending practices. He learned that even though they were there mostly for fun, they did incorporate a couple days a week in the weight room, and two to three times a week ran 2–3 miles around the track. At first, he was quite sore and exhausted. He realized just how unfit he was. As the weeks progressed, he not only began to feel physically better, he realized that his mood felt better too. As he worked on both his strength and his endurance, he was eating a lot more than he usually had but was only putting on lean muscle mass. He did not bulk up but saw greater muscle definition throughout his body. He also realized he was getting better sleep and overall felt more energized.

His friends and people he did not know well at school started noticing the change in his body. He also noticed he was getting more attention from women who seemed interested in him. He felt flattered and for a while got caught up how great it felt to have people notice how he looked; however, he realized that he enjoyed simply working out, practicing, and hanging out with his teammates, a few of whom were becoming good friends. He also knew that he enjoyed learning and started to really think about what subject areas were interesting to him and why.

Overall, Lamar felt much more comfortable with who he was, and felt like he fit in with the friends he was making both on the tennis court, and in the classroom. He also felt more confident asking out a fellow student he met in one of his classes, and who came to watch him play in local tennis competitions. They started dating and found they had a lot in common and shared many of the same interests. By the end of Lamar's first year in college, he felt confident that he was closer to narrowing down what he thought he wanted to do as a career and was deciding between being a psychology major or a social work major.

Analysis

Lamar is like a lot of adolescents or emerging adults who can't find their way when it comes to a career path. It is not uncommon, for example, that one's family will have spoken or unspoken expectations about what someone's life should or should not look like. This can feel like a lot of pressure and may contribute to some pursuing a path that is not really a good fit for them, but that makes the family happy. Lamar felt not only as though he did not really fit in anywhere he also identified a career path that made his family happy and proud, but was not a good fit for him. His awareness of this lack of fit, however, was made more complicated by the fact that he continued to tell his family members that his plans had not changed, which he knew was not true.

Lamar entered college with this uncertainty and sense of alienation until he was introduced to others who were in the same position as he was. He learned that his experience was common and that in order to really know what was important to him and what he wanted to spend his time on, he had to explore as many things as possible to find out what felt like a good fit for him and what did not.

Lamar found a club sport team that fit with him because he remembered enjoying it as a child, and because he realized he wanted to enjoy playing and not be on a team that was super competitive. Lamar seemed to reap many of the benefits associated with participating in sport and being physically active. He noticed, of course, the physical changes his body went through as a result of being regularly physically active, and he noticed that he felt better overall. He felt more rested and did not feel his mood dip very low any more. He started developing more confidence in himself as he learned more and more about himself, but he felt more confident letting people into his life who got to know who he really was. He also had the camaraderie of competing with a team and gathering for team meals or celebrations. As Lamar continued to learn more about himself and make decisions based on what was important to him, he was close to choosing a career path that would be selected based on what he truly wanted rather than what his family wanted or expected. Lamar may or may not benefit from the support of a licensed mental health professional who can help him figure out how to inform his family about his goals. He may also need to learn skills to manage or cope with his family's reaction, particularly if they are not supportive of his decisions.

Directory of Resources

Books

Brown, Tiffany & Steele, Katie (with Erin Strout)—*The Price She Pays: Confronting the Hidden Mental Health Crisis in Women's Sports—from the Schoolyard to the Stadium*

This book discusses the issues specific to women's and girl's sports that contribute to mental health concerns among those who participate. They encourage readers how to find enjoyment playing any sport despite the myriad mixed messages girls and women typically receive (e.g., "Be aggressive, but not too aggressive.").

Buck, Misty—*Athlete Mental Health Playbook: A Guide to Mental Wellness for Athletes*

Written by a former cheerleader, sibling to an athlete, and daughter of a coach, the author noticed the importance of addressing mental health since it has historically been overlooked and undervalued in the context of sport culture (e.g., do not show "weakness" of any kind). She indicates that this a "beginner's resource" for athletes themselves along with their coaches, teammates, and family members. She has written this like a "playbook" including worksheets and practical tips that can be implemented immediately.

Downey, Allan—*The Creator's Game: Lacrosse, Identity, and Indigenous Nationhood*

The author centers Indigenous cultures in the context of lacrosse explaining how this sport was used by Indigenous peoples to resist forced governmental structures, and discusses how lacrosse was appropriate by non-Indigenous people.

Fagan, Kate—*What Made Maddy Run: The Secret Struggles and Tragic Death of an All-American Teen*

A New York Times #1 best seller, this book chronicles Maddy Holleran's life in and outside of sport. The author carefully discusses the mental health issues that seemed to impact Maddy and how those struggles and the pressures of being a student-athlete at a Division I university contributed to her untimely death by suicide at the age of nineteen. The author seemed to have unprecedented access to Maddy's family, friends, and correspondences so that not only Maddy's story could be told but so that her story could serve as a warning sign that student-athletes need more support than is believed necessary by many.

King, Billie Jean (with Johnette Howard & Maryanne Vollers)—*All In: An Autobiography*

Billie Jean King, an icon in professional tennis and considered to be one of the greatest players of all time, recounts how she started in the game of tennis and what it was like for her playing a sport as a woman and as someone who ultimately came out as lesbian in the early 1980s. She famously won the *Battle of the Sexes* in the early 1970s in the midst of advocating for gender equality in sports. She defeated Bobby Riggs who infamously indicated that women's tennis was "inferior" to men's tennis.

Wilson, Godfrey—*Adaptive Sports for the Disabled: Your Guide to Accessible Activities and Events*

This book, published in 2023, begins its introduction with "Welcome to a world where barriers dissolve and limitations are liquidated." The author provides an overview of the history of adaptive sports, how sports in general can be adapted for a wide range of disabilities (e.g., physical, visual, hearing, etc.), how to find adaptive sports in your area, and how fitness-related activities can be adapted.

Websites

Athletes for Hope: Mental Health Resource Hub

https://www.athletesforhope.org/what-we-do/afh-mental-health/whole-being-athlete-resource-hub/

Athletes for Hope was founded by a group of elite athletes in 2006 for the purpose of helping others. Despite this origin, Athletes for Hope is designed to welcome athletes at all levels of competition. Their website includes a page entitled "Whole Being Athlete Education" which includes a section called the "Mental Health Resource Hub" that provides access to various resource guides.

Combating Racism and Racial Discrimination in the Field of Sport

https://rm.coe.int/ecri-general-policy-recommendation-no-12-key-topics-combating-racism-a/16808d28f3

This document prepared by the *European Commission Against Racism and Intolerance* (ECRI) provides numerous recommendations for reducing and eliminating racism and intolerance in sport. This resource also provides links to other resources related to racism in sport.

Concussion Alliance

https://www.concussionalliance.org/

The Concussion Alliance notes that they are "helping solve the hidden concussion epidemic." They provide information and educational resources to those who sustained a concussion, continuing education for those who work with individuals who have sustained a concussion, and provide support for research endeavors that examine the nature of concussion as well as its identification, prevention, and treatment. Searching for "sport" or "athlete" on their website yields myriad articles on concussion as it relates to this population and setting.

Exercise Is Medicine®

https://www.exerciseismedicine.org/

Exercise Is Medicine® (EIM) was founded by the American College of Sports Medicine and the American Medical Association in 2007. Although developed in the United States, it is identified as a "global initiative" with the purpose of making the assessment and promotion of physical activity the standard of care in health-related practices.

Human Rights Campaign

https://www.hrc.org/

The Human Rights Campaign (HRC) notes that it "envisions a world where every member of the LGBTQ+ family has the freedom to live their truth without fear, and with equality under the law." Their website has over 200 results related to sport much of which is focused on transgender athletes in sport.

International Masters Games Association

https://imga.ch/

The International Masters' Games Association (IMGA) was founded in 1985 as a non-profit organization. They reflect the "Olympic movement and 'sport for all' philosophy" noting that sport participation should not and does not stop as we age.

Jed Foundation

https://jedfoundation.org/

The Jed Foundation is a non-profit organization focused on preventing suicide among teens and young adults in the United States. Searching for "sport" or "athlete" on their website yields numerous pages that provide information about suicide in the context of sport and resources to help young athletes cope with sport- and life-related stressors that may contribute to feeling hopeless and helpless about life.

Mental Health in Athletes: 45 Resources to Help You Cope

https://www.onlinemswprograms.com/resources/mental-health-resources-for-athletes/

This page includes forty-five different athlete-related resources (i.e., other organizations and sites on the internet) specifically designed to help educate and support athlete mental health.

North American Indigenous Games Council

http://www.naigcouncil.com/

The North American Indigenous Games Council is a non-profit entity that oversees the North American Indigenous Games. This Council focuses on realizing the potential of the mind, body, and spirit of people through games that reflect the "cultural, spiritual and traditional values of the peoples it represents."

US Center for Mental Health & Sport

https://mentalhealthandsport.org/

This organization is designed to help ensure that all sport-related environments are supportive of mental health. They provide online resources, mental health awareness training, training on coaching practices that support mental-health, and group and individual counseling sessions provided by licensed mental health professionals.

US Center for SafeSport

https://uscenterforsafesport.org/

The US Center for SafeSport, sometimes referred to as "SafeSport," is a non-profit organization devoted to ensuring athletes can participate in sport "free from emotional, physical, and sexual abuse and misconduct." They provide support directly to athletes and training for those who work directly with athletes.

Why Trauma-Informed Sport Is Vital: A White Paper

https://chjs.org/wp-content/uploads/2022/02/CHJS-WhitePaper.pdf

Prepared by the Center for Healing and Justice Through Sport (CJHS), this document explains the prevalence of trauma and its impact on survivors. The document also provides recommendations for anyone working with young people since they will be working with someone who has a trauma history.

World Anti-Doping Code

https://www.wada-ama.org/en/what-we-do/world-anti-doping-code

This code was first published in 2003 by the World Anti-Doping Agency in order to establish a set of rules to be followed by all athletes competing in all sports regardless of the country for which they compete. The current Code reflects eight International Standards that include standards on testing, managing results, and protection of personal information.

World Indigenous Games

https://mastersindigenousgames.ca/

These games, held "every few years," are designed to "celebrate the rich heritage of Indigenous communities across the world." These games are also referred to as the "Indigenous Olympics" and include both Western-style sports and Indigenous sports. These games also involved cultural demonstrations that are non-competitive in nature, including music and dance.

Glossary

Adaptive athlete is an athlete with a disability who competes in sport against others who also have a disability and may use special or modified equipment allowing for their participation.

Adaptive sport is sports that are modified so that athletes with a disability (see also adaptive athlete) can compete in sport.

Autonomy is one of three basic psychological needs associated with Self-Determination Theory and refers to the need to feel like one has the ability to make decisions that reflect the person's values and interests; the freedom to choose.

Autonomy support is providing support to another person that encourages them to make choices that reflects their values and interests.

Biopsychosocial approach is an approach used to understand a person's behavior by considering the impact of biological, psychological, and socio-cultural factors.

BIPOC is an acronym that stands for Black, Indigenous, and Persons of Color.

Competence is one of three basic psychological needs associated with Self-Determination Theory and refers to a person's need to feel that they can effectively develop specific skills and accomplish tasks.

Computer vision syndrome is problems with one's eyes and vision associated with overuse of devices with screens (e.g., smartphones, computers, tablets).

Cyberbullying is a form of bullying that takes place electronically (e.g., via email, texting, social media posts).

Digital literacy is the ability to effectively find, understand, use, and critically evaluate information found via digital technologies.

E'athletes are those who engage in formal esport competitions or who try to improve their in-game ranking (i.e., video games).

Emotional intelligence is the degree to which a person can manage and use their own emotions, and understand the emotions of others.

Epigenetics is the examination of how one's genes get expressed due to one's own behaviors or environmental factors.

Esports are video game competitions by professional or amateur e'athletes, and often have spectators.

Fight or flight response is a physiological reaction in the brain that mobilizes the mind and body to "fight" or "flight" and that can also result in freezing up when we perceive a threat of any kind.

Food insecurity is not having adequate food or good quality food to meet one's nutritional needs.

Higher level of care in the treatment of mental health disorders, refers to more intensive treatment often in a community mental health center, hospital or residential facility setting.

Hypervigilance is exceptionally alert to potential dangers or threats.

Intergenerational trauma is the distress (emotional, physical, or social) that is passed down from one generation to the next. Descendants of a trauma survivor may experience similar reactions to the traumatic event as the survivor of the trauma (i.e., the survivor is the person who directly experienced the trauma).

Media literacy is a person's ability to critically consume information via any form of media to determine if the information presented is accurate or credible.

Mental health literacy is the ability to recognize, manage, and prevent mental health challenges.

Mental toughness in sport is the ability to be resilient despite facing challenges (e.g., mistakes, failures).

Metabolic syndrome is diagnosed when someone has at least three of five markers for this syndrome: high blood pressure, high blood sugar, high triglycerides, low HDL (one type of cholesterol), and a large abdomen.

Microaggressions are any form of subtle or unintentional discrimination or prejudice against a historically marginalized group.

Moral injury is the impact of witnessing or participating in something that goes against a person's moral beliefs.

Name, image, and likeness (NIL) refers to the legal right afforded to a person (in this case athletes) to control how their name, image, and likeness (i.e., something that resembles the person) are used by others.

Neurodivergent/Neurodiversity is the term used to describe a person's brain that works differently than what is expected.

Overtraining syndrome (OTS) occurs when someone exercises or works out too much without sufficient recovery time resulting in predictable physical and mental symptoms.

Recovery paradox is a phenomenon that occurs when recovery and rest are needed a person will be less likely to engage in recovery due to increased levels of stress; the more recovery needed, the less likely it is that the person will engage in restorative activities.

Relatedness is one of three basic psychological needs of Self-Determination Theory that refers to the need to feel connected to other people and to have a sense of belonging.

Social media literacy is the ability to effectively access, evaluate, and create social media-related content.

Stressor, in the context of trauma, refers to a severe experience that significantly affects a person so that their mental health may be significantly impacted.

Title IX refers to a federal civil rights law impacting institutions and programs that receive federal funding, prohibiting discrimination based on sex.

Transfer portal, in the context of collegiate sports, refers to an online system allowing college student-athletes to indicate they want to transfer to and compete at another institution.

Trauma-informed refers to understanding that trauma is common and can affect people in myriad ways, and efforts are made to avoid re-traumatizing someone with a trauma history.

Vicarious trauma refers to having a strong emotional response to hearing about or witnessing someone else's traumatic experience(s).

Bibliography

Chapter 1

American College of Sports Medicine (2021). *Rx for health series: A series on today's most common chronic conditions and their exercise prescriptions.* Exercise Is Medicine, February 8. https://www.exerciseismedicine.org/eim-in-action/health-care/resources/rx-for-health-series/.

American College of Sports Medicine (2024). *Being active for a better life.* Exercise Is Medicine. https://www.exerciseismedicine.org/wp-content/uploads/2021/04/EIM_Rx-for-Health_Being-Active-for-a-Better-Life.pdf.

Badura, P., Geckova, A. M., Sigmundova, D., van Dijk, J. P., & Reijneveld, S. A. (2015). When children play, they feel better: Organized activity participation and health in adolescents. *BMC Public Health, 15*(1), 1090. https://doi.org/10.1186/s12889-015-2427-5.

Bedard, C., Hanna, S., & Cairney, J. (2020). A longitudinal study of sport participation and perceived social competence in youth. *Journal of Adolescent Health, 66*(3), 352–9. https://doi.org/10.1016/j.jadohealth.2019.09.017.

Benefits of exercise (2022). NHS.Uk, January 25. https://www.nhs.uk/live-well/exercise/exercise-health-benefits/.

Brymer, E., Davids, K., & Mallabon, L. (2014). Understanding the psychological health and well-being benefits of physical activity in nature: An ecological dynamics analysis. *Ecopsychology, 6*(3), 189–97.

Carek, P. J., Laibstain, S. E., & Carek, S. M. (2011). Exercise for the treatment of depression and anxiety. *International Journal of Psychiatry in Medicine, 41*(1), 15–28. https://doi.org/10.2190/PM.41.1.c.

Caspersen, C. J., Powell, K. E., & Christenson, G. M. (1985). Physical activity, exercise, and physical fitness: Definitions and distinctions for health-related research. *Public Health Reports, 100*(2), 126–31.

Chen, J.-H., Tsai, P.-H., Lin, Y.-C., Chen, C.-K., & Chen, C.-Y. (2018). Mindfulness training enhances flow state and mental health among baseball players in Taiwan. *Psychology Research and Behavior Management, 12*, 15–21. https://doi.org/10.2147/PRBM.S188734.

Csíkszentmihályi, M. (2008). *Flow: The psychology of optimal experience.* Harper Perennial Modern Classics.

Eime, R. M., Young, J. A., Harvey, J. T., Charity, M. J., & Payne, W. R. (2013). A systematic review of the psychological and social benefits of participation in sport for adults: Informing development of a conceptual model of health through sport. *The International Journal of Behavioral Nutrition and Physical Activity, 10*, 135.

Gothe, N. P., Erlenbach, E., & Engels, H.-J. (2022). Exercise and self-esteem model: Validity in a sample of healthy female adolescents. *Current Psychology: A Journal for Diverse Perspectives on Diverse Psychological Issues, 41*(12), 8876–84. https://doi.org/10.1007/s12144-021-01390-7.

Holt, N. L., Kingsley, B. C., Tink, L. N., & Scherer, J. (2011). Benefits and challenges associated with sport participation by children and parents from low-income families. *Psychology of Sport and Exercise, 12*(5), 490–9. https://doi.org/10.1016/j.psychsport.2011.05.007.

Jackman, P. C., Swann, C., & Crust, L. (2016). Exploring athletes' perceptions of the relationship between mental toughness and dispositional flow in sport. *Psychology of Sport and Exercise, 27*, 56–65. https://doi.org/10.1016/j.psychsport.2016.07.007.

Love, S., Kannis-Dymand, L., & Lovell, G. P. (2021). Sports-specific metacognitions: Associations with flow state in triathletes. *Australian Journal of Psychology, 73*(2), 167–78. https://doi.org/10.1080/00049530.2021.1882267.

Machado-Oliveira, L., Oliveira da Silva, A., Farah, B. Q., Leão, I. C. S., Souza, F. T. C., Santiago, F. L., Machado, L., & Diniz, P. R. B. (2023). Team sports as a protective factor against mental health problems and suicidal ideation in adolescents. *Salud Mental, 46*(4), 177–84.

Mahindru, A., Patil, P., & Agrawal, V. (n.d.). Role of physical activity on mental health and well-being: A review. *Cureus, 15*(1), e33475. https://doi.org/10.7759/cureus.33475.

Malm, C., Jakobsson, J., & Isaksson, A. (2019). Physical activity and sports—Real health benefits: A review with insight into the public health of Sweden. *Sports, 7*(5), 127, Article 5. https://doi.org/10.3390/sports7050127.

Mayo Clinic (2023). *Depression and anxiety: Exercise eases symptoms*. Mayo Clinic, December 23. https://www.mayoclinic.org/diseases-conditions/depression/in-depth/depression-and-exercise/art-20046495.

Mortimer, P., Lowell, J., & Rosen, N. (Directors). (2010). *Alone on the wall* [Film]. Reel Rock.

Nakamura, J., & Csikszentmihalyi, M. (2021). The experience of flow: Theory and research. In C. R. Snyder, S. J. Lopez, L. M. Edwards, & S. C. Marques (Eds.), *The Oxford handbook of positive psychology* (3rd ed., pp. 279–96). Oxford University Press.

Paluska, S. A., & Schwenk, T. L. (2000). Physical activity and mental health: Current concepts. *Sports Medicine (Auckland, N.Z.), 29*(3), 167–80. https://doi.org/10.2165/00007256-200029030-00003.

President's Council on Sports, Fitness & Nutrition Science Board (2020). *Benefits of youth sports*. Office of Disease Prevention and Health Promotion, September 17. https://odphp.health.gov/sites/default/files/2020-09/YSS_Report_OnePager_2020-08-31_web.pdf.

Richman, E., & Shaffer, D. (2000). "If you let me play sports:" How might sport participation influence the self-esteem of adolescent females? *Psychology of Women Quarterly*, *24*(2), 189–99. https://doi.org/10.1111/j.1471-6402.2000.tb00200.x.

Rocliffe, P., Adamakis, M., O'Keeffe, B. T., Walsh, L., Bannon, A., Garcia-Gonzalez, L., Chambers, F., Stylianou, M., Sherwin, I., Mannix-mcnamara, P., & MacDonncha, C. (2023). The impact of typical school provision of physical education, physical activity and sports on adolescent mental health and wellbeing: A systematic literature review. *Adolescent Research Review*, *9*, 339–64. https://doi.org/10.1007/s40894-023-00220-0.

Sancassiani, F., Machado, S., & Preti, A. (2018). Physical activity, exercise and sport programs as effective therapeutic tools in psychosocial rehabilitation. *Clinical Practice and Epidemiology in Mental Health : CP & EMH*, *14*, 6–10. https://doi.org/10.2174/1745017901814010006.

Sanders, C. E., Field, T. M., Diego, M., & Kaplan, M. (2000). Moderate involvement in sports is related to lower depression levels among adolescents. *Adolescence*, *35*(140), 793–7.

Schweickle, M. J., Graupensperger, S., Liddelow, C., Sutcliffe, J. T., Swann, C., & Vella, S. A. (2024). Potential moderators and mediators of intervention effects in a sport-based mental health literacy and resilience program for adolescent men. *Journal of Applied Sport Psychology*, *36*(1), 119–38. https://doi.org/10.1080/10413200.2023.2208632.

Slutzky, C. B., & Simpkins, S. D. (2009). The link between children's sport participation and self-esteem: Exploring the mediating role of sport self-concept. *Psychology of Sport and Exercise*, *10*(3), 381–9. https://doi.org/10.1016/j.psychsport.2008.09.006.

Sonstroem, R. J., & Morgan, W. P. (1989). Exercise and self-esteem: Rationale and model. *Medicine and Science in Sports and Exercise*, *21*(3), 329–37.

Sood, S., & Puri, D. (2022). Psychological capital and positive mental health of student-athletes: Psychometric properties of the sport psychological capital questionnaire. *Current Psychology: A Journal for Diverse Perspectives on Diverse Psychological Issues*, *42*, 21759–74. https://doi.org/10.1007/s12144-022-03272-y.

Thompson, W. R., Sallis, R., Joy, E., Jaworski, C. A., Stuhr, R. M., & Trilk, J. L. (2020). Exercise is medicine. *American Journal of Lifestyle Medicine*, *14*(5), 511–23. https://doi.org/10.1177/1559827620912192.

Vella, S. A., Aidman, E., Teychenne, M., Smith, J. J., Swann, C., Rosenbaum, S., White, R. L., & Lubans, D. R. (2023). Optimising the effects of physical activity on mental health and wellbeing: A joint consensus statement from Sports Medicine Australia and the Australian Psychological Society. *Journal of Science and Medicine in Sport*, *26*(2), 132–9. https://doi.org/10.1016/j.jsams.2023.01.001.

Wann, D. L. (2006). Understanding the positive social psychological benefits of sport team identification: The team identification-social psychological health model. *Group Dynamics: Theory, Research, and Practice*, *10*(4), 272–96. https://doi.org/10.1037/1089-2699.10.4.272.

Wann, D. L. (2013). The Head & Shoulders sport confidence project: An examination of the confidence of novice, intermediate, & advanced skill level amateur athletes. *North American Journal of Psychology, 15*(3), 623–34.

Waters, A. M., Sluis, R. A., Usher, W., Farrell, L. J., Donovan, C. L., Modecki, K. L., Zimmer-Gembeck, M. J., Castle, M., & Hinchey, J. (2024). Reaching young people in urban and rural communities with mental health and wellbeing support within a youth sports development program: Integrating in-person and remote modes of service delivery. *Child Psychiatry and Human Development*, 1–11. https://doi.org/10.1007/s10578-023-01647-1.

World Health Organization (2023). *Stress*. World Health Organization, February 21. https://www.who.int/news-room/questions-and-answers/item/stress.

Chapter 2

Åkesdotter, C., Select Kenttä, G., Eloranta, S., & Franck, J. (2020). The prevalence of mental health problems in elite athletes. *Journal of Science and Medicine in Sport, 23*(4), 329–35. https://doi.org/10.1016/j.jsams.2019.10.022.

Allport, G. W. (1937). *Personality: A psychological interpretation*. Holt, Rinehart & Winston.

American Psychiatric Association (2022). *Diagnostic and statistical manual of mental disorders* (5th ed., text rev.). https://doi.org/10.1176/appi.books.9780890425787.

American Psychological Association (2022). *Increased need for mental health care strains capacity*, November 15. https://www.apa.org/news/press/releases/2022/11/mental-health-care-strains.

Anbouba, M. (2024). Olympian Ilona Maher's BMI says she's "overweight"—Is it time to ditch the test? *Vogue*, August 2. https://www.vogue.com/article/olympian-ilona-mahers-bmi.

Arslan, M., Ayhan, N. Y., Sarıyer, E. T., Çolak, H., & Çevik, E. (2022). The effect of bigorexia nervosa on eating attitudes and physical activity: A study on university students. *International Journal of Clinical Practice, 2022*, 6325860. https://doi.org/10.1155/2022/6325860.

Baghurst, T., & Lirgg, C. (2009). Characteristics of muscle dysmorphia in male football, weight training, and competitive natural and non-natural bodybuilding samples. *Body Image*, 6(3), 221–7. https://doi.org/10.1016/j.bodyim.2009.03.002.

Bu, D., Han, Z., Zhang, C., Liu, J., Huang, Z., Liang, W., Wang, A., & Su, N. (2023). The effect of a mental health literacy intervention on Chinese team officials and staff in elite sports: A two-arm non-randomised controlled trial. *International Journal of Sport and Exercise Psychology, 22*(9), 2151–68. https://doi.org/10.1080/1612197X.2023.2269156.

Chen, A. (2016). *If BMI is the test of health, many pro athletes would flunk*. NPR, February 4. https://www.npr.org/sections/health-shots/2016/02/04/465569465/if-bmi-is-the-test-of-health-many-pro-athletes-would-flunk.

Crust, L. (2007). Mental toughness in sport: A review. *International Journal of Sport and Exercise Psychology*, *5*(3), 270–90. https://doi.org/10.1080/1612197X.2007.9671836.

Derevensky, J. L., McDuff, D., Reardon, C. L., Hainline, B., Hitchcock, M. E., & Richard, J. (2019). Problem gambling and associated mental health concerns in elite athletes: A narrative review. *British Journal of Sports Medicine*, *53*(12), 761–6. https://doi.org/10.1136/bjsports-2019-100668.

Dimailig, G. (n.d.). *How to recognize depression and anxiety in young athletes and how to help*. American Psychiatric Association. https://www.psychiatry.org:443/news-room/apa-blogs/depression-and-anxiety-in-young-athletes.

Dougherty, J. W., 3rd, & Baron, D. (2022). Substance use and addiction in athletes: The case for neuromodulation and beyond. *International Journal of Environmental Research and Public Health*, *19*(23), 16082. https://doi.org/10.3390/ijerph192316082.

González-Martí, I., Bustos, J. G. F., Hernández-Martínez, A., & Jordán, O. R. C. (2014). Physical perceptions and self-concept in athletes with muscle dysmorphia symptoms. *The Spanish Journal of Psychology*, *17*, E43.

Håkansson, A., Durand-Bush, N., & Kenttä, G. (2021). Problem gambling and problem gaming in elite athletes: A literature review. *International Journal of Mental Health and Addiction*, *23*, 1837–53. https://doi.org/10.1007/s11469-021-00692-y.

Holt, R. I. G., Erotokritou-Mulligan, I., & Sönksen, P. H. (2009). The history of doping and growth hormone abuse in sport. *Growth Hormone & IGF Research*, *19*(4), 320–6. https://doi.org/10.1016/j.ghir.2009.04.009.

Hughes, L., & Leavey, G. (2012). Setting the bar: Athletes and vulnerability to mental illness. *The British Journal of Psychiatry*, *200*(2), 95–6. https://doi.org/10.1192/bjp.bp.111.095976.

Hurley, D., Allen, M. S., Swann, C., & Vella, S. A. (2021). A matched control trial of a mental health literacy intervention for parents in community sports clubs. *Child Psychiatry and Human Development*, *52*(1), 141–53. https://doi.org/10.1007/s10578-020 00998 3.

Keyes, C. L. M. (2002). The mental health continuum: From languishing to flourishing in life. *Journal of Health and Social Behavior*, *43*(2), 207–22. https://doi.org/10.2307/3090197.

Laus, M. F., Junqueira, A. C. P., Almeida, S. S., Costa, T. M. B., & Swami, V. (2022). Body image, muscle dysmorphia, and muscularity concerns: A comparison of crossfit athletes, weight-trainers, and non-athletes. *Motricidade*, *18*(1), 50–60. https://doi.org/10.6063/motricidad.25584.

Moesch, K., Kenttä, G., Kleinert, J., Quignon-Fleuret, C., Cecil, S., & Bertollo, M. (2018). FEPSAC position statement: Mental health disorders in elite athletes and models of service provision. *Psychology of Sport and Exercise*, *38*, 61–71. https://doi.org/10.1016/j.psychsport.2018.05.013.

Papageorgiou, K. A., Mutz, J., Lin, Y., & Clough, P. J. (2018). Mental toughness: A personality trait that is relevant across achievement contexts and mental health outcomes. In V. Zeigler-Hill, & T. K. Shackelford (Eds.), *The SAGE handbook of personality and individual differences: Applications of personality and individual differences* (pp. 588–604). Sage Reference. https://doi.org/10.4135/9781526451248.n26.

Patafio, B., Skvarc, D., Miller, P., & Hyder, S. (2021). Evaluating a sport-based mental health literacy intervention in Australian amateur sporting adolescents. *Journal of Youth and Adolescence*, *50*(12), 2501–18. https://doi.org/10.1007/s10964-021-01513-0.

Plateau, C. R., Shanmugam, V., Duckham, R. L., Goodwin, H., Jowett, S., Brooke-Wavell, K. S. F., Laybourne, A., Arcelus, J., & Meyer, C. (2014). Use of the compulsive exercise test with athletes: Norms and links with eating psychopathology. *Journal of Applied Sport Psychology*, *26*(3), 287–301. https://doi.org/10.1080/10413200.2013.867911.

Reardon, C. L., & Factor, R. M. (2010). Sport psychiatry: A systematic review of diagnosis and medical treatment of mental illness in athletes. *Sports Medicine*, *40*(11), 961–80. https://doi.org/10.2165/11536580-000000000-00000.

Rice, S. M., Purcell, R., De Silva, S., Mawren, D., McGorry, P. D., & Parker, A. G. (2016). The mental health of elite athletes: A narrative systematic review. *Sports Medicine*, *46*(9), 1333–53. https://doi.org/10.1007/s40279-016-0492-2.

Sampaio, F., Gonçalves, P., & Sequeira, C. (2022). Mental health literacy: It is now time to put knowledge into practice. *International Journal of Environmental Research and Public Health*, *19*(12), 7030. https://doi.org/10.3390/ijerph19127030.

Sandgren, S. S., & Lavallee, D. (2018). Muscle dysmorphia research neglects DSM-5 diagnostic criteria. *Journal of Loss and Trauma*, *23*(3), 211–43. https://doi.org/10.1080/15325024.2018.1428484.

Sandgren, S. S., & Lavallee, D. (2023). Intervention development for people with muscle dysmorphia symptoms: Best practice and future recommendations. *Journal of Loss and Trauma*, *28*(4), 315–26. https://doi.org/10.1080/15325024.2022.2119718.

Sandhu, A. K., Islam, M., Edirisinghe, I., & Burton-Freeman, B. (2023). Phytochemical composition and health benefits of figs (fresh and dried): A review of literature from 2000 to 2022. *Nutrients*, *15*(11), 2623. https://doi.org/10.3390/nu15112623.

Schwenk, T. (2000). The stigmatisation and denial of mental illness in athletes. *British Journal of Sports Medicine*, *34*(1), 4–5. https://doi.org/10.1136/bjsm.34.1.4.

Sullivan, P., Murphy, J., & Blacker, M. (2019). The level of mental health literacy among athletic staff in intercollegiate sport. *Journal of Clinical Sport Psychology*, *13*(3), 440–50. https://doi.org/10.1123/jcsp.2018-0052.

Weber, S. R., Winkelmann, Z. K., Monsma, E. V., Arent, S. M., & Torres-McGehee, T. M. (2023). An examination of depression, anxiety, and self-esteem in collegiate student-athletes. *International Journal of Environmental Research and Public Health*, *20*(2), 1211. https://doi.org/10.3390/ijerph20021211.

World Anti-Doping Agency (n.d.). *The world anti-doping code.* WADA-AMA.org. https://www.wada-ama.org/en/what-we-do/world-anti-doping-code.

World Health Organization (2022). *Mental health,* June 17. https://www.who.int/news-room/fact-sheets/detail/mental-health-strengthening-our-response.

Wynters, R., Liddle, S. K., Swann, C., Schweickle, M. J., & Vella, S. A. (2021). Qualitative evaluation of a sports-based mental health literacy program for adolescent males. *Psychology of Sport and Exercise, 56.* https://doi.org/10.1016/j.psychsport.2021.101989.

Chapter 3

Alvarez Pires, D., Isoard-Gautheur, S., Madigan, D. J., Smith, A. L., & Gustafsson, H. (2024). Five unsolved issues concerning burnout in athletes: An expert perspective. *Sports Psychiatry: Journal of Sports and Exercise Psychiatry, 3*(1), 39–46. https://doi.org/10.1024/2674-0052/a000074.

American Psychological Association (2023). *Health advisory on social media use in adolescence.* https://www.apa.org/topics/social-media-internet/health-advisory-adolescent-social-media-use.

American Psychological Association (n.d.). *Psychological capital: What it is and why employers need it now.* https://www.apa.org/topics/healthy-workplaces/psychological-capital.

Arvinen-Barrow, M., & Clement, D. (2017). Preliminary investigation into sport and exercise psychology consultants' views and experiences of an interprofessional care team approach to sport injury rehabilitation. *Journal of Interprofessional Care, 31*(1), 66–74. https://doi.org/10.1080/13561820.2016.1235019.

Bär, K.-J., & Markser, V. Z. (2013). Sport specificity of mental disorders: The issue of sport psychiatry. *European Archives of Psychiatry and Clinical Neuroscience, 263 Suppl 2,* S205–S210. https://doi.org/10.1007/s00406-013-0458-4.

Bird, M. D., Simons, E. E., & Jackman, P. C. (2021). Mental toughness, sport-related well-being, and mental health stigma among National Collegiate Athletic Association Division I student-athletes. *Journal of Clinical Sport Psychology, 15*(4), 306–22. https://doi.org/10.1123/jcsp.2020-0043.

Brewer, B. W., Selby, C. L., Linder, D. E., & Petitpas, A. J. (1999). Distancing oneself from a poor season: Divestment of athletic identity. *Journal of Personal and Interpersonal Loss, 4*(2), 149–62. https://doi.org/10.1080/10811449908409723.

Brewer, B. W., Van Raalte, J. L., & Linder, D. E. (1993). Athletic identity: Hercules' muscles or Achilles heel? *International Journal of Sport Psychology, 24*(2), 237–54.

Carrard, J., Rigort, A.-C., Appenzeller-Herzog, C., Colledge, F., Königstein, K., Hinrichs, T., & Schmidt-Trucksäss, A. (2021). Diagnosing overtraining syndrome: A scoping review. *Sports Health, 14*(5), 665–73. https://doi.org/10.1177/19417381211044739.

Centers for Disease Control and Prevention (2020). *Sleep in middle and high school students*, September 10. https://www.cdc.gov/healthyschools/features/students-sleep.htm.

Chang, W. H., Wu, C.-H., Kuo, C.-C., & Chen, L. H. (2018). The role of athletic identity in the development of athlete burnout: The moderating role of psychological flexibility. *Psychology of Sport and Exercise, 39*, 45–51. https://doi.org/10.1016/j.psychsport.2018.07.014.

Charest, J., & Grandner, M. A. (2020). Sleep and athletic performance: Impacts on physical performance, mental performance, injury risk and recovery, and mental health. *Sleep Medicine Clinics, 15*(1), 41–57. https://doi.org/10.1016/j.jsmc.2019.11.005.

Crust, L. (2007). Mental toughness in sport: A review. *International Journal of Sport and Exercise Psychology, 5*(3), 270–90. https://doi.org/10.1080/1612197X.2007.9671836.

DeFreese, J. D., & Shannon, J. (2022). The role of athletic identity foreclosure in the development of poor athlete mental health. In N. Campbell, A. Brady, & A. Tincknell-Smith (Eds.), *Developing and supporting athlete wellbeing: Person first, athlete second* (pp. 239–56). Routledge/Taylor & Francis Group.

de Souza, N. L., Esopenko, C., Conway, F. N., Todaro, S. M., & Buckman, J. F. (2021). Patterns of health behaviors affecting mental health in collegiate athletes. *Journal of American College Health, 69*(5), 495–502. https://doi.org/10.1080/07448481.2019.1682591.

di Luzio, S. S., Martinent, G., Guillet-Descas, E., & Daigle, M.-P. (2020). Exploring the role of sport sense of community in perceived athlete burnout, sport motivation, and engagement. *Journal of Applied Sport Psychology, 32*(5), 513–28. https://doi.org/10.1080/10413200.2019.1575298.

Fogaca, J. L. (2021). Combining mental health and performance interventions: Coping and social support for student-athletes. *Journal of Applied Sport Psychology, 33*(1), 4–19. https://doi.org/10.1080/10413200.2019.1648326.

Foster, S. J. L., & Huml, M. R. (2017). The relationship between athletic identity and academic major chosen by student-athletes. *International Journal of Exercise Science, 10*(6), 915–25.

Gavrilova, Y., Donohue, B., & Galante, M. (2017). Mental health and sport performance programming in athletes who present without pathology: A case examination supporting optimization. *Clinical Case Studies, 16*(3), 234–53. https://doi.org/10.1177/1534650116689302

Gerber, M., Bianchi, R., Madigan, D., Jonsdottir, I. H., Claussen, M. C., & Gustafsson, H. (2024). Burnout and overtraining in elite athletes: Unresolved issues and avenues for future research. *Sports Psychiatry: Journal of Sports and Exercise Psychiatry, 3*(1), 1–3. https://doi.org/10.1024/2674-0052/a000073.

Gerber, M., Gygax, B., & Cody, R. (2024). Coach-athlete relationship and burnout symptoms among young elite athletes and the role of mental toughness as a moderator. *Sports Psychiatry: Journal of Sports and Exercise Psychiatry*, *3*(1), 5–14. https://doi.org/10.1024/2674-0052/a000071.

Gledhill, A. (2021). The downside of sports injury: Poor mental health in injured athletes. In A. Gledhill, & D. Forsdyke (Eds.), *The psychology of sports injury: From risk to retirement* (pp. 63–75). Routledge/Taylor & Francis Group. https://doi.org/10.4324/9780429019227-4.

Godinho, D. B., Fighera, M. R., & Freire Royes, L. F. (2024). Exercise and the brain–gut axis. In N. Hyland, & C. Stanton (Eds.), *The gut-brain axis* (2nd ed., pp. 241–59). Academic Press. https://doi.org/10.1016/B978-0-323-99971-7.00019-9.

Goolsby, M. A. (2021). *Overtraining: What it is, symptoms, and recovery*, August 16. https://www.hss.edu/article_overtraining.asp.

Grandner, M. A., Hall, C., Jaszewski, A., Alfonso-Miller, P., Gehrels, J.-A., & Killgore, W. D. S. (2021). Mental health in student athletes: Associations with sleep duration, sleep quality, insomnia, fatigue, and sleep apnea symptoms. *Athletic Training & Sports Health Care*, *13*(4), e159–e167. https://doi.org/10.3928/19425864-20200521-01.

Gucciardi, D. F., Hanton, S., & Fleming, S. (2017). Are mental toughness and mental health contradictory concepts in elite sport? A narrative review of theory and evidence. *Journal of Science and Medicine in Sport*, *20*(3), 307–11. https://doi.org/10.1016/j.jsams.2016.08.006.

Haghighat, N., & Stull, T. (2024). Up-to-date understanding of overtraining syndrome and overlap with related disorders. *Sports Psychiatry*, *3*(1), 31–8. https://doi.org/10.1024/2674-0052/a000072.

Harvard Medical School (2020, May 21). *The gut-brain connection*. https://www.health.harvard.edu/diseases-and-conditions/the-gut-brain-connection.

Heaney, C. (2021). Understanding mental health and wellbeing in sport. In C. Heaney, N. Kentzer, & B. Oakley (Eds.), *Athletic Development* (1st ed., pp. 185–201). Routledge. https://doi.org/10.4324/9781003153450-15.

Hu, Q., Li, P., Jiang, B., & Liu, B. (2023). Impact of a controlling coaching style on athletes' fear of failure: Chain mediating effects of basic psychological needs and sport commitment. *Frontiers in Psychology*, *14*, 1106916. https://doi.org/10.3389/fpsyg.2023.1106916.

Ivarsson, A., Johnson, U., Andersen, M. B., Tranaeus, U., Stenling, A., & Lindwall, M. (2017). Psychosocial factors and sport injuries: Meta-analyses for prediction and prevention. *Sports Medicine*, *47*(2), 353–65. https://doi.org/10.1007/s40279-016-0578-x.

Jackman, P. C., Swann, C., & Crust, L. (2016). Exploring athletes' perceptions of the relationship between mental toughness and dispositional flow in sport. *Psychology of Sport and Exercise*, *27*, 56–65. https://doi.org/10.1016/j.psychsport.2016.07.007.

Kavussanu, M., Zhang, S., Tang, Q., Cumming, J., & Mackman, T. (2024). Mental health in athletes: Does authentic leadership matter? *Psychology of Sport and Exercise*, *73*, 102617. https://doi.org/10.1016/j.psychsport.2024.102617.

Machado-Oliveira, L., Oliveira da Silva, A., Farah, B. Q., Leão, I. C. S., Souza, F. T. C., Santiago, F. L., Machado, L., & Diniz, P. R. B. (2023). Team sports as a protective factor against mental health problems and suicidal ideation in adolescents. *Salud Mental*, *46*(4), 177–84.

Mahoney, J. W., Gucciardi, D. F., Ntoumanis, N., & Mallet, C. J. (2014). Mental toughness in sport: Motivational antecedents and associations with performance and psychological health. *Journal of Sport & Exercise Psychology*, *36*(3), 281–92. https://doi.org/10.1123/jsep.2013-0260.

Marx, W., Manger, S. H., Blencowe, M., Murray, G., Ho, F. Y.-Y., Lawn, S., Blumenthal, J. A., Schuch, F., Stubbs, B., Ruusunen, A., Desyibelew, H. D., Dinan, T. G., Jacka, F., Ravindran, A., Berk, M., & O'Neil, A. (2023). Clinical guidelines for the use of lifestyle-based mental health care in major depressive disorder: World Federation of Societies for Biological Psychiatry (WFSBP) and Australasian Society of Lifestyle Medicine (ASLM) taskforce. *The World Journal of Biological Psychiatry*, *24*(5), 333–86. https://doi.org/10.1080/15622975.2022.2112074.

McCabe, E. M., Ketcham, C. J., & Hall, E. E. (2021). Good food, good mood: Perspectives on the relationship between nutrition and mental health with division I collegiate athletic programs. *Frontiers in Sports and Active Living*, *3*. https://doi.org/10.3389/fspor.2021.692601

Meeusen, R., & De Pauw, K. (2019). Overreaching and overtraining syndrome: Causes, prevention, and remedy. In M. H. Anshel, S. J. Petruzzello, & E. E. Labbé (Eds.), *APA handbook of sport and exercise psychology: Exercise psychology* pp. 147–57). American Psychological Association. https://doi.org/10.1037/0000124-008.

Merrill, S., & Faustin, M. (2023). Likes and hashtags: Influence of athlete social media use. *Sports Psychiatry: Journal of Sports and Exercise Psychiatry*, *2*(4), 153–6. https://doi.org/10.1024/2674-0052/a000060.

National Cancer Institute (n.d.). *Definition of immune system*. https://www.cancer.gov/publications/dictionaries/cancer-terms/def/immune-system.

National Collegiate Athletic Association (2024). *Mental health best practices: Understanding and supporting student-athlete mental health* (2nd ed.). https://ncaaorg.s3.amazonaws.com/ssi/mental/SSI_MentalHealthBestPractices.pdf.

National Institute of Mental Health (2024). *Looking at my genes: What can they tell me about my mental health*. https://www.nimh.nih.gov/health/publications/looking-at-my-genes.

Ng, T., Sanders, H., Merrill, S., & Faustin, M. (2024). Media's effect on athletes' mental health. *Clinics in Sports Medicine*, *43*(1), 187–98. https://doi.org/10.1016/j.csm.2023.06.022.

Pereira Vargas, M. L. F., Papathomas, A., Williams, T. L., Kinnafick, F.-E., & Rhodes, P. (2021). Diverse paradigms and stories: Mapping "mental illness" in athletes through meta-study. *International Review of Sport and Exercise Psychology*, *17*(1), 343–69. https://doi.org/10.1080/1750984X.2021.2001840.

Polanco-Levicán, K., & Salvo-Garrido, S. (2022). Understanding social media literacy: A systematic review of the concept and its competences. *International Journal of Environmental Research and Public Health, 19*(14), 8807. https://doi.org/10.3390/ijerph19148807.

Reardon, C. L., & Factor, R. M. (2010). Sport psychiatry: A systematic review of diagnosis and medical treatment of mental illness in athletes. *Sports Medicine, 40*(11), 961–80. https://doi.org/10.2165/11536580-000000000-00000.

Renoir, T., Hasebe, K., & Gray, L. (2013). Mind and body: How the health of the body impacts on neuropsychiatry. *Frontiers in Pharmacology, 4*, 158. https://doi.org/10.3389/fphar.2013.00158.

Rice, S. M., Purcell, R., De Silva, S., Mawren, D., McGorry, P. D., & Parker, A. G. (2016). The mental health of elite athletes: A narrative systematic review. *Sports Medicine, 46*(9), 1333–53. https://doi.org/10.1007/s40279-016-0492-2.

Ríos, X., Ventura, C., & Mateu, P. (2022). "I gave up football and I had no intention of ever going back": Retrospective experiences of victims of bullying in youth sport. *Frontiers in Psychology, 13*. https://doi.org/10.3389/fpsyg.2022.819981.

Scamardella, F., Russo, N., & Napolitano, F. (2020). The phenomenon of load management. *Journal of Physical Education and Sport, 20*(4), 2306–9. https://doi:10.7752/jpes.2020.s4310.

Schellenberg, B. J. I., Verner-Filion, J., & Gaudreau, P. (2022). Savoring sport: Connections with athlete passion and burnout. *Journal of Clinical Sport Psychology, 16*(1), 23–41. https://doi.org/10.1123/jcsp.2021-0031.

Schneeberger, A. R., Sudano, L., Leu, A., Claussen, M. C., & Taylor, K. (2023). The complexity of sports psychiatry and sports medicine: Looking beyond the biopsychosocial model. *Sports Psychiatry: Journal of Sports and Exercise Psychiatry, 2*(3), 79–80. https://doi.org/10.1024/2674-0052/a000053.

Selhub, E. (2015). *Nutritional psychiatry: Your brain on food.* Harvard Health, November 16. https://www.health.harvard.edu/blog/nutritional-psychiatry-your-brain-on-food-201511168626.

Simon, M. B., Barczak-Scarboro, N. E., Pexa, B., Register-Mihalik, J., Kerr, Z. Y., & DeFreese, J. D. (2024). Collegiate student-athlete mental health symptom trajectories across a competitive season: Do training load and resilience matter? *International Journal of Sport and Exercise Psychology, 23*(3), 501–19. https://doi.org/10.1080/1612197X.2024.2324433.

Soligard, T., Schwellnus, M., Alonso, J.-M., Bahr, R., Clarsen, B., Dijkstra, H. P., Gabbett, T., Gleeson, M., Hägglund, M., Hutchinson, M. R., van Rensburg, C. J., Khan, K. M., Meeusen, R., Orchard, J. W., Pluim, B. M., Raftery, M., Budgett, R., & Engebretsen, L. (2016). How much is too much? (Part 1) International Olympic Committee consensus statement on load in sport and risk of injury. *British Journal of Sports Medicine, 50*(17), 1030–41. https://doi.org/10.1136/bjsports-2016-096581.

Stamatis, A., Deal, P. J., Morgan, G. B., Forsse, J. S., Papadakis, Z., McKinley-Barnard, S., Scudamore, E. M., & Koutakis, P. (2020). Can athletes be tough yet compassionate to themselves? Practical implications for NCAA mental health best practice no 4. *PLoS ONE, 15*(12), e0244579. https://doi.org/10.1371/journal.pone.0244579.

Stanford Medicine (n.d.). *Sports injury statistics.* https://www.stanfordchildrens.org/en/topic/default?id=sports-injury-statistics-90-P02787.

Stomp Out Bullying (n.d.). *Bullying in sports: Is it competition or bullying?* https://www.stompoutbullying.org/bullying-and-sports.

Straw, E. (2023). *10 things mental toughness is NOT*, November 10. https://www.successstartswithin.com/sports-psychology-articles/athlete-mental-toughness/10-things-mental-toughness-is-not/.

Ströhle, A. (2019). Sports psychiatry: Mental health and mental disorders in athletes and exercise treatment of mental disorders. *European Archives of Psychiatry and Clinical Neuroscience, 269*(5), 485–98. https://doi.org/10.1007/s00406-018-0891-5.

Sudano, L. E., Collins, G., & Miles, C. M. (2017). Reducing barriers to mental health care for student-athletes: An integrated care model. *Families, Systems, & Health, 35*(1), 77–84. https://doi.org/10.1037/fsh0000242.

Vealey, R. S. (2024). A framework for mental training in sport: Enhancing mental skills, wellbeing, and performance. *Journal of Applied Sport Psychology, 36*(2), 365–84. https://doi.org/10.1080/10413200.2023.2274459.

Vento, K. A., Delgado, F., Skinner, J., & Wardenaar, F. (2021). Funding and college-provided nutritional resources on diet quality among female athletes. *Journal of American College Health, 71*(6), 1732–9. https://doi.org/10.1080/07448481.2021.1947301.

Wadey, R., Evans, L., Hanton, S., Sarkar, M., & Oliver, H. (2019). Can preinjury adversity affect postinjury responses? A 5-year prospective, multi-study analysis. *Frontiers in Psychology, 10*, 1411. https://doi.org/10.3389/fpsyg.2019.01411.

Walton, C. C., & Liknaitzky, P. (2020). Advancing elite athlete mental health treatment with psychedelic-assisted psychotherapy. *Journal of Applied Sport Psychology, 34*(3), 605–23. https://doi.org/10.1080/10413200.2020.1848941.

Washington University School of Medicine (2021, October 10). *Three aspects of health and healing: The biopsychosocial model in medicine.* https://surgery.wustl.edu/three-aspects-of-health-and-healing-the-biopsychosocial-model/.

Werner, E. N., Robinson, C. A., Kerver, J. M., & Pivarnik, J. M. (2024). Diet quality of NCAA Division I athletes assessed by the healthy eating index. *Journal of American College Health, 72*(4), 1309–15. https://doi.org/10.1080/07448481.2022.2076102.

Wilson, A., Gicas, K., Stevens, W. D., Sergio, L., & Wojtowicz, M. (2021). Substance use is associated with worse mental health and altered resting state functional connectivity in female university athletes at baseline: A pilot study. *PLoS ONE, 16*(6), e0253261. https://doi.org/10.1371/journal.pone.0253261.

Woods, S., Dunne, S., Gallagher, P., & McNicholl, A. (2022). A systematic review of the factors associated with athlete burnout in team sports. *International Review of Sport and Exercise Psychology*, https://doi.org/10.1080/1750984X.2022.2148225.

World Health Organization (2022). *ICD-11: International classification of diseases* (11th ed.). https://icd.who.int/.

Chapter 4

Baron, D. A., Baron, S. H., Tompkins, J., & Polat, A. (2013). Assessing and treating depression in athletes. In D. A. Baron, C. L. Reardon, & S. H. Baron (Eds.), *Clinical sports psychiatry: An international perspective.* (pp. 65–78). Wiley Blackwell. https://doi.org/10.1002/9781118404904.ch7.

Bender, A. M., Lawson, D., Werthner, P., & Samuels, C. H. (2018). The clinical validation of the athlete sleep screening questionnaire: An instrument to identify athletes that need further sleep assessment. *Sports medicine—open, 4*(1), 23.https://doi.org/10.1186/s40798-018-0140-5.

Brown, R. L., Leonard, T., Saunders, L. A., & Papasouliotis, O. (1998). The prevalence and detection of substance use disorder among inpatients ages 18 to 49: An opportunity for prevention. *Preventive Medicine, 27*(1), 101–10.

Edwards, C. D. (2024). Management of mental health challenges in athletes: Screening, pharmacology, and behavioral approaches. *Clinics in Sports Medicine, 43*(1), 13–31. https://doi.org/10.1016/j.csm.2023.06.006.

Ewing, J. A. (1984). Detecting alcoholism: The CAGE questionnaire. *Journal of the American Medical Association, 252*(14), 1905–7.

Gouttebarge, V., Bindra, A., Blauwet, C., Campriani, N., Currie, A., Engebretsen, L., Hainline, B., Kroshus, E., McDuff, D., Mountjoy, M., Purcell, R., Putukian, M., Reardon, C. L., Rice, S. M., & Budgett, R. (2021). International Olympic Committee (IOC) Sport Mental Health Assessment Tool 1 (SMHAT-1) and Sport Mental Health Recognition Tool 1 (SMHRT-1): Towards better support of athletes' mental health. *British Journal of Sports Medicine, 55*(1), 30–7. https://doi.org/10.1136/bjsports-2020-102411.

Harenberg, S., Keenan, L., Ingram, Y., Wilson, S., Vosloo, J., & Kaye, M. (2024). Factorial validity and gender invariance of the Patient Health Questionnaire (PHQ-9) in student-athletes. *Journal of American College Health*, 1–7. https://doi.org/10.1080/07448481.2024.2317184.

Hughes, L., & Leavey, G. (2012). Setting the bar: Athletes and vulnerability to mental illness. *The British Journal of Psychiatry, 200*(2), 95–6. https://doi.org/10.1192/bjp.bp.111.095976.

Kroenke, K., Spitzer, R. L., & Williams, J. B. W. (1999). Patient Health Questionnaire-9 (PHQ-9) [Database record]. APA PsycTests. https://doi.org/10.1037/t06165-000.

Martinsen, M., Holme, I., Pensgaard, A. M., Torstveit, M. K., & Sundgot-Borgen, J. (2014). The development of the brief eating disorder in athletes questionnaire. *Medicine & Science in Sports & Exercise, 46*(8), 1666–75. https://doi.org/10.1249/MSS.0000000000000276.

Morgan, J. F., Reid, F., & Lacey, J. H. (1999). The SCOFF questionnaire: Assessment of a new screening tool for eating disorders. *British Medical Journal, 319*(7223), 1467–8. https://doi.org/10.1136/bmj.319.7223.1467.

National Collegiate Athletic Association (2024). *Mental health best practices: Understanding and supporting student-athlete mental health* (2nd ed.). https://ncaaorg.s3.amazonaws.com/ssi/mental/SSI_MentalHealthBestPractices.pdf.

Plateau, C. R., Shanmugam, V., Duckham, R. L., Goodwin, H., Jowett, S., Brooke-Wavell, K. S. F., Laybourne, A., Arcelus, J., & Meyer, C. (2014). Use of the compulsive exercise test with athletes: Norms and links with eating psychopathology. *Journal of Applied Sport Psychology*, *26*(3), 287–301. https://doi.org/10.1080/10413200.2013.867911.

Saunders, J. B., Aasland, O. G., Babor, T. F., de la Fuente, J. R., & Grant, M. (1993). Development of the alcohol use disorders identification test (AUDIT): WHO collaborative project on early detection of persons with harmful alcohol consumption–II. *Addiction (Abingdon, England)*, *88*(6), 791–804. https://doi.org/10.1111/j.1360-0443.1993.tb02093.x.

Selby, C. L. B., & Reel, J. J. (2011). A coach's guide to identifying and helping athletes with eating disorders. *Journal of Sport Psychology in Action*, *2*(2), 100–12. https://doi.org/10.1080/21520704.2011.585701.

Society for Sport, Exercise, & Performance Psychology (2012). *APA Sport Psychology Proficiency*. https://www.apadivisions.org/division-47/about/sport-proficiency.

Spitzer, R. L., Kroenke, K., Williams, J. B., & Löwe, B. (2006). A brief measure for assessing generalized anxiety disorder: the GAD-7. *Archives of internal medicine*, *166*(10), 1092–7. https://doi.org/10.1001/archinte.166.10.1092.

Taranis, L., Touyz, S., & Meyer, C. (2011). Disordered eating and exercise: Development and preliminary validation of the Compulsive Exercise Test (CET). *European Eating Disorders Review*, *19*(3), 256–68. https://doi.org/10.1002/erv.1108.

Tran, A. G. T. T. (2020). Using the GAD-7 and GAD-2 generalized anxiety disorder screeners with student-athletes: Empirical and clinical perspectives. *The Sport Psychologist*, *34*(4), 300–9. https://doi.org/10.1123/tsp.2020-0028.

Chapter 5

Association for Applied Sport Psychology (2021). *AASP statement on the continuum of mental health & relationship to performance: A response to the conversation supporting Naomi Osaka and Simone Biles*, August 17. https://appliedsportpsych.org/media/news-releases-and-association-updates/aasp-statement-on-the-continuum-of-mental-health-and-relationship-to-performance-a-response-to-the-conversation-supporting/.

Barker, J. (2021). *Not just a physical thing: The psychology of sports injuries and recovery*. Boston Children's Answers, September 9. https://answers.childrenshospital.org/psychology-sports-injury-recovery/.

Brewer, B. W., & Petitpas, A. J. (2017). Athletic identity foreclosure. *Current Opinion in Psychology*, *16*, 118–22. https://doi.org/10.1016/j.copsyc.2017.05.004.

Chang, C. J., Putukian, M., Aerni, G., Diamond, A. B., Hong, E. S., Ingram, Y. M., Reardon, C. L., & Wolanin, A. T. (2020). Mental health issues and psychological factors in athletes: Detection, management, effect on performance, and prevention: American medical society for sports medicine position statement. *Clinical Journal of Sport Medicine*, *30*(2), e61. https://doi.org/10.1097/JSM.0000000000000817.

Christino, M. A., Pluhar, E. I., & Micheli, L. J. (2023). *Psychological considerations in the young athlete: A multidisciplinary approach* (M. A. Christino, E. I. Pluhar, & L. J. Micheli (Eds.)). Springer Nature Switzerland AG. https://doi.org/10.1007/978-3-031-25126-9

Courtney, K., Dial, B., & Yanos, P. T. (2024). "Suck it up, go play": Mental health stigma in college coaches and their use of mental illness microaggressions. *Journal of American College Health*, 1–10. https://doi.org/10.1080/07448481.2024.2400101.

Daley, M. M., Shoop, J., & Meehan, W. P. I. (2023). Psychological consequences of concussion. In M. A. Christino, E. I. Pluhar, & L. J. Micheli (Eds.), *Psychological considerations in the young athlete: A multidisciplinary approach* (pp. 117–34). Springer Nature Switzerland AG. https://doi.org/10.1007/978-3-031-25126-9_6

Deck, S., Doherty, A., Hall, C., Schneider, A., Patil, S., & Belfry, G. (2021). Perceived time, frequency, and intensity of engagement and older masters athletes' subjective experiences. *Frontiers in Sports and Active Living*, *3*, 653590. https://doi.org/10.3389/fspor.2021.653590

Edison, B. R., & Rizzone, K. (2023). Benefits of sport and athletic identity. In M. A. Christino, E. I. Pluhar, & L. J. Micheli (Eds.), *Psychological considerations in the young athlete: A multidisciplinary approach* (pp. 1–19). Springer Nature Switzerland AG. https://doi.org10.1007/978-3-031-25126-9_1.

Erikson, E. H. (1968). *Identity: Youth and crisis*. Norton.

Fralick, M., Sy, E., Hassan, A., Burke, M. J., Mostofsky, E., & Karsies, T. (2019). Association of concussion with the risk of suicide a systematic review and meta-analysis. *JAMA Neurology*, *76*(2), 144–51. https://doi.org/10.1001/jamaneurol.2018.3487

Geard, D., Rebar, A. L., Dionigi, R. A., & Reaburn, P. R. J. (2021). Testing a model of successful aging on masters athletes and non-sporting adults. *Research Quarterly for Exercise and Sport*, *92*(1), 11–20. https://doi.org/10.1080/02701367.2019.1702146.

Gornall, A., Takagi, M., Morawakage, T., Liu, X., & Anderson, V. (2021). Mental health after paediatric concussion: A systematic review and meta-analysis. *British Journal of Sports Medicine*, *55*(18), 1048–58. https://doi.org/10.1136/bjsports-2020-103548.

Heller, H. C., Herzog, E., Brager, A., Poe, G., Allada, R., Scheer, F., Carskadon, M., de la Iglesia, H. O., Jang, R., Montero, A., Wright, K., Mouraine, P., Walker, M. P., Goel, N., Hogenesch, J., Van Gelder, R. N., Kriegsfeld, L., Mah, C., Colwell, C., & Paul, K. (2024). The negative effects of travel on student athletes through sleep and circadian disruption. *Journal of Biological Rhythms, 39*(1), 5–19. https://doi.org/10.1177/07487304231207330.

Henriksen, K., Schinke, R., Moesch, K., McCann, S., Parham, W. D., Larsen, C. H., & Terry, P. (2020). Consensus statement on improving the mental health of high performance athletes. *International Journal of Sport and Exercise Psychology, 18*(5), 553–60. https://doi.org/10.1080/1612197X.2019.1570473.

Horton, S., Dionigi, R. A., & Bellamy, J. (2013). Canadian women aged 75 and over: Attitudes towards health related role models and female masters athletes. *The International Journal of Interdisciplinary Social and Community Studies. 7(3)*, 33–47.

International Masters Games Association (2024). *Want to take part in the World Masters Games Taipei 2025 ? Find your sport !*, September 3. https://imga.ch/2024/09/03/want-to-take-part-in-the-world-masters-games-taipei-2025-find-your-sport/.

Jayanthi, N. A., Post, E. G., Laury, T. C., & Fabricant, P. D. (2019). Health Consequences of Youth Sport Specialization. *Journal of Athletic Training, 54*(10), 1040–9. https://doi.org/10.4085/1062-6050-380-18.

Jewett, R., Sabiston, C. M., Brunet, J., O'Loughlin, E. K., Scarapicchia, T., & O'Loughlin, J. (2014). School sport participation during adolescence and mental health in early adulthood. *Journal of Adolescent Health, 55*(5), 640–4. https://doi.org/10.1016/j.jadohealth.2014.04.018.

Küettel, A., & Larsen, C. H. (2020). Risk and protective factors for mental health in elite athletes: A scoping review. *International Review of Sport and Exercise Psychology, 13*(1), 231–65. https://doi.org/10.1080/1750984X.2019.1689574.

Ledoux, A.-A., Webster, R. J., Clarke, A. E., Fell, D. B., Knight, B. D., Gardner, W., Cloutier, P., Gray, C., Tuna, M., & Zemek, R. (2022). Risk of mental health problems in children and youths following concussion. *JAMA Network Open, 5*(3), e221235. https://doi.org/10.1001/jamanetworkopen.2022.1235.

Lundqvist, C., Schary, D. P., Eklöf, E., Zand, S., & Jacobsson, J. (2023). Elite lean athletes at sports high schools face multiple risks for mental health concerns and are in need of psychosocial support. *PLoS ONE, 18*(4), e0284725. https://doi.org/10.1371/journal.pone.0284725.

MacCallum, L., Howson, N., & Gopu, N. (2012). *Designed to move: A physical activity action agenda.* Nike. https://www.sportsthinktank.com/uploads/designed-to-move-full-report-13.pdf.

Marcia, J. E. (1966). Development and validation of ego-identity status. *Journal of Personality and Social Psychology, 3*(5), 551–8.

McCormick, B. F., & Glenn, A. L. (2024). Youth with low pre-injury mental health symptoms are at a higher risk for symptoms following mild traumatic brain injury. *Child Psychiatry and Human Development, 55*(2), 488–96. https://doi.org/10.1007/s10578-022-01433-5.

Murray, R. M., Sabiston, C. M., Doré, I., Bélanger, M., & O'Loughlin, J. L. (2021). Association between pattern of team sport participation from adolescence to young adulthood and mental health. *Scandinavian Journal of Medicine & Science in Sports*, *31*(7), 1481–8. https://doi.org/10.1111/sms.13957.

Patankar, A. G., Milewski, M. D., & Christino, M. A. (2023). Psychological considerations for surgical outcomes in the pediatric and adolescent athlete. In M. A. Christino, E. I. Pluhar, & L. J. Micheli (Eds.), *Psychological considerations in the young athlete: A multidisciplinary approach* (pp. 135–53). Springer Nature Switzerland AG. https://doi.org/10.1007/978-3-031-25126-9_7.

Reardon, C. L., Hainline, B., Aron, C. M., Baron, D., Baum, A. L., Bindra, A., Budgett, R., Campriani, N., Castaldelli-Maia, J. M., Currie, A., Derevensky, J. L., Glick, I. D., Gorczynski, P., Gouttebarge, V., Grandner, M. A., Han, D. H., McDuff, D., Mountjoy, M., Polat, A., & Engebretsen, L. (2019). Mental health in elite athletes: International Olympic Committee consensus statement. *British Journal of Sports Medicine*, *53*(11), 667–99. https://doi.org/10.1136/bjsports-2019-100715.

Royal Bank of Canada: Wealth Management (n.d.). *Professional athletes need a retirement game plan*. https://www.rbcwealthmanagement.com/en-us/insights/professional-athletes-need-a-retirement-game-plan.

Schinke, R. J., Henriksen, K., Moore, Z. E., Stambulova, N., Bartley, J., Cosh, S., Wagstaff, C. R. D., Quartiroli, A., Wylleman, P., Maher, C. A., Zhang, L., Si, G., Kentta, G., Zhang, C.-Q., Li, Y., Kuettel, A., Brandao, R., & Wong, R. (2024). International society of sport psychology position stand: Elite athlete mental health revisited. *International Journal of Sport and Exercise Psychology*, *22*(4), 775–801. https://doi.org/10.1080/1612197X.2024.2359872.

Schinke, R. J., Stambulova, N. B., Si, G., & Moore, Z. (2018). International society of sport psychology position stand: Athletes' mental health, performance, and development. *International Journal of Sport and Exercise Psychology*, *16*(6), 622–39. https://doi.org/10.1080/1612197X.2017.1295557.

Smith, A., & Hardin, R. (2020). The transition experiences of division I and III collegiate athletes. *Journal of Athlete Development and Experience*, *2*(3), 142–61. https://doi.org/10.25035/jade.02.03.01

Stanford Medicine: Children's Health (n.d.). *Sports Injury Statistics*. https://www.stanfordchildrens.org/en/topic/default%3Fid%3Dsports-injury-statistics-90-P02787.

Tayrose, G. A., Beutel, B. G., Cardone, D. A., & Sherman, O. H. (2015). The masters athlete. *Sports Health*, *7*(3), 270–6. https://doi.org/10.1177/1941738114548999.

U.S. Bureau of Labor Statistics (2024, August 29). *Athletes and sports competitors*. https://www.bls.gov/ooh/entertainment-and-sports/athletes-and-sports-competitors.htm.

Veliz, P., Ryan, J., & Eckner, J. T. (2021). Head, neck, and traumatic brain injury among children involved in sports: Results from the adolescent brain cognitive development study. *Journal of Adolescent Health*, *68*(2), 414–18. https://doi.org/10.1016/j.jadohealth.2020.06.004.

Voorheis, P., Silver, M., & Consonni, J. (2023). Adaptation to life after sport for retired athletes: A scoping review of existing reviews and programs. *PLoS ONE, 18*(9), e0291683. https://doi.org/10.1371/journal.pone.0291683.

Weber, S. R., Winkelmann, Z. K., Monsma, E. V., Arent, S. M., & Torres-McGehee, T. M. (2023). An examination of depression, anxiety, and self-esteem in collegiate student-athletes. *International Journal of Environmental Research and Public Health, 20*(2), 1211. https://doi.org/10.3390/ijerph20021211.

Weiser, S., & Wilson, J. (2024). *The NCAA gave mental health the old college try and failed: Why federal regulation of student athletes' mental health should be enacted.* Michigan State Law Review, January 13. https://www.michiganstatelawreview.org/vol-20222023/2023/1/12/the-ncaa-gave-mental-health-the-old-college-try-and-failed-why-federal-regulation-of-student-athletes-mental-health-should-be-enacted

Whitney, K. E., d'Hemecourt, P. A., & Stracciolini, A. (2023). Youth sport specialization: Risks, benefits, and mental health considerations. In M. A. Christino, E. I. Pluhar, & L. J. Micheli (Eds.), *Psychological considerations in the young athlete: A multidisciplinary approach* (pp. 179–91). Springer Nature Switzerland AG. https://doi.org/10.1007/978-3-031-25126-9_9.

Wood, C., & Bryant, K. (2019). *Challenges of mental-health issues in high school athletics.* National Federation of State High School Associations, February 5. https://www.nfhs.org/articles/challenges-of-mental-health-issues-in-high-school-athletics

Wooten, S. V., Mittag, U., Alvero Cruz, J. R., Stray-Gundersen, S., Hoffmann, F., Michély, S., Möstl, S., Sies, W., Mulder, E., Rauschendorfer, P., Chilibeck, P. D., Rittweger, J., & Tanaka, H. (2021). Life satisfaction, positive affect, and sleep impairment in masters athletes: Modulation by age, sex, and exercise type. *Frontiers in Physiology, 12*, 101164. https://doi.org/10.3389/fphys.2021.634433.

Yang, Y., Li, Y., & Yu, J. (2021). The influence of personal factors on adolescents' physical and mental health: From the perspective of sports commitment. *Revista de Psicología Del Deporte, 30*(4), 96–104.

Chapter 6

Aitchison, B., Rushton, A. B., Martin, P., Barr, M., Soundy, A., & Heneghan, N. R. (2022). The experiences and perceived health benefits of individuals with a disability participating in sport: A systematic review and narrative synthesis. *Disability and Health Journal, 15*(1). https://doi.org/10.1016/j.dhjo.2021.101164.

ALSO (2024). *5 common misconceptions about people with disabilities.* ALSO, February 1. https://alsoweb.org/nonprofit-blog/5-common-misconceptions-about-people-with-disabilities/

American Foundation for Suicide Prevention (n.d.). *Suicide statistics.* American Foundation for Suicide Prevention. https://afsp.org/suicide-statistics/.

Begel, D. (2023). Tackling racism in sports psychiatry. *Sports Psychiatry: Journal of Sports and Exercise Psychiatry, 2*(3), 109–18. https://doi.org/10.1024/2674-0052/a000041.

Botha, M., Chapman, R., Giwa Onaiwu, M., Kapp, S. K., Stannard Ashley, A., & Walker, N. (2024). The neurodiversity concept was developed collectively: An overdue correction on the origins of neurodiversity theory. *Autism: The International Journal of Research and Practice, 28*(6), 1591–4. https://doi.org/10.1177/13623613241237871.

Carbone, P. S., Smith, P. J., Lewis, C., & LeBlanc, C. (2021). Promoting the participation of children and adolescents with disabilities in sports, recreation, and physical activity. *Pediatrics, 148*(6), 1–18. https://doi.org./10.1542/peds.2021-054664.

Centers for Disease Control and Prevention (2024, July 15). *Disability impacts all of us.* https://www.cdc.gov/ncbddd/disabilityandhealth/infographic-disability-impacts-all.html.

DeChants, J. P., Green, A. E., Price, M. N., & Davis, C. K. (2024). "I get treated poorly in regular school—Why add to it?": Transgender girls' experiences choosing to play or not play sports. *Transgender Health, 9*(1), 61–7.

Eisenmenger, A. (2020). *Five things you didn't know about invisible disabilities.* Access Living, September 14. https://www.accessliving.org/newsroom/blog/five-things-you-didnt-know-about-invisible-disabilities/.

Human Rights Campaign (n.d.). *Get the facts about transgender & non-binary athletes.* Human Rights Campaign. https://www.hrc.org/resources/get-the-facts-about-transgender-non-binary-athletes.

Hoare, E., Reyes, J., Olive, L., Willmott, C., Steer, E., Berk, M., & Hall, K. (2023). Neurodiversity in elite sport: A systematic scoping review. *British Medicine Journal Open Sport & Exercise Medicine, 9*(2), e001575. https://doi.org/10.1136/bmjsem-2023-001575.

International Olympic Committee (n.d.). *IOC mission.* Olympics.com. https://www.olympics.com/ioc/mission.

International Paralympic Committee (n.d.). *IPC classification—Paralympic categories & how to qualify.* International Paralympic Committee. https://www.paralympic.org/classification.

McCavanagh, T. M., & Cadaret, M. C. (2022). Creating safe spaces for lesbian, gay, bisexual, transgender, and queer (LGBTQ+) student–athletes. In D. P. Rivera, R. L. Abreu, & K. A. Gonzalez (Eds.), *Affirming LGBTQ+ students in higher education* (pp. 141–59). American Psychological Association. https://doi.org/10.1037/0000281-009.

Meyer, I. H. (2003). Prejudice, social stress, and mental health in lesbian, gay, and bisexual populations: Conceptual issues and research evidence. *Psychological Bulletin, 129*(5), 674–97. doi: 10.1037/0033-2909.129.5.674.

Miller, B., Barker, J., Hunton, E., & Plateau, C. (2024). Understanding experiences of and influences on well-being in elite para-sport: A qualitative exploration of UK para-athletes. *Sport, Exercise, and Performance Psychology, 13*(2), 126–43. https://doi.org/10.1037/spy0000342.

Mortillaro, G. (2024). Paris 2024 Olympics: One step forward and two steps back for sexual minority and gender diverse athletes. *Sports Psychiatry: Journal of Sports and Exercise Psychiatry*. https://doi.org/10.1024/2674-0052/a000091.

National Collegiate Athletic Association. (2025). *Participation policy for transgender student-athletes*. NCAA, February 6. https://www.ncaa.org/sports/2022/1/27/transgender-participation-policy.aspx.

Pagani, L. S., Harbec, M.-J., Fortin, G., & Barnett, T. A. (2020). Childhood exercise as medicine: Extracurricular sport diminishes subsequent ADHD symptoms. *Preventive Medicine: An International Journal Devoted to Practice and Theory*, *141*, 106256. https://doi.org/10.1016/j.ypmed.2020.106256.

Palofox, S. (2023). *17 popular wheelchair sports: A guide on adaptive athletics*. Spinergy, August 28. https://wheelchair.spinergy.com/blogs/from-where-we-sit-blog/popular-wheelchair-sports-a-guide-on-adaptive-athletics.

Press, T. A. (2024). Florida teachers can discuss LGBTQ topics under "Don't Say Gay" law, settlement says. *NPR*, March 11. https://www.npr.org/2024/03/11/1237730819/florida-dont-say-gay-law-settlement-lgbtq.

Ramos, N., Burgess, A., & Ollen, E. (2022). The current status of sociopolitical and legal issues faced by lesbian, gay, bisexual, transgender, queer, and questioning youth. *Adolescent Psychiatry (Hilversum, Netherlands)*, *12*(3), 180. https://doi.org/10.2174/2210676611666211105120645.

Reyes, M. E. S., Chua, K. Z. R., Jambonganan, R. N. V., Mayor, T. R., Repoquit, C. M. A., Roxas, K. L. A., Tubale, A. L., Cayubit, R. F. O., & Trinidad, K. K. V. (2023). Disclosure & concealment: Outness and its relationship to mental health among selected filipino LGB athletes. *North American Journal of Psychology*, *25*(4), 637–58.

Strong Education (n.d.). *What is an adaptive athlete & how can you get involved?* Strong Education. https://www.certifystrong.com/what-is-an-adaptive-athlete-and-how-can-you-get-involved/.

Virupaksha, H. G., Muralidhar, D., & Ramakrishna, J. (2016). Suicide and suicidal behavior among transgender persons. *Indian Journal of Psychological Medicine*, *38*(6), 505. https://doi.org/10.4103/0253-7176.194908.

Zborowska, A. M. (2024). The role of physical activity and sport in children and adolescents with autism spectrum disorder (ASD): A narrative review. *Sports Psychiatry: Journal of Sports and Exercise Psychiatry*. https://doi.org/10.1024/2674-0052/a000075.

Chapter 7

ABC News Australia (2017). *Dan Vickerman spoke of difficulties he faced before his death, Owen Finegan says*. ABC News, February 19. https://www.abc.net.au/news/2017-02-20/dan-vickerman-struggled-after-retirement-from-rugby-owen-finegan/8285644.

Bailey, A. L., Capron, D. W., Buerke, M. L., & Bauer, B. W. (2023). The associations between sport- and physical activity-related concussions and suicidality, suicide capability, and hopelessness among high school adolescents. *Journal of Adolescence*, *95*(6), 1116–26. https://doi.org/10.1002/jad.12179.

Baron, D. A., Reardon, C. L., & Baron, S. H. (2013). *Clinical sports psychiatry: An international perspective*. John Wiley & Sons, Incorporated.

Baum, A. L. (2013). Suicide in athletes. In D. A. Baron, C. L. Reardon, & S. H. Baron (Eds.), *Clinical sports psychiatry: An international perspective* (pp. 79–88). Wiley Blackwell. https://doi.org/10.1002/9781118404904.ch8.

Belson, K. (2021). *Elegy for a heartbroken medalist*. The New York Times, July 18. https://www.nytimes.com/2021/07/18/sports/olympics/kokichi-tsuburaya-japanese-marathon-suicide.html.

Centers for Disease Control and Prevention (n.d.). *Injuries and violence are leading causes of death*. https://www.cdc.gov/injury/wisqars/animated-leading-causes.html.

Dodd, D. R., Harris, K., Allen, K., Velkoff, E. A., & Smith, A. R. (2021). No pain, no gain? Associations of athletic participation with capability for suicide among college students. *Suicide and Life-Threatening Behavior*, *51*(6), 1117–25. https://doi.org/10.1111/sltb.12794.

Dye, N. (2023). *Michael Phelps opens up about "Looking suicide in the eye" and managing his mental health*. Peoplemag, May 9. https://people.com/sports/michael-phelps-on-looking-suicide-in-the-eye-mental-health-exclusive/.

Edmonds, W. A., Craig, L. L., Christopher, R., Kennedy, T. D., & Mann, D. T. Y. (2022). Adolescent athletes and suicide: A model for treatment and prevention. *Aggression and Violent Behavior*, *64*, 101580. https://doi.org/10.1016/j.avb.2021.101580.

Fagan, K. (2015). *Split image*. ESPN.Com, May 7. https://www.espn.com/espn/feature/story/_/id/12833146/instagram-account-university-pennsylvania-runner-showed-only-part-story.

Gill, V. S., Sullivan, G., Stearns, H., Tummala, S. V., Haglin, J. M., Economopoulos, K. J., Marks, L., & Chauhan, M. (2024). Mental health in elite athletes: A systematic review of suicidal behaviour as compared to the general population. *Sports Medicine (Auckland, N.Z.)*, *54*(6), 1–18. https://doi.org/10.1007/s40279-024-01998-2.

Harris, M. (2023). *College student-athletes are dying in mental health crisis*. Psychology Today, July 5. https://www.psychologytoday.com/us/blog/letters-from-your-therapist/202212/college-student-athletes-are-dying-in-mental-health-crisis.

Harvard University (n.d.). *Football players health study*. Footballplayershealth.com. https://footballplayershealth.harvard.edu/.

Iverson, G. L. (2014). Chronic traumatic encephalopathy and risk of suicide in former athletes. *British Journal of Sports Medicine*, *48*(2), 162–4. https://doi.org/10.1136/bjsports-2013-092935.

Kleen, B. (2023). *Women student athletes still face high risk of suicidality*. Global Sport Matters, July 3. https://globalsportmatters.com/research/2023/07/03/despite-benefits-sport-participation-women-student-athletes-risks-suicide-persist/.

Krumer, A., Shavit, T., & Rosenboim, M. (2011). Why do professional athletes have different time preferences than non-athletes? *Judgment and Decision Making*, *6*(6), 542–51. https://doi.org/10.1017/S1930297500002503.

Lester, D. (2013). The effect of retirement on athletes. In D. Lester, & J. F. I. Gunn (Eds.), *Suicide in professional and amateur athletes: Incidence, risk factors, and prevention.* (pp. 132–44). Charles C Thomas Publisher.

Lester, D., Battuello, M., Falcone, I., Simone, E., Berry, I., Innamorati, M., Tatarelli, R., & Pompili, M. (2009). Does participation in sports activities prevent suicide? *Policlinico—Sezione Medica*, *115*(1), 1–12.

Lester, D., & Gunn, J. F. (2013). *Suicide in professional and amateur athletes: Incidence, risk factors, and prevention.* Charles C Thomas Publisher.

Lopez, A. (2024). *New report shows increased NCAA athlete suicides*, April, 29. https://spectrumlocalnews.com/nc/charlotte/news/2024/04/29/news-ncaa-athlete-report-

McDermid, B. (2018). *Victim of ex-USA gymnastics doctor says abuse led to dad's suicide.* Reuters, January 16. https://www.reuters.com/article/sports/victim-of-ex-usa-gymnastics-doctor-says-abuse-led-to-dads-suicide-idUSKBN1F52MS/.

National Collegiate Athletic Association (2018). *Panel discusses realities of student-athlete well-being.* NCAA.Org, January 26. https://www.ncaa.org/news/2018/1/26/panel-discusses-realities-of-student-athlete-well-being.aspx

National Collegiate Athletic Association (2022). *NCAA student-athletes surpass 520,000, set new record.* NCAA.Org, December 5. https://www.ncaa.org/news/2022/12/5/media-center-ncaa-student-athletes-surpass-520-000-set-new-record.aspx

Olympedia (n.d.) *Olympians who committed suicide.* https://www.olympedia.org/lists/55/manual.

Pfeffer, S. E. (2022). *Michael Phelps says therapy "saved" him during his darkest moment: "I didn't want to be alive."* People.Com, May 3. https://people.com/health/michael-phelps-says-therapy-saved-him-in-darkest-moment/.

Pichler, E., Ewers, S., Ajdacic-Gross, V., Deutschmann, M., Exner, J., Kawohl, W., Seifritz, E., & Claussen, M. C. (2023). Athletes are not at greater risk for death by suicide: A review. *Scandinavian Journal of Medicine & Science in Sports*, *33*(5), 569–85. https://doi.org/10.1111/sms.14316.

Pilkington, C. (2017). "*What made Maddy run" is about much more than suicide.* Women's Running, July 13. https://www.womensrunning.com/culture/what-made-maddy-run-suicide/.

Rao, A. L., Asif, I. M., Drezner, J. A., Toresdahl, B. G., & Harmon, K. G. (2015). Suicide in National Collegiate Athletic Association (NCAA) athletes. *Sports Health*, *7*(5), 452–7. https://doi.org/10.1177/1941738115587675.

Rao, A. L., & Hong, E. S. (2016). Understanding depression and suicide in college athletes: Emerging concepts and future directions. *British Journal of Sports Medicine*, *50*(3), 136–7. https://doi.org/10.1136/bjsports-2015-095658.

Sabo, D., Miller, K. E., Melnick, M. J., Farrell, M. P., & Barnes, G. M. (2005). High school athletic participation and adolescent suicide: A nationwide US study. *International Review for the Sociology of Sport*, *40*(1), 5–23. https://doi.org/10.1177/1012690205052160.

Substance Abuse and Mental Health Services Administration (2016). *Substance use and suicide: A nexus requiring a public health approach*. https://store.samhsa.gov/sites/default/files/sma16-4935.pdf.

Teasley, M. L., & Gill, E. (2015). School sports, sexual abuse, and the utility of school social workers. *Children & Schools*, *37*(1), 4–7. https://doi.org/10.1093/cs/cdu032.

Timpka, T., Spreco, A., Dahlstrom, O., Jacobsson, J., Kowalski, J., Bargoria, V., Mountjoy, M., & Svedin, C. G. (2021). Suicidal thoughts (ideation) among elite athletics (track and field) athletes: Associations with sports participation, psychological resourcefulness and having been a victim of sexual and/or physical abuse. *British Journal of Sports Medicine*, *55*(4), 198–205. https://doi.org/10.1136/bjsports-2019-101386.

Waldman, D. (2023). *Student-athletes aren't immune from suicide risk. Colleges are taking notice*. CBS News, March 24. https://www.cbsnews.com/news/student-athletes-suicide-risk-colleges-mental-health/.

Weisholtz, D. (2024). *Michael Phelps shares the "great" learning that came out of his experience with depression*. TODAY.Com, May 10. https://www.today.com/health/michael-phelps-shares-great-change-came-experience-depression-rcna151620

Whelan, B. M., Kliethermes, S. A., Schloredt, K. A., Rao, A., Harmon, K. G., & Petek, B. J. (2024). Suicide in National Collegiate Athletic Association athletes: A 20-year analysis. *British Journal of Sports Medicine*, *58*(10), 531–7. https://doi.org/10.1136/bjsports-2023-107509.

Woodyatt, A. (2023). *These young female athletes died by suicide. They all had head injuries in common*. CNN, February 6. https://www.cnn.com/2023/02/05/sport/head-injury-suicide-female-athletes-intl-spt-cmd/index.html

Chapter 8

ABC News (2023). *Damar Hamlin opens up about surviving on field scare | Nightline* [Video]. YouTube, February 14. https://www.youtube.com/watch?v=LtYvbn8mAVs

Administration for Children & Families (n.d.). *Trauma: What is historical trauma?* https://www.acf.hhs.gov/trauma-toolkit/historical-trauma-concept.

Allan, V. (2018). *A surprising number of elite athletes faced childhood trauma*. The Dallas Morning News, December 9. https://www.dallasnews.com/opinion/commentary/2018/12/09/a-surprising-number-of-elite-athletes-faced-childhood-trauma/.

Aron, C. M., Harvey, S., Hainline, B., Hitchcock, M. E., & Reardon, C. L. (2019). Post-traumatic stress disorder (PTSD) and other trauma-related mental disorders in elite athletes: A narrative review. *British Journal of Sports Medicine*, *53*(12), 779–84. https://doi.org/10.1136/bjsports-2019-100695.

Barbash, E. (2017). *Different types of trauma: Small "t" versus large "T": An accumulation of smaller or less pronounced events can still be traumatic.* Psychology Today, March 13. https://www.psychologytoday.com/us/blog/trauma-and-hope/201703/different-types-trauma-small-t-versus-large-t.

Bellis, M. A., Hughes, K., Ford, K., Ramos Rodriguez, G., Sethi, D., & Passmore, J. (2019). Life course health consequences and associated annual costs of adverse childhood experiences across Europe and North America: A systematic review and meta-analysis. *The Lancet. Public Health*, *4*(10), e517–e528. https://doi.org/10.1016/S2468-2667(19)30145-8.

Bergholz, L., Stafford, E., & D'Andrea, W. (2016). Creating trauma-informed sports programming for traumatized youth: Core principles for an adjunctive therapeutic approach. *Journal of Infant, Child & Adolescent Psychotherapy*, *15*(3), 244–53. https://doi.org/10.1080/15289168.2016.1211836.

Bremmer, J. (2021). *Simone Biles urges Congress to remove top US Olympic bosses.* The Independent, October 14. https://www.the-independent.com/news/world/americas/simone-biles-olympics-bosses-congress-b1938584.html

Center for Healing and Justice Through Sport (2022). *Why trauma-informed sport is vital: A white paper.* https://chjs.org/wp-content/uploads/2022/02/CHJS-WhitePaper.pdf.

Centers for Disease Control and Prevention (n.d.). *About adverse childhood experiences.* CDC. https://www.cdc.gov/aces/about/index.html.

Day, M. C., Bond, K., & Smith, B. (2013). Holding it together: Coping with vicarious trauma in sport. *Psychology of Sport and Exercise*, *14*(1), 1–11. https://doi.org/10.1016/j.psychsport.2012.06.001.

Day, M. C., & Schubert, N. (2012). The impact of witnessing athletic injury: A qualitative examination of vicarious trauma in artistic gymnastics. *Journal of Sports Sciences*, *30*(8), 743–53. https://doi.org/10.1080/02640414.2012.671530.

Edwards, C., Claussen, M. C., & Schmidt, R. E. (2023). Mental health impacts of interpersonal violence in sports. *Sports Psychiatry: Journal of Sports and Exercise Psychiatry*, *2*(1), 1–2. https://doi.org/10.1024/2674-0052/a000039.

Folco, M. (2023). The neurobiological impact of trauma on youth development: Restoring relationships and regulation through sport. *Child and Adolescent Social Work Journal*, *41*, 907–17. https://doi.org/10.1007/s10560-023-00937-w.

Forte, T. (2022). *It didn't start with you: How to understand and heal from intergenerational trauma.* Forte Labs, August 22. https://fortelabs.com/blog/it-didnt-start-with-you-how-to-understand-and-heal-from-intergenerational-trauma/

Hepburn, S. (2022). Former professional rugby player Joe Williams on self compassion and intergenerational trauma. #CrisisTalk, June 7. https://talk.crisisnow.com/former-professional-rugby-player-joe-williams-on-self-compassion-and-intergenerational-trauma/.

Krug, G. E., Dahlberg, L. L., Mercy, J. A., Zwi, A. B., & Lozano, R. (2002). *World report on violence and health.* World Health Organization. https://www.who.int/publications/i/item/9241545615.

Martinelli, L., & Day, M. (2021). "It's impacted me too": Where does vicarious growth fit in? In R. Wadey, M. Day, & K. Howells (Eds.), *Growth following adversity in sport: A mechanism to positive change.* (pp. 47–58). Routledge/Taylor & Francis Group.

Mercy, J. A., Hillis, S. D., Butchart, A., Bellis, M. A., Ward, C. L., Fang, X., & Rosenberg, M. L. (2017). Interpersonal violence: Global impact and paths to prevention. In C. N. Mock, R. Nugent, O. Kobusingye, & K. R. Smith (Eds.), *Injury Prevention and Environmental Health* (3rd ed.). (pp. 71–96). The International Bank for Reconstruction and Development / The World Bank.

Misra, A. (2014). *Common sports injuries: Incidence and average charges.* Office of the Assistant Secretary for Planning and Evaluation (ASPE), March 16. https://aspe.hhs.gov/reports/common-sports-injuries-incidence-average-charges-0.

Morris, J. (2021). *Indigenous athletes contend with numerous barriers en route to Olympic qualification.* CBC Sports, June 11. https://www.cbc.ca/sports/indigenous-athletes-barriers-olympics-1.6061509.

Mountjoy, M., Brackenridge, C., Arrington, M., Blauwet, C., Carska-Sheppard, A., Fasting, K., Kirby, S., Leahy, T., Marks, S., Martin, K., Starr, K., Tiivas, A., & Budgett, R. (2016). International Olympic Committee consensus statement: Harassment and abuse (non-accidental violence) in sport. *British Journal of Sports Medicine, 50*(17), 1019–29. https://doi.org/10.1136/bjsports-2016-096121.

National Public Radio (2024). *Justice Department pays $138 million over FBI failures in Larry Nassar case.* NPR, April 23. https://www.npr.org/2024/04/23/1246647531/doj-settles-larry-nassar-usa-gymnastics-sexual-assault-victims.

Noel-London, K., Ortiz, K., & BeLue, R. (2021). Adverse childhood experiences (ACEs) & youth sports participation: Does a gradient exist? *Child Abuse & Neglect, 113*, 104924. https://doi.org/10.1016/j.chiabu.2020.104924.

Papathomas, A., & Lavallee, D. (2012). Narrative constructions of anorexia and abuse: An athlete's search for meaning in trauma. *Journal of Loss and Trauma, 17*(4), 293–318. https://doi.org/10.1080/15325024.2011.616740.

Parent, S., Vaillancourt-Morel, M.-P., & Gillard, A. (2022). Interpersonal Violence (IV) in sport and mental health outcomes in teenagers. *Journal of Sport and Social Issues, 46*(4), 323–37. https://doi.org/10.1177/01937235211043652.

Shaikh, M., Bean, C., Bergholz, L., Rojas, M., Ali, M., & Forneris, T. (2021). Integrating a sport-based trauma-sensitive program in a national youth-serving organization. *Child & Adolescent Social Work Journal, 38*(4), 449–61. https://doi.org/10.1007/s10560-021-00776-7.

Sommerlad, J., & Baio, A. (2023). *Larry Nassar: A timeline of the sexual abuse allegations against the former USA Gymanstics team doctor.* The Independent, July 10. https://www.the-independent.com/news/world/americas/crime/larry-nassar-now-abuse-timeline-b1920783.html.

Substance Abuse and Mental Health Services Administration (2014). *SAMHSA's concept of trauma and guidance for a trauma-informed approach.* https://ncsacw.acf.hhs.gov/userfiles/files/SAMHSA_Trauma.pdf.

The Athletic (2023). NFL players on Damar Hamlin, football safety and what they wish fans knew. The Athletic, January 5. https://www.nytimes.com/athletic/4059265/2023/01/05/damar-hamlin-nfl-player-reaction/.

Toyoda, H., Ishikawa, K., Omi, Y., Kado, T., Iizuka, S., & Endo, T. (2023). Psychological violence victimization with moral injury in sports exacerbates PTSD symptoms. *Sports Psychiatry, 2*(1), 3–12. https://doi.org/10.1024/2674-0052/a000034.

Vertommen, T., Kampen, J., Schipper-van Veldhoven, N., Uzieblo, K., & Van Den Eede, F. (2018). Severe interpersonal violence against children in sport: Associated mental health problems and quality of life in adulthood. *Child Abuse & Neglect, 76*, 459–68. https://doi.org/10.1016/j.chiabu.2017.12.013.

Wang, X., Lee, M. Y., & Quinn, C. R. (2023). Intergenerational transmission of trauma: Unpacking the effects of parental adverse childhood experiences. *Journal of Family Studies, 29*(4), 1687–703. https://doi.org/10.1080/13229400.2022.2073903.

World Health Organization (n.d.). *The violence prevention alliance (VPA) approach.* https://www.who.int/groups/violence-prevention-alliance/approach.

Zogg, C. K., Runquist, E. B., III, Amick, M., Gilmer, G., Milroy, J. J., Wyrick, D. L., Grimm, K., & Tuakli-Wosornu, Y. A. (2024). Experiences of interpersonal violence in sport and perceived coaching style among college athletes. *JAMA Network Open, 7*(1), e2350248. https://doi.org/10.1001/jamanetworkopen.2023.50248.

Chapter 9

Alipon, S. (2023). *E-health of esports.* Medium, May 25. https://medium.com/@shainna.alipon/e-health-of-esports-45aad2a3ea8d.

Alshehri, A. G., & Mohamed, A. M. A. S. (2019). The relationship between electronic gaming and health, social relationships, and physical activity among males in Saudi Arabia. *American Journal of Men's Health, 13*(4), 1557988319873512. https://doi.org/10.1177/1557988319873512.

American Optometric Association (n.d.). *Computer vision syndrome.* AOA.org. https://www.aoa.org/healthy-eyes/eye-and-vision-conditions/computer-vision-syndrome?sso=y

American Psychiatric Association (2022). Conditions for further study. In American Psychiatric Association, *Diagnostic and statistical manual of mental disorders* (5th ed.). American Psychiatric Association Publishing. https://doi.org/10.5555/appi.books.9780890425787.

Badillo, K. (2024). *The great debate: Legal status of esports betting in the US.* PlayToday, March 19. https://playtoday.co/blog/guides/is-esports-betting-legal-in-us/.

Bányai, F., Griffiths, M. D., Demetrovics, Z., & Király, O. (2019). The mediating effect of motivations between psychiatric distress and gaming disorder among esport gamers and recreational gamers. *Comprehensive Psychiatry, 94*, 152117. https://doi.org/10.1016/j.comppsych.2019.152117

Bányai, F., Griffiths, M. D., Király, O., & Demetrovics, Z. (2019). The psychology of esports: A systematic literature review. *Journal of Gambling Studies, 35*(2), 351–65. https://doi.org/10.1007/s10899-018-9763-1.

Bányai, F., Zsila, Á., Griffiths, M. D., Demetrovics, Z., & Király, O. (2020). Career as a professional gamer: Gaming motives as predictors of career plans to become a professional esport player. *Frontiers in Psychology, 11*, 1866. https://doi.org/10.3389/fpsyg.2020.01866.

Bonnar, D., Lee, S., Gradisar, M., & Suh, S. (2019). Risk factors and sleep intervention considerations in esports: A review and practical guide. *Sleep Medicine Research, 10*(2), 59–66. https://doi.org/10.17241/smr.2019.00479.

Bubna, K., Trotter, M. G., Polman, R., & Poulus, D. R. (2023). Terminology matters: Defining the esports athlete. *Frontiers in Sports and Active Living, 5*, 1232028. https://doi.org/10.3389/fspor.2023.1232028.

Complete Sports (2023). *The psychology of esports: Unleashing the power of the mind.* Completesports.com, May 30. https://www.completesports.com/the-psychology-of-esports-unleashing-the-power-of-the-mind/.

Cottrell, C., McMillen, N., & Harris, B. S. (2019). Sport psychology in a virtual world: Considerations for practitioners working in eSports. *Journal of Sport Psychology in Action, 10*(2), 73–81. https://doi.org/10.1080/21520704.2018.1518280.

Cullen, J. (2019). *TSM announces construction of new esports practice facility in Los Angeles.* Yahoo Finance, September 12. https://finance.yahoo.com/news/tsm-announces-construction-esports-practice-215200658.html.

Duarte, F. (2024). *Top 23 esports statistics in 2024.* Exploding Topics, April 29. https://explodingtopics.com/blog/esports-statistics.

Harvard International Review (2020). *Esports part 1: What are esports?* Harvard International Review, April 24. https://hir.harvard.edu/esports-part-1-what-are-esports/

Hyrliková, H. (2022). *The journey ahead for mental health support in esports—Digital Isle of Man.* ESI Esports Insider, April 26. https://esportsinsider.com/2022/04/mental-health-support-esports-digital-isle-of man.

Idaho State University (2023). *Esports research aimed to understand burnout.* Idaho State University, March 6. https://www.isu.edu/news/2023-spring/esports-research-aimed-to-understand-burnout.html.

Jeong, M. (2020). *What to do about the increasing problem of player burnout in esports.* Esports.Net, August 31. https://www.esports.net/news/self-care-and-burnout-in-esports/.

Kalro, N. (2022). *Dev1ce probing teams for return this fall after extended hiatus from play.* Esports.Net, August 29. https://www.esports.net/news/dev1ce-probing-teams-for-return-to-competition/.

Kaspersky (2022). *Self-care matters—42% of professional gamers worry about their mental health condition.* Kaspersky.Com, October 17. https://www.kaspersky.com/about/press-releases/2022_self-care-matters—42-of-professional-gamers-worry-about-their-mental-health-condition.

Kaspersky Daily (2022). *Performance addicted: Exploring gamers' priorities*. Kaspersky.com. https://www.kaspersky.com/blog/gamers-report-2022/.

Kegelaers, J., Trotter, M. G., Watson, M., Pedraza-Ramirez, I., Bonilla, I., Wylleman, P., Mairesse, O., & Van Heel, M. (2024). Promoting mental health in esports. *Frontiers in Psychology*, *15*, 1342220. https://doi.org/10.3389/fpsyg.2024.1342220.

Madden, D., & Casper, H. (2021, May 8). *"Constant pressure of having to perform": Exploring player health concerns in esports*. [Conference presentation, May 8]. Association for Computing Machinery Conference, Yokohama, Japan.

Mangat, H. S., Griffiths, M. D., Yu, S. M., Felvinczi, K., Ngetich, R. K., Demetrovics, Z., & Czakó, A. (2024). Understanding esports-related betting and gambling: A systematic review of the literature. *Journal of Gambling Studies*, *40*(2), 893–914. https://doi.org/10.1007/s10899-023-10256-5.

Martin-Niedecken, A. L., & Schättin, A. (2020). Let the body'n'brain games begin: Toward innovative training approaches in eSports athletes. *Frontiers in Psychology*, *11*, 138. https://doi.org/10.3389/fpsyg.2020.00138.

May, E. (2022). *What studies show about the effects of stress in gaming and esports*. Streamlabs, May 5. https://streamlabs.com/content-hub/post/what-studies-show-about-the-effects-of-stress-in-gaming-and-esports.

Mistry, J. (2023). *The hidden struggles of esports: LOL pros in a mental health crisis*. Esports.Net, July 18. https://www.esports.net/news/industry/hidden-struggles-of-esports-athletes-mental-health-crisis/.

Ohno, S. (2022). The link between battle royale games and aggressive feelings, addiction, and sense of underachievement: Exploring esports-related genres. *International Journal of Mental Health and Addiction*, *20*(3), 1873–81. https://doi.org/10.1007/s11469-021-00488-0.

Paaßen, B., Morgenroth, T., & Stratemeyer, M. (2017). What is a true gamer? The male gamer stereotype and the marginalization of women in video game culture. *Sex Roles*, *76*(7–8), 421–35. https://doi.org/10.1007/s11199-016-0678-y.

Palanichamy, T., Sharma, M. K., Sahu, M., & Kanchana, D. M. (2020). Influence of esports on stress: A systematic review. *Industrial Psychiatry Journal*, *29*(2), 191–9. https://doi.org/10.4103/ipj.ipj_195_20.

Pedraza-Ramirez, I., Musculus, L., Raab, M., & Laborde, S. (2020). Setting the scientific stage for esports psychology: A systematic review. *International Review of Sport and Exercise Psychology*, *13*(1), 319–352. https://doi.org/10.1080/1750984X.2020.1723122.

Ruvalcaba, O., Shulze, J., Kim, A., Berzenski, S. R., & Otten, M. P. (2018). Women's experiences in eSports: Gendered differences in peer and spectator feedback during competitive video game play. *Journal of Sport & Social Issues*, *42*(4), 295–311.https://doi.org/10.1177/0193723518773287.

Sayyed, R. (2023). *Sports psychologist weighs in on the mental health toll of high-stakes esports and its impact on performance*. IGN India, January 18. https://in.ign.com/

esports/178040/interview/sports-psychologist-weighs-in-on-the-mental-health-toll-of-high-stakes-esports-and-its-impact-on-per

Seffah, K. D., Salib, K., Dardari, L., Taha, M., Dahat, P., Toriola, S., Satnarine, T., Zohara, Z., Adelekun, A., Ahmed, A., Gutlapalli, S. D., Patel, D., & Khan, S. (2023). Health benefits of esports: A systematic review comparing the cardiovascular and mental health impacts of esports. *Cureus, 15*(6), e40705. https://doi.org/10.7759/cureus.40705.

Sharma, M. K., Anand, N., & Mathew, V. (2018). Case report on implication of e-sport for changing platform of expression of bullying. *Asian Journal of Psychiatry, 34*, 16–17. https://doi.org/10.1016/j.ajp.2018.03.019

Smith, M., Sharpe, B., Arumuham, A., & Birch, P. (2022). Examining the predictors of mental Ill health in esport competitors. *Healthcare (Basel, Switzerland), 10*(4), 626. https://doi.org/10.3390/healthcare10040626.

Smith, M. J., Birch, P. D. J., & Bright, D. (2019). Identifying stressors and coping strategies of elite esports competitors. *International Journal of Gaming and Computer-Mediated Simulations, 11*(2), 22–39. https://doi.org/10.4018/IJGCMS.2019040102.

Stubbs, M. (2021). *Why esports team Misfits is prioritizing mental health for players and staff*. Forbes, June 9. https://www.forbes.com/sites/mikestubbs/2021/06/09/why-esports-team-misfits-is-prioritizing-mental-health-for-players-and-staff/.

Chapter 10

American Psychological Association (2024). *Barriers to care in a changing practice environment: 2024 practitioner pulse survey*. American Psychological Association, December. https://www.apa.org/pubs/reports/practitioner/2024/practitioner-pulse-2024-full-report.pdf.

Anyan, F., Hjemdal, O., Ernstsen, L., & Havnen, A. (2020). Change in physical activity during the coronavirus disease 2019 lockdown in Norway: The buffering effect of resilience on mental health. *Frontiers in Psychology, 11*. https://doi.org/10.3389/fpsyg.2020.598481.

Barbee, P. H. (2023). *A post pandemic analysis of COVID-19 and the impact on mental health of high school student-athletes—Today, more than ever minds matter*. (Publication no. 87) [Doctoral dissertation, University of Washington Tacoma]. UW Tacoma Digital Commons.

Bareis, N., Tepper, M. C., Wang, R., Tang, F., Olfson, M., Dixon, L. B., Kimhy, D., Wall, M. M., Medalia, A., Finnerty, M. T., Anderson, A., & Smith, T. E. (2023). Engagement of individuals with serious mental illness in outpatient mental health services and telehealth use during the COVID-19 pandemic. *Psychiatry Research, 329*, 115497. https://doi.org/10.1016/j.psychres.2023.115497.

Bertollo, M., Forzini, F., Biondi, S., Di Liborio, M., Vaccaro, M. G., Georgiadis, E., & Conti, C. (2021). How does a sport psychological intervention help professional cyclists to cope with their mental health during the COVID-19 lockdown? *Frontiers in Psychology, 12*, 607152. https://doi.org/10.3389/fpsyg.2021.607152.

Burke, M. (2020). *Maine teen dies by suicide after struggling to cope with pandemic, father says.* NBC News, December 8. https://www.nbcnews.com/news/us-news/teen-dies-suicide-after-struggling-cope-pandemic-father-says-n1250442.

Centers for Disease Control and Prevention (2024). *The changing threat of COVID-19.* National Center for Immunization and Respiratory Diseases, February 12. https://www.cdc.gov/ncird/whats-new/changing-threat-covid-19.html.

Centers for Disease Control and Prevention (2024). *Clinical overview of long COVID.* CDC.gov, July 15. https://www.cdc.gov/covid/hcp/clinical-overview/index.html

Christ, M., & Rim, C. (2024). *2024 Paris Olympics hit by early COVID cases, but organizers don't seem worried by risk of major outbreak.* CBSNews.com, July 24. https://www.cbsnews.com/news/2024-paris-olympics-covid-cases-organizers-seem-unfazed-outbreak-risk/.

Coleman, M. (2021). *NCAA survey examines impact of COVID-19 on athletes.* Sports Illustrated, February 16. https://www.si.com/college/2021/02/17/ncaa-fall-survey-shows-rise-mental-health-struggles.

Collins, D. P., Jagim, A. R., Sowders, J. P., Blessman, J. D., McLachlan, M. L., Miller, N. E., Garrison, E. G., Kuisle, M., Asplund, C. A., & Garrison, G. M. (2022). Athletic disruptions caused by the COVID-19 pandemic negatively affect high school student-athletes social-emotional well-being. *Medicine, 101*(51), e31890. https://doi.org/10.1097/MD.0000000000031890.

Corrales, A. (2023). *Youth sports are more important than ever for kids' mental health.* Global Sport Matters, April 12. https://globalsportmatters.com/health/2023/04/12/youth-sports-programs-more-important-than-ever-kids-mental-health/.

Davis, P. A., Gustafsson, H., Callow, N., & Woodman, T. (2020). Written emotional disclosure can promote athletes' mental health and performance readiness during the COVID-19 pandemic. *Frontiers in Psychology, 11*, 599925. https://doi.org/10.3389/fpsyg.2020.599925.

Facer-Childs, E. R., Hoffman, D., Tran, J. N., Drummond, S. P. A., & Rajaratnam, S. M. W. (2022). Sleep and mental health in athletes during COVID-19 lockdown. *Sleep, 44*(5), zsaa261. https://doi.org/10.1093/sleep/zsaa261.

Graupensperger, S., Benson, A. J., Kilmer, J. R., & Evans, M. B. (2020). Social (Un) distancing: Teammate interactions, athletic identity, and mental health of student-athletes during the COVID-19 pandemic. *Journal of Adolescent Health, 67*(5), 662–70. https://doi.org/10.1016/j.jadohealth.2020.08.001.

Jia, L., Carter, M. V., Cusano, A., Li, X., Kelly, J. D., Bartley, J. D., & Parisien, R. L. (2023). The effect of the COVID-19 pandemic on the mental and emotional health of athletes: A systematic review. *The American Journal of Sports Medicine, 51*(8), 2207–215. https://doi.org/10.1177/03635465221087473.

Johnson, G. (2021). *Pandemic continues to impact student-athlete mental health.* NCAA.org, February 16. https://www.ncaa.org/news/2021/2/16/pandemic-continues-to-impact-student-athlete-mental-health.aspx.

Karrer, Y., Fröhlich, S., Iff, S., Spörri, J., Scherr, J., Seifritz, E., Quednow, B. B., & Claussen, M. C. (2022). Training load, sports performance, physical and mental health during the COVID-19 pandemic: A prospective cohort of Swiss elite athletes. *PLoS ONE, 17*(12), e0278203. https://doi.org/10.1371/journal.pone.0278203.

Kass, P., & Morrison, T. E. (2023). The impact of COVID-19 restrictions on youth athlete mental health: A narrative review. *Current Psychiatry Reports, 25*(5), 193–9. https://doi.org/10.1007/s11920-023-01422-y.

Laurier, C., Pascuzzo, K., & Beaulieu, G. (2021). Uncovering the personal and environmental factors associated with youth mental health during the COVID-19 pandemic: The pursuit of sports and physical activity as a protective factor. *Traumatology, 27*(4), 354–64. https://doi.org/10.1037/trm0000342.

Lee, M. (2021). *Slowed and sidelined, some athletes struggle to return from long-haul covid. Washington Post*, April 19. https://www.washingtonpost.com/sports/2021/04/19/athletes-long-haul-covid-justin-foster/.

Levy, J. J., Tarver, T. L., & Douglas, H. R. (2021). Examining the impact of gym closures due to the COVID-19 pandemic on combat sport athletes' mental health. *Journal of Clinical Sport Psychology, 15*(4), 289–305. https://doi.org/10.1123/jcsp.2021-0078.

Lillehei, A. (2022). The second pandemic: Mental health. *Explore (New York, N.Y.), 18*(3), 257–8. https://doi.org/10.1016/j.explore.2022.03.007.

Lim, H. B. T., Malhotra, N., Lou, S., & Pillai, J. (2023). The impact of the COVID-19 pandemic on Singapore national youth athletes' mental health and potential protective factors. *International Journal of Sport and Exercise Psychology 22*(7), 1569–87. https://doi.org/10.1080/1612197X.2023.2235593.

Mehrsafar, A. H., Gazerani, P., Zadeh, A. M., & Sánchez, J. C. J. (2020). Addressing potential impact of COVID-19 pandemic on physical and mental health of elite athletes. *Brain, Behavior, and Immunity, 87*, 147–8. https://doi.org/10.1016/j.bbi.2020.05.011.

Mehrsafar, A. H., Moghadam Zadeh, A., Gazerani, P., Jaenes Sanchez, J. C., Nejat, M., Rajabian Tabesh, M., & Abolhasani, M. (2021). Mental health status, life satisfaction, and mood state of elite athletes during the COVID-19 pandemic: A follow-up study in the phases of home confinement, reopening, and semi-lockdown condition. *Frontiers in Psychology, 12*, 630414. https://doi.org/10.3389/fpsyg.2021.630414.

Newman, T. J., Turgeon, S., Moore, M., Bean, C., Lee, L., Knuettel, M., & Osmers Rahill, C. (2022). The dual pandemic: Covid-19, systemic racism, and college student-athletic mental health. *International Journal of Sport and Exercise Psychology, 21*(1), 156–73. https://doi.org/10.1080/1612197X.2022.2026997.

Panchal, N., Saunders, H., Rudowitz, R., & Cox, C. (2023). *The implications of COVID-19 for mental health and substance use.* KFF, March 20. https://www.kff.org/

mental-health/issue-brief/the-implications-of-covid-19-for-mental-health-and-substance-use/

Pfizer (2023). *Global and U.S. agencies declare end of COVID-19 emergency*. Pfizer.com, May 11. https://www.pfizer.com/news/announcements/global-and-us-agencies-declare-end-covid-19-emergency.

Pons, J., Ramis, Y., Alcaraz, S., Jordana, A., Borrueco, M., & Torregrossa, M. (2020). Where did all the sport go? Negative impact of COVID-19 lockdown on life-spheres and mental health of Spanish young athletes. *Frontiers in Psychology, 11*, 611872. https://doi.org/10.3389/fpsyg.2020.611872.

Schary, D. P., & Lundqvist, C. (2021). Mental health in times of the COVID-19 pandemic: Exploring the impact on well-being across the athlete-collegiate career. *Journal of Clinical Sport Psychology, 15*(3), 249–67. https://doi.org/10.1123/jcsp.2021-0041.

Shepherd, H. A., Evans, T., Gupta, S., McDonough, M. H., Doyle-Baker, P., Belton, K. L., Karmali, S., Pawer, S., Hadly, G., Pike, I., Adams, S. A., Babul, S., Yeates, K. O., Kopala-Sibley, D. C., Schneider, K. J., Cowle, S., Fuselli, P., Emery, C. A., & Black, A. M. (2021). The impact of COVID-19 on high school student-athlete experiences with physical activity, mental health, and social connection. *International Journal of Environmental Research and Public Health, 18*(7), 3515. https://doi.org/10.3390/ijerph18073515.

Shukla, A., Dogra, D. K., Bhattacharya, D., Gulia, S., & Sharma, R. (2023). Impact of COVID-19 outbreak on the mental health in sports: A review. *Sport Sciences for Health, 19*(4) 1–15. https://doi.org/10.1007/s11332-023-01063-x.

Simons, C., Martin, L. A., Balcombe, L., Dunn, P. K., & Clark, R. A. (2021). Mental health impact on at-risk high-level athletes during COVID-19 lockdown: A pre-, during and post-lockdown longitudinal cohort study of adjustment disorder. *Journal of Science and Medicine in Sport, 24*(4), 329–31. https://doi.org/10.1016/j.jsams.2020.12.012.

Sky Sports (2023). *"Covid-19 ruined our dreams" | Two athletes who retired due to long Covid diagnosis* [Video recording, April 11]. https://www.youtube.com/watch?v=IRdXFgkbQOU.

Strauser, C. M., Chavez, V., Lindsay, K. R., Figgins, M. M., & DeShaw, K. J. (2023). College student athlete versus nonathlete mental and social health factors during the COVID-19 pandemic. *Journal of American College Health, 73*(1), 97–102. https://doi.org/10.1080/07448481.2023.2201853.

Watson, D. (2022). *COVID-19 pandemic cancellations took harsh toll on teen athletes, whose mental and physical health improved significantly after sports resumed* [Paper presentation]. American Academy of Pediatrics National Conference and Exhibition, Anaheim, CA. https://www.aap.org/en/news-room/news-releases/conference-news-releases/covid-19-pandemic-cancellations-took-harsh-toll-on-teen-athletes-whose-mental-and-physical-health-improved-significantly-after-sports-resumed/.

Wessner, D. (2024). *Covid outbreak among Olympic athletes serves as a pandemic reminder*. Forbes, July 25. https://www.forbes.com/sites/davewessner/2024/07/25/covid-outbreak-among-olympic-athletes-serves-as-a-pandemic-reminder/.

Wezenbeek, E., Denolf, S., Bourgois, J. G., Philippaerts, R. M., De Winne, B., Willems, T. M., Witvrouw, E., Verstockt, S., & Schuermans, J. (n.d.). Impact of (long) COVID on athletes' performance: A prospective study in elite football players. *Annals of Medicine*, *55*(1), 2198776. https://doi.org/10.1080/07853890.2023.2198776.

Zipp, S., & Nauright, J. (2024). Global sport in the post-COVID era. *Sport in Society*, *27*(2), 185–90. https://doi.org/10.1080/17430437.2024.2298022.

Chapter 11

André-Morin, D., Caron, J. G., & Bloom, G. A. (2017). Exploring the unique challenges faced by female university athletes experiencing prolonged concussion symptoms. *Sport, Exercise, and Performance Psychology*, *6*(3), 289–303. https://doi.org/10.1037/spy0000106

Baiden, P., Morgan, M. A., & Logan, M. W. (2022). Sports- and physical activity-related concussions, binge drinking and marijuana use among adolescents: The mediating role of depression and suicidal ideation. *Substance Use & Misuse*, *57*(4), 504–15. https://doi.org/10.1080/10826084.2021.2019779.

Bailey, A. L., Capron, D. W., Buerke, M. L., & Bauer, B. W. (2023). The associations between sport- and physical activity-related concussions and suicidality, suicide capability, and hopelessness among high school adolescents. *Journal of Adolescence*, *95*(6), 1116–26. https://doi.org/10.1002/jad.12179.

Bloom, G. A., Trbovich, A. M., Caron, J. G., & Kontos, A. P. (2020). Psychological aspects of sport-related concussion: An evidence-based position paper. *Journal of Applied Sport Psychology*, *23*(3), 495–517. https://doi.org/10.1080/10413200.2020.1843200.

Concussion Alliance (n.d.). *A brief history of concussion as a public health issue*. Concussion Alliance.org. https://www.concussionalliance.org/history-of-concussion.

Ellis, M. J., Ritchie, L. J., McDonald, P. J., Cordingley, D., Reimer, K., Nijjar, S., Koltek, M., Hosain, S., Johnston, J., Mansouri, B., Sawyer, S., Silver, N., Girardin, R., Larkins, S., Vis, S., Selci, E., Davidson, M., Gregoire, S., Sam, A., & Russell, K. (2017). Multidisciplinary management of pediatric sports-related concussion. *Canadian Journal of Neurological Sciences*, *44*(1), 24–34. https://doi.org/10.1017/cjn.2016.312.

Finkbeiner, N. W., Max, J. E., Longman, S., & Debert, C. (2016). Knowing what we don't know: Long-term psychiatric outcomes following adult concussion in sports. *Canadian Journal of Psychiatry*, *61*(5), 270–6. https://doi.org/10.1177/0706743716644953.

Gornall, A., Takagi, M., Morawakage, T., Liu, X., & Anderson, V. (2021). Mental health after paediatric concussion: A systematic review and meta-analysis. *British Journal of Sports Medicine, 55*(18), 1048–58. https://doi.org/10.1136/bjsports-2020-103548.

Gouttebarge, V., & Kerkhoffs, G. M. M. J. (2021). Sports career-related concussion and mental health symptoms in former elite athletes. *Neurochirurgie, 67*(3), 280–2. https://doi.org/10.1016/j.neuchi.2020.01.001.

Haarbauer-Krupa, J., Arbogast, K. B., Metzger, K. B., Greenspan, A. I., Kessler, R., Curry, A. E., Bell, J. M., DePadilla, L., Pfeiffer, M. R., Zonfrillo, M. R., & Master, C. L. (2018). Variations in mechanisms of injury for children with concussion. *The Journal of Pediatrics, 197*, 241–8.e1. https://doi.org/10.1016/j.jpeds.2018.01.075.

Ianof, J. N., Freire, F. R., Calado, V. T. G., Lacerda, J. R., Coelho, F., Veitzman, S., Schmidt, M. T., Machado, S., Velasques, B., Ribeiro, P., Basile, L. F. H., Paiva, W. S., Amorim, R., & Anghinah, R. (2014). Sport-related concussions. *Dementia & Neuropsychologia, 8*(1), 14–19. https://doi.org/10.1590/S1980-57642014DN81000003.

Iverson, G. L., Williams, M. W., Gardner, A. J., & Terry, D. P. (2020). Systematic review of preinjury mental health problems as a vulnerability factor for worse outcome after sport-related concussion. *Orthopaedic Journal of Sports Medicine, 8*(10), 2325967120950682. https://doi.org/10.1177/2325967120950682.

Kirschen, M. P., Tsou, A., Nelson, S. B., Russell, J. A., Larriviere, D., & Ethics, Law, and Humanities Committee, a Joint Committee of the American Academy of Neurology, American Neurological Association, and Child Neurology Society (2014). Legal and ethical implications in the evaluation and management of sports-related concussion. *Neurology, 83*(4), 352–8. https://doi.org/10.1212/WNL.0000000000000613.

Kontos, A. P. (2023). Concussion and CTE: Separating the facts from the fear and its impact on athletes' mental health [Presentation]. In C. Selby (Chair) *The mental health of athletes: General considerations and contemporary issues.* American Psychological Association, August.

Kontos, A. P., Deitrick, J. M., & Reynolds, E. (2016). Mental health implications and consequences following sport-related concussion. *British Journal of Sports Medicine, 50*(3), 139–40. https://doi.org/10.1136/bjsports-2015-095564.

Kontos, A. P., Pan, R., & Emami, K. (2020). Mental health manifestations of concussion. In E. Hong & A. L. Rao (Eds.), *Mental health in the athlete: modern perspectives and novel challenges for the sports medicine provider* (pp. 149–63). Springer International Publishing. https://doi.org/10.1007/978-3-030-44754-0_12.

Ledoux, A.-A., Webster, R. J., Clarke, A. E., Fell, D. B., Knight, B. D., Gardner, W., Cloutier, P., Gray, C., Tuna, M., & Zemek, R. (2022). Risk of mental health problems in children and youths following concussion. *JAMA Network Open, 5*(3), e221235. https://doi.org/10.1001/jamanetworkopen.2022.1235.

Mayo Clinic (n.d.). *Chronic traumatic encephalopathy.* Mayo Clinic. https://www.mayoclinic.org/diseases-conditions/chronic-traumatic-encephalopathy/symptoms-causes/syc-20370921.

McGivern, A., Shannon, S., & Breslin, G. (2021). Resilience, well-being, depression symptoms and concussion levels in equestrian athletes. *Journal of Public Mental Health, 20*(3), 172–81. https://doi.org/10.1108/JPMH-08-2020-0110.

Merrill, E., (2024). *Dolphins QB Tua Tagovailoa still faces concussion concerns.* ESPN, October 22. https://www.espn.com/nfl/story/_/id/41927160/tua-tagovailoa-miami-dolphins-quarterback-concussions.

National Institutes of Health (2013). *A bang to the brain: What we know about concussions.* NIH News in Health, May. https://newsinhealth.nih.gov/2013/05/bang-brain

National Institutes of Health (2019). *Mental health disorders common following mild head injury.* National Institutes of Health, January 30. https://www.nih.gov/news-events/news-releases/mental-health-disorders-common-following-mild-head-injury

Ott, S. D., Bailey, C. M., & Broshek, D. K. (2018). An interdisciplinary approach to sports concussion evaluation and management: The role of a neuropsychologist. *Archives of Clinical Neuropsychology, 33*(3), 319–29. https://doi.org/10.1093/arclin/acx132.

Peskind, E. R., Brody, D., Cernak, I., McKee, A., & Ruff, R. L. (2013). Military- and sports-related mild traumatic brain injury: Clinical presentation, management, and long-term consequences (CME commentary). *The Journal of Clinical Psychiatry, 74*(02), 180–8. https://doi.org/10.4088/JCP.12011co1c.

Rice, S. M., Parker, A. G., Rosenbaum, S., Bailey, A., Mawren, D., & Purcell, R. (2018). Sport-related concussion and mental health outcomes in elite athletes: A systematic review. *Sports Medicine, 48*(2), 447–65. https://doi.org/10.1007/s40279-017-0810-3.

Sarmiento, K., Miller, G. F., & Jones, S. E. (2022). Sports- or physical activity–related concussions and feelings of sadness or hopelessness among US High school students: Results from the 2017 Youth Behavior Risk Survey. *The Journal of School Nursing, 38*(2), 203–9. https://doi.org/10.1177/1059840520945389.

Selemon, L. D. (2013). A role for synaptic plasticity in the adolescent development of executive function. *Translational Psychiatry, 3*(3), e238–e238. https://doi.org/10.1038/tp.2013.7.

Senecal, G., Gurchiek, E., & Slattery, E. (2017). The brain and beyond in the aftermath of head trauma—A systems view of development for contact sport athletes. *Cogent Psychology, 4*(1). https://doi.org/10.1080/23311908.2017.1330935.

Sheldrake, E., Al-Hakeem, H., Lam, B., Goldstein, B. I., Wheeler, A. L., Burke, M., Dunkley, B. T., Reed, N., & Scratch, S. E. (2022). Mental health outcomes across the lifespan in individuals with persistent post-concussion symptoms: A scoping review. *Frontiers in Neurology, 13*, 850590. https://doi.org/10.3389/fneur.2022.850590

Torres, D. M., Galetta, K. M., Phillips, H. W., Dziemianowicz, E. M. S., Wilson, J. A., Dorman, E. S., Laudano, E., Galetta, S. L., & Galcer, L. J. (2013). Sports-related concussion: Anonymous survey of a collegiate cohort. *Neurology Clinical Practice, 3*(4), 279–87. https://doi.org/10.1212/CPJ.0b013e3182a1ba22.

Tracey, A. J., Bateman, A. G., Baez, S. E., & Covassin, T. (2023). Effectiveness of interventions for the improvement of mental health and well-being post-concussion: A systematic review. *Brain Injury*, *37*(10), 1135–58. https://doi.org/10.1080/02699052.2023.2219901.

Wadhawan, A., Stiller, J., Potocki, E., Okusaga, O., Dagdag, A., Lowry, C., Benros, M., & Postolache, T. (2019). Traumatic brain injury and suicidal behavior: A review. *Journal of Alzheimer's Disease*, *68*(4), 1339–70. https://doi.org/10.3233/JAD-181055.

Yang, M. N., Clements-Nolle, K., Parrish, B., & Yang, W. (2019). Adolescent concussion and mental health outcomes: A population-based study. *American Journal of Health Behavior*, *43*(2), 258–65. https://doi.org/10.5993/AJHB.43.2.3.

Ziminski, D., Szlyk, H. S., Baiden, P., Okine, L., Onyeaka, H. K., Muoghalu, C., & Cavazos-Rehg, P. (2022). Sports- and physical activity-related concussion and mental health among adolescents: Findings from the 2017 and 2019 Youth Risk Behavior Survey. *Psychiatry Research*, *312*, 114542. https://doi.org/10.1016/[[j.psychres.2022.114542.

Chapter 12

Aronson, K. (2022). The current state of student-athlete NIL rights: How congress should respond to the rapidly changing landscape of inter-collegiate sports. *Journal of the National Association of Administrative Law Judiciary*, *43*(1), 249–93.

Business of College Sports (2024). *Current college sports television contracts.* Business of College Sports.com, March 19. https://businessofcollegesports.com/current-college-sports-television-contracts/

Butler, D. (2022). *The highest paid college athletes.* Icon Source, October 24. https://iconsource.com/blog/highest-paid-college-athletes/.

Claybourn, C. (2024). *Name, image, likeness: What college athletes should know about NCAA rules.* US News and World Report, February 8. https://www.usnews.com/education/best-colleges/articles/name-image-likeness-what-college-athletes-should-know-about-ncaa-rules.

Coyle, P. (2022). *Social media, NIL demands can take toll on college athlete mental health.* Sportico.com, April 27. https://www.sportico.com/leagues/college-sports/2022/social-media-nil-demands-hurt-mental-health-1234673562/.

Curington, R. J. (2020). The importance of NCAA student-athletes' financial literacy and mental health in anticipation of the historic fair pay to play act. *DePaul Journal of Sports Law*, *16*(1), 74–92.

Eating Disorder Care (2023). *Student-athletes & body image: How ED can develop with the new NCAA name, image & likeness rules.* Eating Disorder Care, March 9. https://eatingdisorder.care/student-athletes-body-image-how-ed-can-develop-with-the-new-ncaa-name-image-likeness-rules/.

Economou, P. J., & Gamble, A. (2024). Navigating an intercollegiate athletes' transition related to the name, image, and likeness (NIL) interim policy. *Journal of Sport Psychology in Action*, 1–10. https://doi.org/10.1080/21520704.2024.2348153.

Effress, S. (2024). *NCAA inks 8-year, $920 million deal with ESPN.* Business of College Sports.com, January 4. https://businessofcollegesports.com/television/ncaa-inks-8-year-920-million-deal-with-espn/.

ESPN (2023). *A $13-million NIL deal gone wrong, a top QB recruit and what happens next.* ESPN.Com, January 20. https://www.espn.com/college-football/story/_/id/35482485/jaden-rashada-faq-top-recruit-nil-deal-florida-football.

Gulavani, S. S., Henry, T. E., Floyd, C., Du, J., Pifer, N. D., & Su, Y. (2023). Putting athletes first: An empirical examination of the hedonic well-being of college student-athletes in response to NIL. *Journal of Issues in Intercollegiate Athletics, 16*(1), 266–89.

Harris, H. A., Brison, N. T., & Dixon, M. A. (2021). Hidden consequences: Examining the impact of NIL on athlete well-being. *Journal of Applied Sport Management, 13*(2), 29–35. https://doi.org/10.7290/jasm13r7xo.

Hosick, M. B. (2021). *NCAA adopts interim name, image and likeness policy.* NCAA.Org, June 30. https://www.ncaa.org/news/2021/6/30/ncaa-adopts-interim-name-image-and-likeness-policy.aspx

Johnson, R. (2019). *A history of skyrocketing college football coach salaries, from Camp to Dabo.* Banner Society, August 15. https://www.bannersociety.com/2019/8/15/20732192/coach-salaries-history-highest.

Kindbridge (2023). *How does NCAA NIL policy grade on athlete mental health?* Kindbridge Behavioral Health, January 27. https://kindbridge.com/mental-health/how-does-the-ncaa-nil-policy-grade-on-college-athlete-mental-health/.

King, A. H. (2022). *Name, image, and likeness in US college athletics: One year later.* The National Law Review, July 11. https://www.natlawreview.com/article/name-image-and-likeness-us-college-athletics-one-year-later.

Kirshner, A. (2020). *Football has been college sports' golden goose since the 1800s.* Banner Society, April 8. https://www.bannersociety.com/2020/4/8/21211241/college-athletic-budgets-football.

Morones, S., & Heldt, P. (n.d.). *Following the money in college sports.* Morones Analytics. https://moronesanalytics.com/following-the-money-in-college-sports/.

National Collegiate Athletics Association (2011). *2011 2012 NCAA Division I manual.* NCAA. http://www.ncaapublications.com/productdownloads/D112.pdf.

National Collegiate Athletics Association (n.d.). *Role of boosters.* NCAA.Org. https://www.ncaa.org/sports/2013/11/27/role-of-boosters.aspx.

Next College Student Athlete (2024). *Name, image, likeness.* NCSA College Recruiting, December 6. https://www.ncsasports.org/name-image-likeness.

Planos, J. (2022). *The NCAA doesn't know how to stop boosters from playing the NIL game.* FiveThirtyEight, May 16. https://fivethirtyeight.com/features/the-ncaa-doesnt-know-how-to-stop-boosters-from-playing-the-nil-game/.

Pope, B., & McMichael, B. (2024). *Highlights of the federal proposals to regulate NIL deals.* Littler Mendelson P.C, February 6. https://www.littler.com/publication-press/publication/highlights-federal-proposals-regulate-nil-deals.

Reader, J., Gordon, B., & Christensen, N. (2022). Food Insecurity among a Cohort of Division I Student-Athletes. *Nutrients, 14*(21), 4703. https://doi.org/10.3390/nu14214703.

Romaine, C. A., & Marsh, B. (2023). *Name, image, and likeness policy challenges.* National Association of Student Personnel Administrators, February 28. https://www.naspa.org/blog/name-image-and-likeness-policy-challenges

Skarecky, H. (2023). *How TV money is gerrymandering college sports.* The Georgetown Voice, September 23. https://georgetownvoice.com/2023/09/23/how-tv-money-is-gerrymandering-college-sports/

Smith, M. (2022). *Social media dominates NIL activity, latest data shows.* Sports Business Journal, February 17. https://www.sportsbusinessjournal.com/Daily/Issues/2022/02/17/Marketing-and-Sponsorship/NIL-data.aspx.

Springgate, J. (2023). *Mental health toll of NIL and heading to college.* WNDU.com, June 6. https://www.wndu.com/2023/06/06/mental-health-toll-nil-heading-college/.

Steele, D. (2023). *Understanding NIL and well-being.* Athletes Connected, July 20. https://athletesconnected.umich.edu/understanding-nil-and-well-being/.

Index

About the Author

Christine L.B. Selby, PhD, earned her doctoral degree in Counseling Psychology at the University of North Texas in 2000 and earned her master's degree in Athletic Counseling in 1994 from Springfield College. Christine is currently an Associate Professor of Psychology at Springfield College and Director of the Athletic Counseling masters degree program. She also maintains a part-time private practice as a licensed counseling and sport psychologist, and certified eating disorder specialist (CEDS) through the International Association of Eating Disorders Professionals. She also has emeritus status as Certified Mental Performance Consultant® (CMPC) through the Association of Applied Sport Psychology (AASP). Christine is also a past-president of and former Council of Representatives member representing the Society for Sport, Exercise, & Performance Psychology, Division 47, of the American Psychological Association (APA). She was also co-founder and past co-chair of the AASP Eating Disorder Special Interest Group, and is a co-founder and current chair of the Eating Disorders and Body Image Interest Group of the Society for Health Psychology, Division 38, of the APA. Christine's publications include articles and book chapters primarily in the area of athletes with eating disorders, and her presentations at local, national, and international meetings focus on eating disorders and the inherent complexity they present.